T0199313

PROCESS MODELING AND MANAGEMENT FOR HEALTHCARE

Chapman & Hall/CRC
Healthcare Informatics Series

Series Editor
Christopher Yang
Drexel University
Philadelphia, PA, USA

Aims and Scope

Healthcare informatics is concerned with the application of computer science principles, information science principles, information technology, and communication technology to address problems in healthcare and everyday wellness. This book series serves as a publication venue for innovative technical contributions in healthcare informatics, highlighting end-to-end applications, systems, and technologies. The series will focus on the three major tracks in healthcare informatics: (1) Systems Track focuses on building healthcare informatics systems (e.g., architecture, framework design, engineering, and application); (2) Analytics Track focuses on data analytics; and (3) Human Factors Track focuses on understanding users or context, interface design, and user studies of healthcare informatics applications.

Published Titles

Process Modeling and Management for Healthcare
Carlo Combi, Giuseppe Pozzi, and Pierangelo Veltri

PROCESS MODELING AND MANAGEMENT FOR HEALTHCARE

Edited by
Carlo Combi
Giuseppe Pozzi
Pierangelo Veltri

CRC Press
Taylor & Francis Group
Boca Raton London New York

CRC Press is an imprint of the
Taylor & Francis Group, an **informa** business

A CHAPMAN & HALL BOOK

CRC Press
Taylor & Francis Group
6000 Broken Sound Parkway NW, Suite 300
Boca Raton, FL 33487-2742

Printed on acid-free paper
Version Date: 20170907

International Standard Book Number-13: 978-1-138-19665-0 (Hardback)

Library of Congress Cataloging-in-Publication Data

Names: Combi, Carlo, editor. | Pozzi, Giuseppe, 1961- editor. | Veltri, Pierangelo, editor.
Title: Process modeling and management for healthcare / [edited by] Carlo Combi, Giuseppe Pozzi, and Pierangelo Veltri.
Other titles: Chapman & Hall/CRC healthcare informatics series.
Description: Boca Raton : Taylor & Francis, 2017. | Series: Chapman & Hall/CRC healthcare informatics series | Includes bibliographical references and index.
Identifiers: LCCN 2017020658 | ISBN 9781138196650 (hardback : alk. paper)
Subjects: | MESH: Health Services Research--organization & administration | Medical Informatics Applications | Research Design | Data Collection
Classification: LCC RA971 | NLM W 84.3 | DDC 362.1068--dc23
LC record available at https://lccn.loc.gov/2017020658

Visit the Taylor & Francis Web site at
http://www.taylorandfrancis.com

and the CRC Press Web site at
http://www.crcpress.com

Printed and bound in the United States of America by
Edwards Brothers Malloy on sustainably sourced paper

To Lella,
C.C.

To Monica,
G.P.

To Fulvia,
P.V.

Contents

Aitor Eguzkitza, Jesús D. Trigo, Miguel
Martínez-Espronceda, Luis Serrano, and José Andonegui

Giuseppe Tradigo, Patrizia Vizza, Pietro Hiram Guzzi,
Andrea Tagarelli, and Pierangelo Veltri

Jan Mendling

Chapter   9 ▪ Temporal Clinical Guidelines   217

Luca Anselma, Luca Piovesan, and Paolo Terenziani

List of Figures

List of Tables

Foreword

It is my great honor to have the opportunity to read this outstanding book before its publication. *Process Modeling and Management for Healthcare*, co-edited by three excellent experts in healthcare informatics, Professors Carlo Combi, Giuseppe Pozzi, and Pierangelo Veltri, covers the most important topics in handling the high level of variability and complicated healthcare processes.

As we know, healthcare processes are far more complicated than many business processes, which can be defined based on the business strategy and operations. Healthcare processes vary substantially from one patient to another patient even though the patients may be diagnosed with the same disease, especially in the precision medicine era. It often requires specific medical domain knowledge before the processes can be defined and modeled. The editors are addressing one of the most difficult challenges we face in healthcare informatics.

This book includes 9 high-quality chapters authored by 26 active and highly reputed researchers in healthcare informatics. It provides a comprehensive overview of the fundamental concepts in healthcare process management as well as some advanced topics in the cutting-edge research of the closely related areas. This book is ideal for graduate students and practitioners who want to build the foundations and develop novel contributions in healthcare process modeling and management.

I would like to congratulate the editors for their excellent work and the authors for their excellent contributions. The concepts, methods, and analytics for process modeling and management collected in this book have tremendous values for students, researchers, and practitioners who are interested in these topics.

Christopher Yang
Drexel University, Pennsylvania

Preface

Process modeling and process management[1] are traversal disciplines which have earned more and more relevance over the last two decades. Several research areas are involved by these traversal disciplines: database systems, database management, and information systems; ERP (Enterprise Resource Planning) and operations research; formal languages and logics, to mention just a few of them.

Process modeling and process management have been covering many applications domains, ranging from the pure and typical business activities (e.g., bank loan, insurance claim, and car rental to mention a few of them) which are more rigorous and strictly invariant from one case to another, to much more complex and variability-prone activities. Bank loan process instances are rigorously the same, no matter who is the applicant or the customer: so too insurance claim, car rental and many other process instances, whose execution schema is customer-invariant.

On the other side, more complex domains, such as healthcare, are more affected by case-to-case variability and do not feature the same exact behaviors for all the cases: one patient may react in a completely different way from the "other" patients; emergency situations can arise at any time, and need to be managed as soon as possible; time-critical situations, i.e., where the correctness of the reaction also depends on the time needed to react to the event, may occur at any stage. Thus, process modeling and management techniques need to be suitably customized, adapted—and sometimes tamed, too—when facing domains which show a very high level of variability from one case to another, or from one patient to another as in healthcare, or which show a time-critical behavior.

This book aims at providing the reader with an in-depth analysis of what process modeling and process management techniques can do in healthcare, of the major challenges faced, and of those challenges still remaining to be faced. In order to cover these major topics, the book collects contributions from the major authors in the field of process modeling and management in healthcare.

---

[1] This book was typeset by LATEX [153].

PREREQUISITES

In order to fully understand the contributions of this book, the reader is expected to own some basic skills in computer science, database and data management systems, information systems and graphical notations. Skills in the field of medical informatics, clinical guidelines, care processes, clinical protocols, recommendations, and best practices will also benefit the reader in better understanding—and, we hope, appreciating—the contents of the book.

BOOK OUTLINE

The book is structured into two main parts: fundamentals and advanced topics.

Part 1 on fundamentals includes Chapters 1 to 5, and it aims at providing the reader with the basic concepts on process management in healthcare. Considered topics deal with: the architecture of a process management environment; the flexibility of a process model (this feature is extremely important when dealing with healthcare, to face the inter-person variability of medical care); the compliance of a process model to the real world; a real application domain of patients suffering from age-related macular degeneration (AMD); and the use of scientific workflows.

Part 2 includes Chapters 6 to 9, and it aims at providing the reader with full details on more advanced topics, typically coming from the leading frontiers of scientific research on process management in general as well as in healthcare. Considered topics deal with: software metrics which help measure some features of the process model considered as a software artifact; process analysis to discover the formal properties of the process model prior to deploying it in the real application domain; exceptions to capture abnormal situations which may occur during the execution of the instances of the process model; and temporal clinical guidelines to properly describe temporal aspects of the clinical guidelines formalized by suitable process models.

In detail, the structure of the book is the following:

i. **Models and Architectures for the Enactment of Healthcare Processes**: Chapter 1 by Carlo Combi, Barbara Oliboni, Francesca Zerbato (University of Verona, Verona, Italy) and Giuseppe Pozzi (Politecnico di Milano, Milano, Italy) introduces the reader to the world of healthcare process management, focusing on modeling approaches and architectures for process enactment. The chapter also includes an overview of the architecture of a typical Workflow Management System (WfMS), also known as Business Process Engine (BPE), describing its software modules, components, and functionalities.

ii. **Flexible Support for Healthcare Processes**: Chapter 2 by Manfred Reichert and Rüdiger Pryss (University of Ulm, Ulm, Germany) deals with the characteristic flexibility needs of both prespecified and loosely specified healthcare processes, and presents fundamental flexibility features required to address these flexibility needs as well as to accommodate them in healthcare practice.

iii. **Process Compliance**: Chapter 3 by Stefanie Rinderle-Ma (University of Wien, Wien, Austria) describes how business process models have to comply with business level rules and policies (i.e., semantic constraints) stemming from real world applications, to ensure error-free executions at the semantic level.

iv. **Modeling a Process for Managing Age-Related Macular Degeneration**: Chapter 4 by Aitor Eguzkitza, Jesús Daniel Trigo, Miguel Martínez-Espronceda, Luis Serrano (Public University of Navarra, Pamplona, Spain), and José Andonegui (Complejo Hospitalario de Navarra, Pamplona, Spain) describes how a previously developed methodology was deployed to formalize the clinical process associated with age-related macular degeneration (AMD), reusing the existing electronic models when possible. The chapter also describes the implementation of the AMD monitoring service in a real healthcare scenario.

v. **Scientific Workflows for Healthcare**: Chapter 5 by Giuseppe Tradigo (University of Calabria, Rende, Italy), Patrizia Vizza (University Magna Græcia of Catanzaro, Catanzaro, Italy), Pietro Hiram Guzzi (University Magna Græcia of Catanzaro, Catanzaro, Italy), Andrea Tagarelli (University of Calabria, Rende, Italy), and Pierangelo Veltri (University Magna Græcia of Catanzaro, Catanzaro, Italy) describes how business process engines can be used to enable the composition and the execution of scientific applications in healthcare. The chapter also presents some applications of scientific workflows in the healthcare scenario.

vi. **Metrics for Processes in Healthcare**: Chapter 6 by Jan Mendling (University of Economics and Business, Wien, Austria) introduces the concept of measurement of processes: measurement is important since a precise understanding of the current situation in a quantitative way provides a solid foundation for taking action in terms of improving the process.

vii. **Healthcare Process Analysis**: Chapter 7 by Robert Andrews, Suriadi Suriadi, Moe Wynn, and Arthur Harry Maria ter Hofstede (Queensland University of Technology, Brisbane, Australia) presents a variety of process mining analysis techniques that can be applied to healthcare processes and discusses, for each type of analysis, the data requirements, available tools, and associated caveats.

viii. **Exception Management in Healthcare Processes**: Chapter 8 by Mor Peleg (University of Haifa, Haifa, Israel, and Stanford University, Stanford, CA) and Giuseppe Pozzi (Politecnico di Milano, Milano, Italy) describes how abnormal events, also known as *exceptions*, can be captured and properly managed within a healthcare process model. The chapter also describes a methodology (i.e., a set of steps, criteria, and good practices to be followed at design time) helpful in defining exceptions and in executing them even if the deployed process engine doesn't come with an exception management unit.

ix. **Temporal Clinical Guidelines**: Chapter 9 by Luca Anselma (Università di Torino, Torino, Italy), and Luca Piovesan and Paolo Terenziani (University of Piemonte Orientale "Amedeo Avogadro", Alessandria, Italy) moves from the temporal aspects of clinical information in general, and focuses on the management (representation and reasoning) of temporal phenomena in clinical guidelines.

ACKNOWLEDGMENTS

The editors express their gratitude to Prof. Chris Yang, who offered them the chance of editing a book on the topics of their major research activities, and to Randi Cohen from Taylor and Francis, who constantly encouraged the editors in continuing the project of the book.

The editors also deeply thank all the authors, who contributed in writing their chapters, and who patiently, carefully, and promptly considered all the requests of modifying their contributions.

Verona   *Carlo Combi*
Como   *Giuseppe Pozzi*
Catanzaro   *Pierangelo Veltri*

Editors' Bios

Carlo Combi is Full Professor at the Department of Computer Science, University of Verona, Verona, Italy. He received the Laurea Degree in Electrical Engineering from the Politecnico of Milano in 1987. He received the Ph.D. degree in Biomedical Engineering in 1993. In 1994 and 1995 he was Post-Doc fellow at the Department of Biomedical Engineering of the Politecnico of Milano. From 1987 to 1996 he worked within the research group in Medical Informatics at the Politecnico of Milan. From April 1996 to October 2001, Carlo Combi was with the Department of Mathematics and Computer Science of the University of Udine, Italy, as Assistant Professor.

Since November 2001, he has been with the Department of Computer Science of the University of Verona, Italy. From November 2001 to February 2005, he was Associate Professor of Computer Science; since March 2005, he has been Professor of Computer Science. From October 2007 to September 2012, he served as head of the Department of Computer Science.

From July 2009 to June 2013 he was chair of the Artificial Intelligence in Medicine Society (AIME). He is author, with Elpida Keravnou (University of Cyprus) and Yuval Shahar (Ben-Gurion University of the Negev) of the book *Temporal Information Systems in Medicine*, Springer, 2010. He is author/co-author of more than 120 papers.

Giuseppe Pozzi is Associate Professor at the Dipartimento di Elettronica, Informazione e Bioingegneria of the Politecnico di Milano, Milano, Italy. He received the Laurea Degree in Electrical Engineering from the Politecnico of Milano on June 1986. He received the Ph.D. degree on July 1992. On December 1992 he received a post-doc fellowship from Politecnico di Milano. From October 1st, 1993 to October 31st, 2002 he served as research assistant at the Dipartimento di Elettronica e Informazione of the Politecnico di Milano. Since November 1st, 2002 he has been associate professor at the Dipartimento di Elettronica, Informazione e Bioingegneria of the Politecnico di Milano.

Giuseppe Pozzi's past interests include computer-based analysis of the electrocardiographical signal, multiservice software for medicine, biomedical image compression, classification of public domain medical software, object-oriented and temporal databases for medicine. At present, his interests are mainly focused on active database systems, their application to WorkFlow Management Systems (WfMS), temporal databases, and the management of temporal aspects in WfMSs.

He is author/co-author of more than 100 papers. He co-authored 4 books.

Pierangelo Veltri is Associate Professor of Bioinformatics and Computer Science at the Medicine and Surgical Science Department, University Magna Græcia of Catanzaro, Catanzaro, Italy. He received the Laurea Degree in Computer Engineering from the University of Calabria in April 1998. He received the Ph.D. degree from the University of Orsay (Paris XI) in 2002. He was researcher with european fellows from 1998 to 2002 at INRIA of Rocquencourt, France working in the Verso Database Group, and contract teacher from 2000 to 2002 at University of Paris XIII, teaching database and programming languages. From 2002 to 2011 was assistant professor at University of Catanzaro, teaching application of computer science in medicine degree. He is currently associate professor at the same University. He teaches Database for computer science and biomedical engineering master students and Advanced database and health informatic systems for biomedical engineering postgraduate students.

His past interests include semistructured and spatial databases. His interests are currently focused on data analytics, proteomics and genomics data management, voice and health-related signal analysis, and health informatics. He is author/co-author of more than 100 papers published in international conference proceedings, and more than 30 international journal papers. He has been editor of the ACM Sigbio (special interest group on bioinformatics, computational biology and biomedical informatics) newsletter since 2013.

Contributors

Carlo Combi
University of Verona
Verona, Italy

Giuseppe Pozzi
Politecnico di Milano
Milano, Italy

Pierangelo Veltri
University Magna Græcia of
    Catanzaro
Catanzaro, Italy

Barbara Oliboni
University of Verona
Verona, Italy

Francesca Zerbato
University of Verona
Verona, Italy

Manfred Reichert
University of Ulm
Ulm, Germany

Rüdiger Pryss
University of Ulm
Ulm, Germany

Stefanie Rinderle-Ma
University of Wien
Wien, Austria

Aitor Eguzkitza
Public University of Navarra
Pamplona, Spain

Jesús Daniel Trigo
Public University of Navarra,
    Institute of Smart Cities
Pamplona, Spain

Miguel Martínez-Espronceda
Public University of Navarra
Pamplona, Spain

Luis Serrano
Public University of Navarra,
    Institute of Smart Cities
Pamplona, Spain

José Andonegui
Complejo Hospitalario de Navarra
Pamplona, Spain

Giuseppe Tradigo
University of Calabria
Rende, Italy

Patrizia Vizza
University Magna Græcia of
    Catanzaro
Catanzaro, Italy

Pietro Hiram Guzzi
University Magna Græcia of
    Catanzaro
Catanzaro, Italy

Andrea Tagarelli
University of Calabria
Rende, Italy

xxviii ■ Contributors

Jan Mendling
University of Economics and
    Business
Wien, Austria

Robert Andrews
Queensland University of Technology
Brisbane, Australia

Suriadi Suriadi
Queensland University of Technology
Brisbane, Australia

Moe Wynn
Queensland University of Technology
Brisbane, Australia

Arthur H.M. ter Hofstede
Queensland University of Technology

Brisbane, Australia

Mor Peleg
University of Haifa
Israel
Stanford University, USA

Luca Anselma
University of Torino
Torino, Italy

Luca Piovesan
University of Piemonte Orientale
    "Amedeo Avogadro"
Alessandria, Italy

Paolo Terenziani
University of Piemonte Orientale
    "Amedeo Avogadro"
Alessandria, Italy

I

Fundamentals

CHAPTER 1

Models and Architectures for the Enactment of Healthcare Processes

Carlo Combi

University of Verona, Verona, Italy

Barbara Oliboni

University of Verona, Verona, Italy

Giuseppe Pozzi

Politecnico di Milano, Milano, Italy

Francesca Zerbato

University of Verona, Verona, Italy

CONTENTS

In those foundations which I build upon

W. Shakespeare

T HIS chapter introduces the reader to the world of healthcare process management, focusing on modeling approaches and architectures for process enactment. First, the need and the application of process design and execution in healthcare is discussed. As for process modeling, the fundamentals of the Business Process Model and Notation, which is the leading standard for process design, are provided. Then, the relationships between organization, process and information perspectives involved in process management are discussed by means of examples taken from the clinical domain. The chapter ends with an overview of the architecture of a typical Workflow Management System (WfMS), also known as Business Process Engine (BPE), describing its software modules, components, and functionalities.

1.1 INTRODUCTION

In the last few decades, the need of representing and managing processes in a suitable manner has become central in most organizations, in order to optimize resource allocation, improve the quality of products, increase business outcomes and standardize daily procedures.

Business processes serve this role and are commonly defined as a collection of interrelated activities that are performed in coordination within an organizational and technical environment to achieve a specific business goal [336]. In general, business processes can be described at different levels of detail, depending on the final purposes of the organizational analysis and on the audience they address. On the one hand, processes are employed to describe the strategic objectives of an organization and its relationships with peers. On the other hand, such high-level processes can be decomposed into more detailed sub-processes, in order to define operational business objectives and procedural steps that are specific of the enactment context.

Process models can be used to design, study and understand processes. A process can be graphically represented in terms of one or more process diagrams, by using a process modeling language, that is, a specialized language tailored for process design. A process diagram is the representation of a process, obtained by combining visual constructs, each one having its own well-defined semantics. Usually, a process diagram fosters the representation of those activities that are necessary to achieve a specific (business) goal and defines the temporal and causal constraints between them.

Sometimes process diagrams are employed to capture a readable and understandable overview of the main business procedures: in this scenario, the main purpose of the process diagram is to document the logical ordering of activities and, therefore, no interaction with users is expected. In other circumstances, business process analysis and execution require representations that are able to detail both dynamic and functional aspects of the designed realities. In such setting, process diagrams are formalized in order to act as a template for the creation and control of process instances during process enactment and to suit simulation or complex what-if analyses.

The term *Business Process Management* (BPM) is often used to identify the large umbrella of methods and tools that support the integrated modeling, administration, enactment and analysis of operational business processes. BPM is a crossroads of disparate viewpoints, as it is the result of the interaction between of IT specialists, business and healthcare managers and industrial engineers, who work together for a common interest.

In the BPM community, international societies such as the Workflow Management Coalition (WfMC) [294] and the Object Management Group (OMG) [293] have been establishing and reviewing process related standards that support process modeling, exchange, simulation, and execution.

The WfMC is a nonprofit organization collecting scientists, developers, users, and consultants in the field of Workflow Management Systems. Major achievements of the WfMC are on the development of glossary, terminology, and language standards, having the aim of improving interoperability between existing systems. In particular, the WfMC has defined *workflows* as the automated version of business processes [60]. This definition encompasses criteria to indicate the process starting and termination times, information about individual activities, such as assigned participants, associated IT applications and manipulated data, and procedural rules that allow for workflow management during process enactment.

Besides, the WfMC proposed a reference architecture for a Workflow Management System, that is, a software system that supports the enactment of a business process by coordinating and supporting executing resources (agents) in performing their activities [294]. Typically, a WfMS takes care of scheduling process activities, assigns work to process agents, handles events occurring within the process execution environment, and deals with the data that are generated during process execution. WfMSs also provide administrative and supervisory functions, to support work reassignment or escalation, and to properly manage information regarding the overall system or single process instances. A WfMS, sometimes called a Business Process Engine (BPE), is a kind of Process-Aware Information System [305].

Especially in the context of healthcare organizations, processes play a crucial role in terms of improving care standardization, interaction between care providers belonging to different functional units, and overall operational efficiency. Indeed, healthcare processes are intrinsically complex and multidisciplinary, and procedural aspects are often intertwined with complex decisional activities that require proper information management [64]. Therefore, healthcare providers are attracted by process technology and process-aware systems are becoming part of healthcare organization assets. In healthcare, the application of BPM techniques is fundamental to address manifold aspects of care delivery. Clinicians take part to different healthcare processes in different roles and their work may be carried out in different facilities or departments [74]. Therefore, combining different roles, process participants (agents) and medical activities assigned to them can become quite cumbersome. In addition, clinical working environments are burdened with frequent context switches and unforeseen events and, therefore, a well-defined organizational structure is required to ensure timely and effective care actions. From an organizational standpoint, deep understanding and supervision of healthcare processes can improve the quality of care in terms of cost reduction, resource planning, and coordination among different functional units within an organization, benefit compliance to clinical guidelines and best practices, guarantee high quality of given care.

This chapter is organized as follows: Section 1.2 provides an overview of business process applications in healthcare; Section 1.3 introduces the Business Process Model and Notation standard and presents examples of BPMN-based approaches for healthcare process management and execution; Section 1.4 outlines the organization, process, and information perspectives of BPM in healthcare; Section 1.5 describes the reference architecture for a Workflow Management System, starting from the reference model proposed by the WfMC.

1.2 HEALTHCARE PROCESS MANAGEMENT

In this section, we introduce healthcare process management, focusing on the organizational challenges imposed by clinical and social care working environments.

Among the various application domains suitable to be addressed by a BPM approach, the healthcare domain is probably the most challenging and important application scenario [74]. Healthcare organizations have grown in size and complexity, and integrated care facilities have been established in order to improve health quality and patient satisfaction in terms of accessibility, cost-effectiveness and participation. Consequently, medical treatments have become predominantly multidisciplinary, encompassing also social and daily life aspects. As a result, the processes used to represent healthcare procedures have to consider numerous organizational factors and must be able to harmonize human, physical and informational resources. Evidence suggests that the understanding of healthcare processes and related information, when combined with proper knowledge management, supports clinicians in scheduling and doing their work and in making the right decisions. Indeed, a lot of clinical tasks, such as clinical diagnosis and drug treatment are knowledge-intensive by nature, that is, medical knowledge plays a pivotal role in driving care providers actions and decisions.

A healthcare process, sometimes called a careflow, is any set of activities performed to provide medical care for one or more patients presenting a specific clinical condition. Healthcare processes integrate medical and organizational tasks, and each one of them is performed by one or more process participants (agents), often covering a medical or administrative role in the organization entitled of care provision.

Healthcare process participants can be directly involved in medical activities, as it is for physicians, nurses and medical personnel, they can indirectly contribute to care delivery, as it is the case of laboratory analysts, pharmacologists and social workers, or they can be responsible for executing different organizational tasks, typically related to logistics, security, IT (Information Technology), and resource administration.

In hospitals, physicians and nurses are often loaded with various and heterogeneous tasks and responsibilities. Besides, multiple organizational roles can be assigned to the same professional figure: a physician that is also the director of a hospital department, must also take care of administrative duties beside medical activities. Moreover, different degrees of expertise contribute to specialize the medical personnel and, consequently, specific hierarchical interactions are defined between roles.

Patient care is often a result of a synergistic interaction between care providers belonging to different functional units and having complimentary medical and organizational expertise and experience. Physicians have to decide which are the most appropriate interventions to schedule, which is their preferred order, and which are the activities to carry out in case of unexpected changes in treatment outcomes. Such delicate, but crucial decisions, typically based on evidence-based knowledge, clinical best-practice or examination results, and guidelines (see Chapter 9), affect the outcomes of the overall care process. Moreover, some medical tasks such as diagnosis and treatment, are inherently complex, thus requiring proper information management and constant coordination in terms of temporal scheduling and resource management.

Such a heterogeneous scenario requires the standardization of patient management and care delivery procedures, and of their decisional counterpart, to guarantee proper information and knowledge sharing. Reaching a standard care plan definition is the first step towards ensuring that all the patients presenting the same clinical conditions benefit from the same care, which must respond to disparate and individual needs and must be compliant with organizational and social objectives. Besides, healthcare processes have to consider best practices as a reference, are often subjected to local policies and regulations and must conform to clinical standards.

In this setting, business process management techniques support the incremental and information-aware design of healthcare processes.

For example, let us consider the following clinical scenario, describing the typical procedure for detecting catheter-related infections involving a patient that is hospitalized in the Intensive Care Unit (ICU), adapted from the well-known IDSA guideline [163].

Example 1.1 *Venous catheters are used in the ICU for the treatment of critically ill patients, in order to permit hemodynamic monitoring and allow reliable access for medications. These catheters are required in the management of life–saving treatments, but, unfortunately, they are often associated with in-*

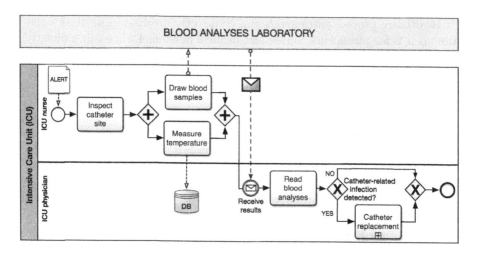

FIGURE 1.1 Simple healthcare process representing detection and confirmation of catheter-related bloodstream infections in Intensive Care Units.

fections, thromboses, and mechanical complications. Trained ICU nurses are usually in charge of catheter placing and monitoring.

Whenever a catheter-related infection is suspected, an ICU nurse inspects the catheter site to see if it requires cleaning and then he or she draws blood samples for culturing, while verifying the patient's temperature. The drawn blood samples are collected and transported to the laboratory by a person that belongs to the hospital logistic system. Then, a lab analyst takes care of culturing and analyzing blood, in order to see if there is evidence of a catheter-related bloodstream infection and to identify the pathogen responsible for it. Blood testing results are sent back to the ICU physician attending the patient, who reads them and decides if the catheter must be replaced. Catheter replacement is a multi-step procedure, requiring specific clinical indications and proper timing.

A possible graphical representation of the healthcare process corresponding to the described clinical scenario is depicted in Figure 1.1, by using the Business Process Model and Notation (BPMN 2.0) [291], the leading standard in the frame of business processes and workflow modeling languages, introduced in Section 1.3.

The viewpoint chosen for the representation is that of the medical personnel working in the intensive care unit and, therefore, the portrayed steps are executed by ICU clinicians. By contrast, the involvement of the patient is not represented in this healthcare process.

1.3 THE BUSINESS PROCESS MODEL NOTATION – BPMN

The Business Process Model and Notation (BPMN 2.0) [291] was proposed by the Object Management Group [293] as a graphical language for process representation. The standard notation is meant to support the design of business processes in a way that is understood by business users of any degree of expertise, starting from the developers in charge of implementing the technology that will enact those processes, to the business managers responsible for monitoring them. BPMN was proposed with the aim of improving business understanding and setting up a standard communication means for organizations to share procedures.

BPMN fosters process representation at two levels of abstraction. On the one hand, the notation supports the definition of executable processes, which behave according to a formal semantics. On the other hand, BPMN can be used to design expressive diagrams that are used for organizational modeling and for documentation purposes. Thus, information needed for execution and details that are relevant for process automation are not included in this case.

BPMN provides three kinds of diagrams, each one delivering suitable information to a specific audience. *Processes* represent the workflow internal to an organization. *Collaborations* outline the interactions between two or more business entities, which are usually process participants or organizational units. *Choreographies* define the expected behavior that participants have to observe within a collaboration.

In BPMN, a *process diagram* is defined as a set of activities or events, connected by a sequence flow, that denotes their ordering relations and whose branching is controlled by gateways. The sequence flow is traversed by a token, that enables process elements and interacts with them according to the behavior of the considered element.

Activities represent work that is carried out during process execution. Tasks are atomic units of work that cannot be broken down to a finer level of abstraction, whereas sub-processes are compound activities whose internal details are modeled using other BPMN elements. Graphically, a task is represented as a rectangle with rounded corners and labeled with the name of the activity. In Figure 1.1, Inspect catheter site, Draw blood samples, Measure temperature, and Read blood analyses are examples of tasks. Sub-processes can be graphically represented in two ways. Collapsed sub-processes are depicted as tasks, with a small " +" sign in the lower-center of the shape that indicates that the activity has a lower level of detail. Expanded sub-processes have an enlarged border that encloses all the visible internal elements. In Figure 1.1, Catheter replacement is a more complex procedure and it is represented through a collapsed sub-process, whose detailed steps remain hidden in the representation.

Events represent facts that occur instantaneously during process execution, such as the receipt of a message or the expiration of a deadline. Graphically, they are depicted as circles, which might contain a marker to diversify the kind of event trigger. Depending on their triggering behavior, events can either "catch" a trigger or "throw" a result, which is possibly caught by another event. Events are also classified according to their position in the process flow. Start events initiate a process instance, whereas end events conclude it. Intermediate events are located at any point in-between start and end events. In Figure 1.1 the intermediate message event `Receive results` is used to represent that the process waits for the results of the blood analyses, sent by the `Blood analyses laboratory`. Events can also be attached to the boundary of an activity to capture exceptions occurring during activity execution. Interrupting intermediate events interrupt the task they are tied to, while non-interrupting ones initiate a parallel exception path.

Gateways are elements in the process used to control the divergence and convergence of the sequence flow, according to data-based conditions or event occurrence. Graphically, they are depicted as diamonds with an internal marker that differentiates their routing behavior. The "+" symbol is used for parallel branching, while the "×" marker identifies an exclusive gateway, i.e., a point in the process where a condition must be evaluated in order to choose one path out of more. In Figure 1.1, the branching point labeled with the question `Catheter-related infection detected?` represents an exclusive gateway, which drives the process flow according to the answer provided by the preceding `Read blood analysis` task.

BPMN defines a few data-aware elements to ease the representation of data involved in a process. Volatile data is represented through *data objects*, which are visually displayed as documents with a bent angle, whereas persistent data sources are modeled as *data stores*. In Figure 1.1 the `Alert` is a data object that initiates the process, while the `DB` represents the ICU health record, belonging to the hospital information system.

Pools and lanes are containers used to identify process participants and roles. Pools represent organizations, while lanes sub-partition the organization into functional units. The participants to the process of Figure 1.1 are the ICU nurse and the ICU physician, whose work is represented in detail, and the lab analyst, whose role is modeled only through interactions with the ICU medical personnel. By contrast, the involvement of the patient is not represented, as the patient is not depicted within the healthcare process model. In particular, a pool is used to represent the `Intensive Care Unit` (`ICU`) department, which is partitioned into two lanes, one for the `ICU Nurse` and the other for the `ICU Physician`. External participants, such as the `Blood Analyses Laboratory`, are represented as collapsed pools, that is, their inner details are hidden.

Interactions between pools are represented through a *message flow*, which denotes communication and possible exchange of physical objects across different functional units. It is depicted as a dashed line, having an empty circle as a start and an empty arrow as an end. Message flows are usually labeled with the content of the exchanged message. In Figure 1.1 the results of the blood cultures are sent from the analyses laboratory to the ICU physician through a message flow.

1.3.1 Applications of BPMN in Healthcare

As for BPMN-based approaches in healthcare, most research proposals focus on extending the notation core to improve expressiveness with respect to healthcare design, often introducing methodological approaches [95] that are tailored for specific clinical circumstances.

In [191], the authors recognize the value of using BPMN in the healthcare domain, and introduce an extension to the notation meta-model having the aim of incorporating role information and easing assignment of tasks. A major BPMN extension developed to systematically support the design of clinical pathways is discussed in [37]. A clinical pathway is a task-oriented description of a clinical procedure that outlines the essential steps and decisions to be taken for offering optimal care to patients presenting a specific clinical condition. This proposal, named BPMN4CP, includes concepts from the context of clinical pathways in order to enhance evidence-based decisional activities related to the considered domain. Diagnosis, support, and therapy tasks are added and data objects are differentiated according to the type of document they represent, such as patient files, results from lab tests, or treatment contracts. In [340], the conceptual modeling of clinical pathways for catheter-related bloodstream infections in ICUs is addressed, by considering also process-related information and temporal constraints. In [64] a methodology for supporting the integrated design of BPMN healthcare processes and clinical decisions is presented. Clinical decisions are represented with the help of the Decision Model and Notation, a standard developed under the OMG umbrella to complement BPMN for decision modeling and execution. The information-aware methodology is applied to the modeling of care pathways for patients affected by Chronic Obstructive Pulmonary Disease within a regional context. Finally, in [253] the design of two clinical pathways for colon and rectum carcinoma is carried out within a pilot project, with the aim of evaluating the benefits of using BPMN for modeling of structured medical procedures. According to the outcomes of the work, BPMN can be successfully applied to the interprofessional analysis and design of medical and organizational processes. Besides, it supports teaching and training of the medical personnel, as well as it enhances patient information sharing and quality management.

1.4 MODELING PERSPECTIVES IN BPM

In this section, we give an overview of the interaction between healthcare processes, their related information, and the organizational resources involved in process enactment and management.

Process, information, and organization are intertwined; in BPM in general, as well as in healthcare process management, we deal with any of the three perspectives.

The organization perspective focuses on the representation of the organization where the healthcare process is enacted. The process perspective is related to the definition of a structure for the managed healthcare process, and the information perspective deals with the representation of the information that is related to a specific application domain, thus encompassing informational aspects related to the organization, its processes, and applications. In Figure 1.2, we show the three dimensions involved in healthcare process management and their relationships.

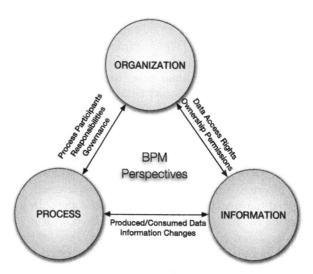

FIGURE 1.2 Relationships between BPM perspectives.

The *organization* dimension describes process participants (agents), their roles and interactions. Sometimes this perspective is also called the *resource perspective*. A resource is anyone or anything that is involved in the performance of a process activity, such as a process participant, i.e., an individual person, a software system or a piece of equipment. Process activities are assigned to participants according to specific criteria, which take into account their skills, their availability in time, and their responsibilities. The latter often depend on the role a participant plays in the considered process, which does not necessarily coincide with the role he or she has within the organizational hierarchy. Participants can also cover multiple roles in the process.

In general, roles are likely to be defined independently from process participants and can refer to one or more process activities. Role definition allows one to maintain the process definition separate from process participants and to redistribute workload among available resources in case of process bottlenecks. Participants can be grouped according to their role and a worklist can be shared between group components.

For instance, let us consider a generic process of patient discharge from the Emergency Room. Whenever a patient is ready to leave the emergency department, a discharge summary must be authored and signed by the attending physician, in order to help clinicians outside the hospital understand what happened to the patient during hospitalization. Often, the discharge summary is the only form of communication that accompanies the patient to the next setting of care. For this reason, high-quality discharge summaries are essential to promote patient safety during transitions between hospital and home care settings.

Example 1.2 *In the hospital Emergency Room, the task of authoring the discharge summary is assigned to a specific person, that is, Doctor Leeds. As Doctor Leeds must take care of all patient discharges, when many patients have to be dismissed, he is overloaded with work and patients complain about discharge delays and poor quality summaries. Besides, whenever Doctor Leeds is involved in an emergency case or he takes a day off, no one can be discharged. As a consequence, the emergency department tends to become more and more crowded. In addition, a few patients have to be readmitted in the hospital, because their safety was compromised by inaccurate discharge summaries. However, if the authoring of the discharge summary is assigned to the role "ER physician", any colleague of Doctor Leeds is also entitled to dismiss patients and, thus, both the timing and quality of the overall discharge process can be improved.*

A healthcare organization can be represented as an organigram, sometimes referred to as an organizational chart. Every hospital, small or large, has its own internal organizational structure that promotes efficient department management. An excerpt of a hospital organigram is depicted in Figure 1.3.

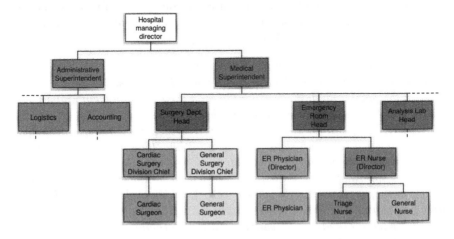

FIGURE 1.3 Excerpt of a hospital organigram.

In the proposed representation, roles are organized in a vertical structure, where the top layers correspond to the figures having higher degrees of decision-making authority and responsibility. In detail, the hospital managing director oversees both administrative and medical areas, which in turn are directed by the corresponding superintendents. Examples of hospital administrative departments are logistics, accounting, security, and informational services, whereas medical departments and wards are usually divided according to the kind of provided care and of associated treatment facilities. In particular, in the emergency room both ER physicians and ER nurses refer to a director and the latter are further specialized into triage nurses and general nurses. Triage nurses are responsible for initiating emergency care, and therefore, they receive special training to be able to develop quick and effective decision-making skills.

The *process* dimension describes the structure of the managed process, by means of a process modeling language, as for instance BPMN, used for designing the process diagram.

In a process diagram, temporal and causality relationships are defined between activities with the help of a process control flow. Elements that allow the branching and merging of the process flow are also part of the process representation. Process participants and roles can also be defined. A participant can be either an entity, such as a hospital department, or an agent, such as a physician or a nurse, which controls or is responsible for the execution of part of the process. In a process diagram, information consumed and produced by the process can be included, and additional data, such as governance rules or compliance guidelines, can be defined to constrain process execution. Usually data flow through the process in the form of a variable, a shared data source, or within a workflow-related document.

As a simple example of healthcare process, consider the following clinical scenario describing the assessment and treatment in the emergency room of a patient with suspected appendicitis [268, 287].

Example 1.3 *A patient is admitted to the Emergency Room (ER) after having experienced acute abdominal pain and fever. First, Miss White, the triage nurse at the admission desk, assesses the conditions of the patient and decides when the patient will be seen by one of the ER physicians available. Patient prioritization is based on a severity index: the triage nurse assigns to the patient an urgency level, which is a measure of how long a patient can safely wait for medical examination and treatment.*

All the information regarding the reported signs and symptoms, acquired during triage, is registered in an ER report, which is later handled to the attending physician during the physical examination of the patient.

After having examined the patient, the ER physician, Mr. Leeds, suspects appendicitis. Therefore, he requests further laboratory exams to be performed and schedules a surgical evaluation. If both the surgeon and the outcomes of the laboratory analyses confirm the inflammation of the appendix, Mr. Leeds diagnoses appendicitis and proceeds with planning the surgical intervention.

Otherwise, the physician suggests the use of diagnostic imaging techniques, such as CT scanning, for further investigations.

The corresponding BPMN process diagram is shown in Figure 1.4. The definition of process roles in the process of Figure 1.4 is highlighted in the previously introduced organigram of Figure 1.3 through the use of the same colors for the roles depicted in the organigram and the process lanes. Interaction with external participants, that is, the clinical laboratory and the surgery department is represented by using a message flow.

As for process-related data, both the ER report and the lab analyses represent worflow-related documents that are exchanged between process activities and participants, respectively. By contrast, the Medical Record (MR) of the patient is modeled through a data store that symbolizes the part of the hospital information system involved in the process. Complex business rules and compliance guidelines are not explicitly displayed in BPMN processes. In the considered scenario, examples of this kind of context-related knowledge are: The fact that the surgical evaluation has to preferably be performed by a senior surgical resident [268]; the triage rules that relate the gravity of the patient with the acuity level that determines when the physical examination is scheduled.

In BPMN, another way to represent communication between different process participants can be achieved through the use of choreographies. A choreography is a type of diagram that formalizes the way business participants coordinate their interactions through the exchange of information in the form of messages [291]. A choreography diagram describes the order of message exchanges between multiple participants and it consists of choreography activities, which are special kinds of tasks and sub-processes, and common BPMN elements, such as gateways and events, that are used in the same way as they are in process diagrams.

Choreography activities, i.e., tasks or sub-processes, represent one or more interactions between at least two process participants. A choreography task is depicted as a BPMN process task with a band labeled with the name of the activity and at least two other bands, each one containing the name of a task participant. The band of the participant that initiates the interaction must be unfilled. Choreographies do not have a mechanism for representing data.

Each choreography is initiated by a message and the initiating participant of each choreography task must be involved in the previous choreography activity. Initiating and return messages are connected to choreography tasks through a dashed line. Initiating messages are unfilled, whereas return messages that respond to other message requests are shaded with a darker fill.

A simple choreography corresponding to the interactions of the ER physician with both the surgery department and the clinical laboratory is represented in Figure 1.5. The ER physician initiates both the Surgery consult and the Laboratory analyses choreography tasks by respectively sending an initiating message Request consult to the surgeon and a message Request

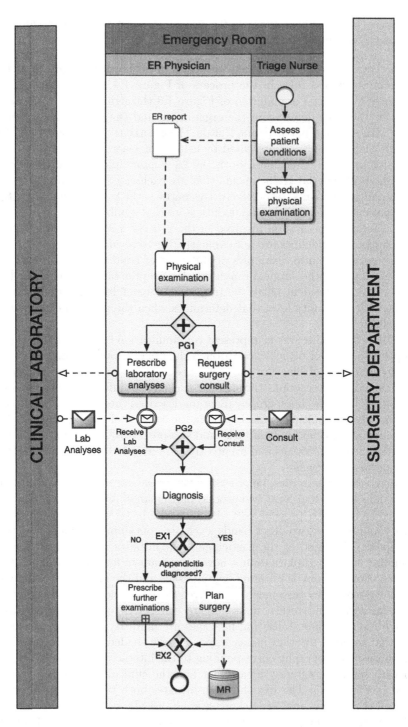

FIGURE 1.4 Example of BPMN process diagram for the assessment and treatment of a patient diagnosed with appendicitis in an emergency room.

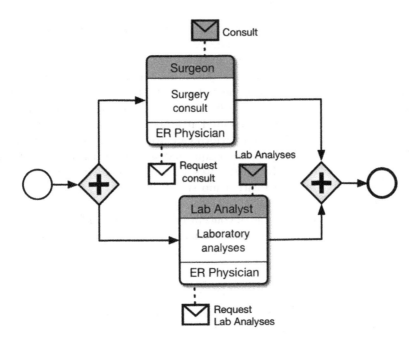

FIGURE 1.5 BPMN choreography model for the interactions between the ER physician, the surgeon, and the lab analyst.

Lab Analyses to the lab analyst. The corresponding return messages Consult and Lab Analyses are received by the physician.

The *information* perspective considers data associated with the specific application domain, data related to the organizational and process structures, and both current and historical data related to process execution [67]. More specifically, three kinds of data can be distinguished. *Process control data* are internal data, managed by the WfMS, and aimed at process management. *Process relevant data* data are generated and produced during process execution and are fundamental for process enactment. Finally, *application data* are managed by domain-specific applications and may not be accessible by the process.

Among the existing approaches suitable to be used as a basis for a unified view of data, the Entity Relationship (E-R) data model is widely adopted in information system design and software engineering.

The Entity-Relationship data model allows one to give a conceptual description of the information of interest for a specific application context, representing the structure of the involved data, their relationships and significant attributes within an *E-R Diagram*. Historically, they have been used to describe the conceptual structure of databases [87].

An *entity* is something that can be distinctly identified, such as a specific person, object or event, about which information is stored. Graphically, an entity is depicted as a rectangle, labeled with its name. A *relationship* is an association among entities and represents how entities share information. Graphically, a relationship is portrayed as a diamond, labeled with its name. In some cases, relationships can be reflexive, that is, they can be related to the same entity with itself. *Attributes* are used to detail entities and/or relationships. Attributes are represented attached to entities or relationships through a line ending with a circle, which can either be empty or filled. Some attributes, called key attributes, are unique and are used as the distinguishing characteristic of the entity. Key attributes are represented with a filled circle. Finally, the *cardinality* of a relationship specifies how many instances of an entity relate to one instance of another entity.

Figure 1.6 shows an example of conceptual representation for the management of data related to the application domain of the clinical process depicted in Figure 1.4.

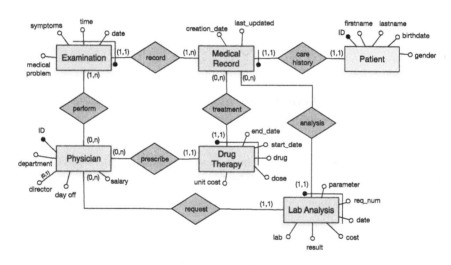

FIGURE 1.6 Entity-Relationship (E-R) diagram representing part of a hospital information system related to the management of patients' examinations and treatment.

In particular, the E-R diagram of Figure 1.6 outlines the information that is relevant for the execution of the aforementioned process and, in general, for other procedures that involve the patient medical record. Specifically, the considered clinical scenario requires the management of information about patients and their health records, and of the related examinations, drug therapies, and lab analyses, all of which are prescribed by one or more physicians.

Example 1.4 *Whenever a physician working in the emergency room requests some lab analyses for a given patient, these must contain a request number,*

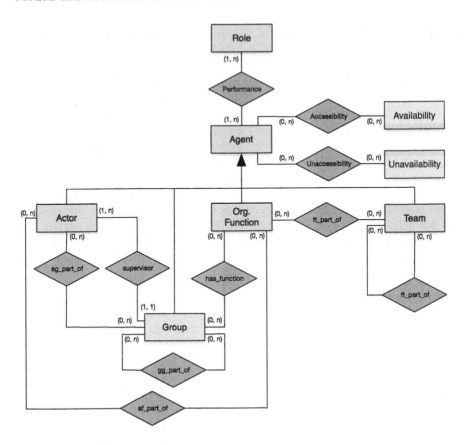

FIGURE 1.7 Entity-Relationship (E-R) diagram representing the main entities involved in the organization (attributes are omitted).

the execution date, and the name of the analyzed parameter, with the relative measured value and total cost. The name of the laboratory is also recorded and each performed analysis is directly attached to the patient medical record.

In Figure 1.6, the entity **Lab Analysis** is uniquely identified by the medical record, the parameter, the request number, and the date, all of which are represented as attributes. Additional attributes are the cost of the analysis, the result and the laboratory in which it is performed. With respect of the discussed data-aware elements of the BPMN process depicted in Figure 1.4, it is assumed that the requested laboratory analyses are recorded in the patient medical record, together with the surgical evaluation, and the various physical examinations performed in the emergency room. A tabular representation of the **Lab Analysis** entity is given in Table 1.1.

Data regarding the structure of the previously discussed process and organization perspectives can also be included in the organization informational patrimony. An E-R representation of the resources involved in an organization is depicted in Figure 1.7. This information perspective of the organization relates (process) roles with agents that are the persons or systems that are assigned a process task to execute. Agents can have specific availability times and can be further discerned in actors, groups, functions, or teams. Actors are individual processing units, of a human or automatized (mechanical or electronic) type. Groups are classes of actors, defined according to common features such as their assignment to a specific project or to a geographical site. Functions define classes either of groups, of actors, or of a team, having common features, based on what they can perform or on what they are enabled to perform. Finally, teams are lists of functions which rely on a part of the organizational structure. A team may include duplicates, e.g., a project team may include one general manager, one technical manager, and two researchers.

Information sources can be accessed by human resources according to their rights. Usually, in large organizations, one or more information systems are used to collect all the information that is used to feed various internal client applications. Application users can operate on subsets of the overall informational patrimony, depending on their role and final objective. Process participants are also application users and, thus, they are allowed to visualize and modify information according to their data access rights, which are not necessarily tied to the role they cover in the process and in the organization. A central concept in relational database theory is that of *database view*. Roughly speaking, a view is a mechanism that allows showing only the subsets of the stored data that are of interest for a specific user or goal. One of the uses of views is to restrict access to a data source, yet allowing users to access data according to their rights and the final use of such information.

Example 1.5 *To confirm the diagnosis of appendicitis, Doctor Leeds requests the following lab analyses for the patient: complete blood count, which includes various parameters, such as white and red blood counts, and C-reactive protein (CRP). Miss Ross, the ER nurse director, has to ensure sure that every patient receives analyses results within time. For this reason, she is allowed to see the list of analyses that have been requested for any patient, that is request number, parameters, time, and date, but she does not have access to the resulting measured values. Mr. Marple works in the accounting department. He does not participate in the care process directly, but instead he takes care of analyzing the monthly costs of all the analyses requested within the hospital. Therefore, he has access to the total cost of each performed analysis, but he cannot see any clinical information, due to privacy restrictions.*

A database instance corresponding to the section of the patient medical record concerning analyses requests is shown in Table 1.1. The conceptual description of the database can be seen in Figure 1.6. Mr. Marple's view of the analyses requests is limited to the costs of the analyses, as summarized in Table 1.2.

TABLE 1.1 Example of instantiated database table for medical analyses.

MR	Req_num	Date	Parameter	Lab	Result	Cost
001	2023WBC	10-05-16	white blood count (WBC)	L1	$10,6 * 10^9 L$	€2,98
001	2023RBC	10-05-16	red blood count (RBC)	L1	$4,7 * 10^{12} L$	€2,92
001	2023Plt	10-05-16	platelet count (Plt)	L1	$200 * 10^9 L$	€4,65
001	2023HGB	10-05-16	hemoglobin	L1	$130 g/L$	€2,85
001	2023HCT	10-05-16	hematocrit (HCT)	L1	40%	€4,50
001	2023CRP	10-05-16	C-reactive protein (CRP)	L1	$100 mg/dL$	€10,73
020	0098HIAA	22-07-16	Urinary 5-HIAA (HIAA)	L2	$8 mg/24h$	€68,85
450	4788WBC	30-10-16	white blood count (WBC)	L1	$7,4 \ 10^9 L$	€2,98

TABLE 1.2 Mr. Marple's view of the medical analyses instantiated table.

Req_num	Cost
2023WBC	€2,98
2023RBC	€2,92
2023Plt	€4,65
2023HGB	€2,85
2023HCT	€4,50
2023CRP	€10,73
0098HIAA	€68,85
4788WBC	€2,98

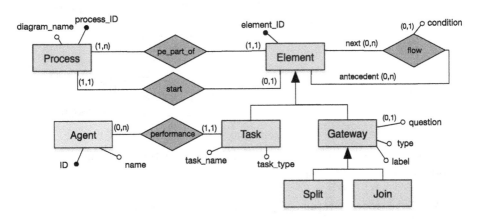

FIGURE 1.8 Entity-Relationship (E-R) diagram representing the main elements of a BPMN process diagram.

Similarly, the E-R diagram of Figure 1.8 describes the main elements used in a process diagram, the relationships allowed between them, and a few basic attributes that can be specified to support process definition and execution. Process agents correspond to the agents of the organization model of Figure 1.7.

In general, several instances or cases of a process can be run, each one owning its specific data [67]. Current process execution data are collected during process enactment, whereas historical data describe past cases managed by the process execution system. Such a system reads the process definition and schedules the activities according to their defined order and assigned agents. An example of an E-R diagram summarizing the main elements needed for process execution is depicted in Figure 1.9. Case History is uniquely identified by an ID and by the process name, and has one agent that is responsible for it. Task History is uniquely distinguished by the case identifier and by the identifier of task that is executed. A task belonging to a process case can be executed by one or more agents.

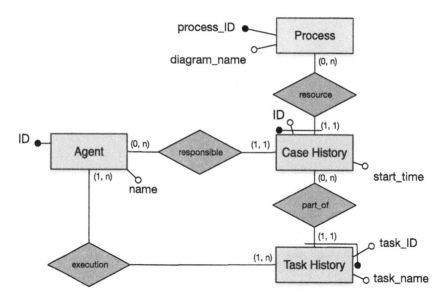

FIGURE 1.9 Entity-Relationship (E-R) diagram representing data related to process execution.

A tabular representation of process execution, based on case and task history, is provided in Table 1.3, where underlined attributes are identifiers for the represented entities.

TABLE 1.3 Example of process execution.

Process

Process ID	Diagram Name	Start Task
P01	ER appendicitis	AssessPatientCondition

Tasks

Task ID	Process ID	TaskName	Role
TEA001	P01	AssessPatientCondition	TriageNurse
TEA002	P01	SchedulePhysicalExamination	TriageNurse
TEA003	P01	PhysicalExamination	ER Physician
TEA004	P01	PrescribeLaboratoryAnalyses	ER Physician
TEA005	P01	RequestSurgeryConsult	ER Physician
TEA006	P01	Diagnosis	ER Physician
TEA007	P01	PrescribeFurtherExaminations	ER Physician
TEA008	P01	PlanSurgery	ER Physician

Gateways

Gateway ID	Process ID	Label	Type	Question
GEA001	ER appendicitis	PG1	ParallelGateway	–
GEA002	ER appendicitis	PG2	ParallelGateway	–
GEA003	ER appendicitis	EX1	ExclusiveGateway	"Appendicitis Diagnosed?"
GEA004	ER appendicitis	EX2	ExclusiveGateway	–

Agents

Agent ID	Name	Role	Availability
MR	Miss Ross	Triage Nurse Director	Mon-Fri
MW	Miss White	Triage Nurse	Sat-Sun
DL	Doctor Leeds	ER Physician	Everyday
DP	Doctor Paul	ER Physician	Fri-Sun
DC	Doctor Carey	ER Physician	Everyday

Case History

Case ID	SchemaName	Responsible
ER01	ER_appendicitis	DL

Task History

Case ID	Task ID	TaskName	State	Agent
ER01	TEA001	AssessPatientCondition	Completed	MM
ER01	TEA002	SchedulePhysicalExamination	Completed	MM
ER01	TEA003	PhysicalExamination	Activated	DL

1.5 WORKFLOW ARCHITECTURES

Workflow Management Systems (WfMS), sometimes referred to as Business Process Engines (BPEs), can boost organizational competitiveness by increasing process efficiency and resource sharing. Basically, such systems support both the management of activities that have to be performed by human resources and the automation of other service tasks. Traditionally, WfMSs present a clear separation between process design time and run time. During process design, the structure of a process is defined, usually with the help of a graphical tool, whereas the enactment of process instances is carried out by a workflow (or process) engine.

The *workflow engine* is the central component of a WfMS and takes care of assigning each process activity to the agent entitled to execute it. A workflow engine handles multiple process and task instances, defined by means of a process diagram. Automated tasks are executed directly by the engine, which transfers data between invoked applications involved in the process. By contrast, when dealing with tasks that require human intervention, the engine relies on client applications that allow agents to interact with the process and to execute work through graphical user interfaces. The basic concept related to client applications is the *worklist*, containing the work items that are to be executed by a specific agent [81].

During process enactment, the WfMS must also provide a means to monitor the state of every running process, to measure its performance, and to set up measures to react to critical situations.

Standardization efforts have been devoted to the specification of a reference architecture for a WfMS. The most known reference model is the *Workflow Reference Architecture* proposed by the WfMC [294] and depicted in Figure 1.10.

The architectural model was intentionally proposed to give an overview of the main components of a WfMS and of their interactions, abstracting from the specific technologies that can be used for implementing the system in a real world scenario.

At the heart of the workflow reference architecture lies the workflow enactment service, encapsulating one or more workflow engines, and five functional interfaces that facilitate information exchange and interoperability between different systems and the workflow enactment service. For each interface, the architectural model describes which is the business goal that is achieved, how it operates, and, in some cases, one or more interface bindings are provided to specify how an interface can be implemented using a particular language or technology.

The *workflow enactment service* consists of one or more workflow engines, responsible for generating and executing a process instance starting from a given process model or definition. A workflow enactment service may consist of several workflow engines, for instance, when it is implemented in a distributed manner [81]. A workflow engine creates work items based on the

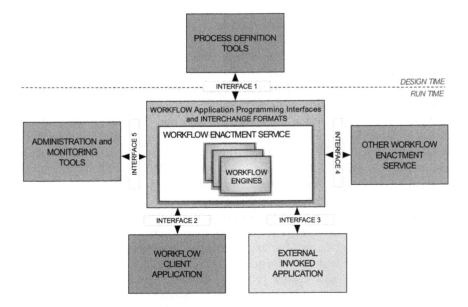

FIGURE 1.10 WfMC Workflow Reference Architecture. The central workflow enactment service interacts with external invoked applications through the five interfaces. *Interface 1* formalizes the separation between process design and run times.

process definition, matches the capabilities of agents, such as skills and experience, with the requirements of each task, and allocates work items to workflow users through the use of worklists. The workflow engine is also responsible for recording data about task and process instances, the so-called task history and case history.

A process definition is a representation of what is intended to happen in the process, in terms of steps and decisions, processing times, and resource assignment and variability. A process definition can be instantiated several times by a workflow engine, and multiple instances may be concurrently active.

Interface 1 in Figure 1.10 supports the exchange, that is, import and export, of process definitions between process modeling tools and the workflow enactment service. A variety of different tools may be used to model, analyze, describe, and document a business process. Modeling tools differ according to the level of support they provide for graphical process modeling, specification of implementation details and resource management. The main objective of this interface is to standardize the representation format of business processes defined with different vendor-specific tools and specified through different languages. In addition, the interface also defines a formal separation between the design and run time environments, enabling a process definition, generated by a design-time modeling tool, to be used as input to a number of different run time products.

Interface 1 is specified by the WfMC as a common meta-model for describing process definition, the XML Process Definition Language (XPDL) which is integrated with an XML schema for the interchange of process definitions [339].

XPDL is the serialization format for BPMN, and both languages address the same modeling problem from different perspectives. On the one side, XPDL provides an XML file format that can be used to interchange process models between tools. On the other side, BPMN provides a graphical notation to facilitate human communication between healthcare users and technical users, of complex care processes.

XPDL is a process definition model that allows defining the main process entities, their attributes and relationships in a common representation and provides a textual grammar for expressing the process definition structure, process-related applications, information contents, and execution properties.

For example, let us consider process activities. An activity is a piece of work, performed by a combination of human resources and/or computer applications. In order to support activity execution, additional information, such as the activity starting and ending times, expected duration, priority, and data usage, can be specified within a process definition. However, as many of such details are only needed during process execution, BPMN diagrams can be drawn and interchanged at design-time without including this information. Conversely, when a process activity is scheduled for execution, the workflow engine reads the corresponding XPDL description, executes the rules associated to the XPDL definition, and assigns the activity to the selected agent.

As an example, let us refer to the BPMN process of Figure 1.4 and let us consider the two tasks Schedule physical examination, performed by a triage nurse and the following Physical examination, performed by an ER physician. An excerpt of the XPDL process definition for the mentioned pair of connected activities is represented in Figure 1.11.

The XPDL Activity node corresponding to task Schedule physical examination is highlighted in blue, whereas the definition of task Physical examination is highlighted in red. Beside their name, each activity is identified by a unique ID, and by the attributes CompletionQuantity and StartQuantity, which set the number of tokens that are expected to complete and, respectively, to start, the activity. The Implementation property allows one defining the kind of expected implementation for the considered activity. Activities not having implementation are presumed to be implemented by manual procedures.

The particular resources that are assigned to perform an activity are specified through the attribute Performers, which links the activity to the set of resources which may be allocated to it. In Figure 1.11, activity performers are highlighted in purple and they correspond to the process lanes. Activities are related to one another via sequence flows (transitions). Each transition has three elementary properties, the from-activity, the to-activity, and the condition under which the transition is made. Finally, the nodes `NodeGraphicsInfo` and `ConnectorGraphicsInfo` include graphic information, which is tool-dependent and it is necessary to provide the graphical portability of the definition.

Interface 2 in Figure 1.10 defines the interaction of the workflow enactment service with various client applications in order to facilitate portability and reuse of the latter with different WfMSs (BPEs). Workflow client applications allow agents to execute the assigned activities that are grouped in a *worklist*, possibly shared between various participants. Interface 2 is specified as a series of workflow Application Programming Interfaces (APIs) that concern the presentation of the worklist, the selection of work items, and the notification of workflow participants in the event of overdue activities and/or processes.

With respect to the considered clinical context, we can suppose that triage in ER is performed with the support of a computerized application. This application allows scheduling physical examinations according to the patient acuity level, assessed by the triage nurse, and it informs ER physicians whenever a patient requires examination. Often, in healthcare, such applications are based on medical vocabularies and ontologies to facilitate data sharing among different hospital units.

Interface 3 in Figure 1.10 provides a standard framework that supports the integration and the communication of the workflow enactment service with domain-specific applications or services that serve a defined goal. This concerns mostly the passing of data between the workflow engine and a remote application, and the corresponding handling of application return codes. Invoked applications may be located on the same platform as the workflow engine or on a separate network-accessible platform. Interface 3 is based on a set of basic application programming interfaces that support common mechanisms for connecting, disconnecting, and calling to heterogeneous third–party software environments.

An example of invoked application for the process of Figure 1.4 could be the database management system and the related data transformation procedures invoked to record the planning of the surgical intervention in the patient medical record. Similarly, it is plausible that an invoked service would allow the planned intervention to be added to the surgery department electronic scheduling system, so that surgeons can see the planned interventions.

Together, Interfaces 2 and 3 form the core of the Workflow API (WAPI) specification, which realizes the communication between the workflow enactment service and external systems. Whereas Interface 2 defines the invocations of a workflow participant that demands a work item from a workflow engine for further processing, Interface 3 specifies the invocations of a workflow engine that demands another application to execute operations [81].

Interface 4 eases process automation across multiple heterogeneous workflow enactment services. It is specified by means of a set of process interoper-

```
<?xml version="1.0" encoding="UTF-8"?>
<Package xmlns="http://www.wfmc.org/2008/XPDL2.1" xmlns:xpdExt="http://www.tibco.com/
XPD/xpdExtension1.0.0" Language="English" Id="canvas">
  <ConformanceClass GraphConformance="NON-BLOCKED"
BPMNModelPortabilityConformance="STANDARD" />
  <Script Type="http://www.w3.org/TR/XPath" />
<WorkflowProcesses>
<WorkflowProcess Adhoc="false" AdhocOrdering="Parallel"
EnableInstanceCompensation="false" ProcessType="None" Status="None"
SuppressJoinFailure="false"
Id="ER_AppendicitisTreatment_02_process">
  <Pools>
    <Pool BoundaryVisible="true" MainPool="false"
          Process="ER_AppendicitisTreatment_02_process" Orientation="HORIZONTAL"
          Id="ER_1" Name="Emergency Room">
      <Lanes>
        <Lane ParentPool="ER_1" Id="ERPyhs_1" Name="ER Physician">
        </Lane>
        <Lane ParentPool="ER_1" Id="TriageNurse_1" Name="Triage nurse">
        </Lane>
      </Lanes>
    </Pool>
  </Pools>
    <Activities>
      <Activity CompletionQuantity="1" StartQuantity="1" Id="id_SchedPhysExam_01"
              Name="Schedule physical examination">
        <Implementation>
          <No />
        </Implementation>
        <Performers>
        <Performer> TriageNurse_1 </Performer>
        </Performers>
        <NodeGraphicsInfos>
          <NodeGraphicsInfo FillColor="#d3d3e3" Height="79.99999999999999"
Width="100.0" BorderColor="#0,0,0" ToolId="Oryx">
            <Coordinates XCoordinate="207.8999993292689"
                         YCoordinate="109.63761467889908" />
          </NodeGraphicsInfo>
        </NodeGraphicsInfos>
      </Activity>
      <Activity CompletionQuantity="1" StartQuantity="1" Id="id_PhysExam_01"
              Name="Physical examination">
        <Implementation>
          <No />
        </Implementation>
         <Performers>
        <Performer> ERPyhs_1 </Performer>
        </Performers>
        <NodeGraphicsInfos>
            . . .
        </NodeGraphicsInfos>
      </Activity>
    <\Activities>
    <Transitions>
      <Transition From="id_SchedPhysExam_01" To="id_PhysExam_01" Id="TR_B66B-B2E6"
              FlowType = "SequenceFlow">
        <ConnectorGraphicsInfos>
          <ConnectorGraphicsInfo BorderColor="#0,0,0" ToolId="Oryx">
            <Coordinates XCoordinate="257.8999993292689"
                         YCoordinate="149.63761467889907" />
            <Coordinates XCoordinate="456.0" YCoordinate="354.63761467889907" />
          </ConnectorGraphicsInfo>
        </ConnectorGraphicsInfos>
      </Transition>
    </Transitions>
      . . .
</WorkflowProcess>
</WorkflowProcesses>
```

FIGURE 1.11 XPDL description of the two connected activities "Schedule physical examination" and "Physical examination", belonging to the process of Figure 1.4.

ability models and an interchange protocol covering basic operations, such as the instantiation of a process.

Interface 4 in Figure 1.10 can be specified in terms of Wf-XML, an interaction protocol that relies on XML message encoding and HTTP as a transport protocol [81]. In other words, Wf-XML is a protocol for standardizing cross-organizational processes that are executed in a web environment.

Wf-XML supports different models of interoperability through message-based interactions that can be either exchanged individually or in batch operations. An *interaction* is the exchange of process-related information between two generic services. Wf-XML uses messages for providing interactions among generic services.

Intuitively, a workflow engine can be seen as a special type of *service*: it has the ability to be started, to involve people in process execution, and to complete, at different times. One of the distinguishing features of Wf-XML is the loose coupling of services. A service does not need to know information about other services, but, instead, it interacts with them by using the standard HTTP operations to gain knowledge about the context in which the other engines operate. Three types of interactions are used in the form of messages exchanged between Wf-XML services. A *Request* is used by a resource to initiate an operation in another resource, and/or to provide input to that resource. An *Acknowledgment* is used by a resource receiving a Wf-XML message to inform the sender that the message has been received. A *Response* is used by an enacting resource to send the results of an operation to its requesting resource, providing output. By means of these basic operations, Wf-XML allows one engine to retrieve the process definition, and to monitor the current state of a process instance running on a different engine.

As an example of healthcare process interoperability, let us consider the scenario of a patient that needs to be carried to the emergency room by ambulance. This process can be implemented by using two engines, one controlling care during ambulance transportation and the other managing patient care in the emergency room. Interaction between such engines is required: while the patient is transported by ambulance to the ER, the engine of the ambulance service has control over the process. However, this engine must send updates to the hospital regarding the patient health status, so that the engine in the ER can allocate the resources needed to properly treat the patient. Upon patient arrival to the hospital, the engine in the ER takes control of the process, and interacts with the other engine to communicate that the patient has been taken in charge by the ER.

Interface 5 in Figure 1.10 provides consistency between the workflow enactment service and those tools that are used for process administration and monitoring. In particular, this interface specifies a common model for audit data that encompasses event identification, data formats, and data recording. Process monitoring allows users to analyze the current status of the running process instances, as well as resource availability and real-time workload. Alerting mechanisms can be set to inform either users or process administrators about the occurrence of critical situations, such as process bottlenecks caused by excessive resource consumption or activity failure.

As an example of a critical situation, let us consider emergency room crowding. Even if the triage procedure is carried out efficiently, it may happen that in some moments ER physicians are not able to handle all the patients promptly. This situation is obviously undesired for a lot of reasons: the ER facility may not be able to welcome any other patient, some patient that was assigned a low gravity level may worsen due to long waiting times, and the probability for the medical personnel to commit mistakes increases.

Process monitoring, simulation, and administration tools should provide a means to identify such critical situations and to properly react to them. Usually, information related to the execution of previous process instances is analyzed in order to extract knowledge about which are the circumstances that can lead to execution bottlenecks and in order to predict potential problems in running processes.

Referring to a simple healthcare process model for the assessment and diagnosis of appendicitis in the ER, we gave an overview of the main components of the WfMC reference architecture and, for each interface, we presented a few examples of possible implementation. Indeed, the implementation of the introduced architectural model can be realized in many different ways, according to the application domain of interest.

Other architectural models, such as service-oriented architectures or data-driven approaches for the enactment of healthcare processes are not discussed in this chapter. For further details, the reader is invited to refer to [80, 81, 336].

1.6 CONCLUSION

This chapter provided the reader with an overview of the main concepts related to healthcare process modeling and architectures. The benefits of applying BPM techniques to support the design and enactment of healthcare processes have been discussed, with particular attention to the organizational complexity of clinical domains. The fundamentals of BPMN have been introduced, mostly focusing on process diagrams, but also giving a broad idea of how choreography diagrams can be used to represent interactions between different processes and, more in general, participants. Independent but intertwined perspectives of healthcare processes are provided, each one addressing a different aspect of the portrayed organizational reality, and the connections between them are explored. Finally, the workflow reference architecture has been introduced, with the help of examples taken from the clinical domain. Indeed, the WfMC model still represents one of the most influential frameworks for process execution.

The main goal of this chapter was to introduce the reader to healthcare process management by introducing some basic terminology, concepts, and architecture related to the world of business process and workflow management that will be addressed more in depth in the following chapters of this book.

EXERCISES

1.1 *Process Modeling.* Consider the sample BPMN process for the detection of catheter-related blood stream infections (CR-BSIs), depicted in Figure 1.1. If an empirical antibiotic therapy is administrated by an ICU nurse while waiting for blood analyses results and also during catheter replacement, how would the diagram of Figure 1.1 change?

1.2 *Information Perspective.* With respect to *Example 1* discuss, with the help of examples, which kinds of data (i.e., process relevant data, process control data, and application data) could be part of the information model for the considered context.

1.3 *Architecture.* Consider the BPMN process of Figure 1.1. Give an example of a client application and one of an invoked application that may be used during process enactment.

  Solution: Client Application: alerting system that instances the process by informing the nurse about a suspected infection, based on set patient parameters. Invoked Application: e-mail based system that automatically delivers the results of the blood analyses to the requesting physician, when these are ready.

GLOSSARY

Actor: An individual processing unit, of a human or automatized (mechanical or electronic) type.

Agent: Individual that conducts the actual operational work during the enactment of a process instance. Specializations of agents are actors, groups, teams, and organizational functions.

Activity: A piece of work that is performed in a process. An activity can be executed by a human resource, i.e., a process participant, possibly with the help of an automatic application.

BPMN: (Business Process Modeling Notation) A standard graphical notation to describe the model of a process.

Business Process Management: The set of concepts, methods, and techniques that support the design, administration, enactment, and analysis of business processes.

Client Application: An application that interacts with a process engine to request facilities and services.

Choreography: In BPMN, a type of process that formalizes the way participants coordinate their interactions, mostly focusing on the exchange of information between them.

Event: An occurrence of a particular condition that has an impact on the flow of the process, usually causing the workflow management system to take one or more actions.

Gateway: In BPMN, a flow element that denotes a point in the process where a specific routing mechanism is invoked to split or merge the process flow, according to data–based conditions or event occurrence.

Group: A class of actors, defined according to common features such as assignment to a specific project or to a geographical site.

Invoked Application: A workflow application that is invoked by the workflow management system to partially or fully automate an activity or to support a participant in processing a work item.

Lane: In BPMN, the graphical representation of a role used to partition processes into sub-classes of participants.

Organizational Function: The definition of a class of groups, of actors, or of a team, with common features based on what they can perform or on what they are enabled to perform.

Participant: See *Agent*.

Pool: In BPMN, the graphical representation of an organization or of a class of participants that acts as the container for a process.

Process: A set of activities that are performed in an organizational and technical environment to jointly realize a particular (business) goal.

Process Diagram: A graphical representation of a process, based on a specific notation or modeling language.

Process Engine: The core component of a workflow management system provides operational functions to support and control the execution of process instances.

Role: A group of participants exhibiting a specific set of attributes, qualifications, and/or skills.

Team: List of possibly duplicate functions, based on a part of the organizational structure.

XPDL: A standard process definition language (XML process definition language) recommended by the Workflow Management Coalition.

Work Item: The representation of the work to be processed (by a participant) in the context of an activity within a process instance.

Workflow: The automation of a business process, in whole or part, during which documents, information or tasks are passed from one participant to another for action, according to a set of procedural rules.

Workflow Enactment Service: A software service that may consist of one or more process engines in order to create, manage, and execute particular workflow instances.

Workflow Management Coalition: An organization collecting users, developers, consultants, and scientists in the field of workflow management.

Workflow Management System: A software system that defines, creates, and manages the execution of processes through the use of software which is able to interpret the process definition, interact with participants, and, where required, invoke the use of IT tools and applications.

Worklist: A list of work items associated with a given participant or with a group of participants.

FURTHER READING

Combi Carlo, Pozzi Giuseppe, *Architectures for a Temporal Workflow Management System*, Proc. of the 19th Symposium on Applied Computing, Nicosia, Cyprus, 2004, pp. 659–666.

Weske Mathias, *Business process management: concepts, languages, architectures*. Springer Publishing Company, 2010.

Pourmirza Shaya, Peters Sander, Dijkman Remco, Grefen Paul, A systematic literature review on the architecture of business process management systems, *Information Systems*, 2017, vol. 66, pp. 43–58.

CHAPTER 2

Flexible Support of Healthcare Processes

Manfred Reichert

Ulm University, Ulm, Germany

Rüdiger Pryss

Ulm University, Ulm, Germany

CONTENTS

> Makes flexible the knees of
> knotted oaks
>
> ──────────────────
>
> W. Shakespeare

T RADITIONALLY, healthcare information systems have focused on the support of predictable and repetitive clinical processes. Even though the latter can be often prespecified in formal process models, process flexibility in terms of dynamic adaptability is indispensable to cope with exceptions and unforeseen situations. Flexibility is further required to accommodate the need for evolving healthcare processes and to properly support healthcare process variability. In addition, process-aware information systems are increasingly used to support less structured healthcare processes (i.e., patient treatment processes), which can be characterized as knowledge-intensive. Healthcare processes of this category are neither fully predictable nor repetitive and, therefore, they cannot be fully prespecified at design time. The partial unpredictability of these processes, in turn, demands a certain amount of looseness. This chapter deals with the characteristic flexibility needs of both prespecified and loosely specified healthcare processes. In addition, it presents fundamental flexibility features required to address these flexibility needs as well as to accommodate them in healthcare practice.

2.1 INTRODUCTION

Traditionally, *process-aware information systems* (PAIS) have focused on the support of predictable and repetitive business processes, which can be fully described prior to their execution in terms of formal process models [336]. Characteristic examples of healthcare processes falling in this category include organizational procedures in hospitals, like medical order entry and result reporting, as well as administrative processes. In spite of several success stories on the uptake of process-aware information systems in healthcare and the growing process-orientation in this domain, *Business Process Management* (BPM) technologies have not been widely adopted in healthcare yet [162, 241].

A major reason for the low use of BPM systems in healthcare has been the rigidity enforced by them, which inhibits the ability of a hospital to respond to process changes and exceptional situations in an agile way [229]. When efforts are taken to improve and automate the flow of healthcare processes, however, it is of utmost importance not to restrict medical staff [74]. First attempts to change the function- and data-centric views on patient treatment processes failed whenever rigidity came with them. Variations in the course of a disease or treatment process are inherent to medicine, and to some degree the unforeseen event constitutes a "normal" phenomenon [210]. Hence, a sufficient degree of flexibility is needed to support dynamic process adaptations in case of such unforeseen situations. Moreover, PAIS *flexibility* is required to accommodate the need for evolving healthcare processes [235], e.g., to integrate new medical devices, implement new laws, or change clinical guidelines (due to new empirical evidence). Finally, support for healthcare process variability is needed [19, 234]. For example, in a particular hospital, different variants of the order entry process may exist whose concrete behavior and structure depends on various contextual factors like the status of the patient, the kind of medical examination ordered, or the concrete provider of the medical service [166].

For several years, BPM technologies have been increasingly used to support less structured business processes as well [223]. The latter include patient treatment processes and are often characterized as knowledge-intensive. Processes of this category feature non-repeatability, i.e., the models of two process instances (e.g., coordinating the treatment of two different patients) do not fully resemble one another. Generally, *knowledge-intensive processes* tend to be *unpredictable* as their exact course of action depends on situation-specific parameters [192, 194]. Usually, the values of the latter are unknown *a priori* and may change during process execution. Moreover, knowledge-intensive processes can be characterized as *emergent*, i.e., knowledge and information gathered during the execution of the process determines its future course of action. Consequently, respective processes cannot be prescribed at a fine-grained level at design time. In addition to *variability, adaptation,* and *evolution,* which are also needed in the context of predictable processes, they require *looseness.*

The vast majority of healthcare processes can be characterized by a combination of predictable and unpredictable elements falling in between the two extremes described above. While procedures for handling single medical orders or examinations are relatively predictable, complex patient treatment processes are rather unpredictable and unfold during process execution [162].

This chapter elaborates on advanced BPM concepts enabling process flexibility at the operational level. Emphasis is put on key features enabling process variability, process adaptation, process evolution, and process looseness. Based on them process-aware healthcare information systems, being able to flexibly cope with real-world exceptions, uncertainty and change, can be realized. Section 2.2 presents the conditions under which a process-aware healthcare information system needs to operate and illustrates the need for flexible healthcare process support in this context. Section 2.3 then discusses and structures the flexibility needs of both prespecified and loosely specified healthcare processes in detail. Sections 2.4 – 2.7 present concepts and techniques for properly addressing these flexibility needs. Section 2.8 deals with other approaches fostering process flexibility, whereas Section 2.9 concludes and summarizes the chapter.

2.2   HEALTHCARE PROCESS CHARACTERISTICS

In the following, an impression of the characteristic properties of hospital working environments is provided to give an idea under which conditions process-aware healthcare information systems need to operate. On one hand, this real-life description confirms the high need for process coordination in healthcare, on the other it emphasizes the non-suitability of rigid approaches when it comes to the automation of healthcare processes.

In a hospital, the work of clinical staff is burdened by numerous organizational as well as medical tasks. Medical procedures must be planned, ordered, and prepared, appointments be made, and results be obtained and evaluated. Usually, in the diagnostic and treatment process of a particular patient various organizationally more or less autonomous units are involved. For a patient treated in a department of internal medicine, for example, medical tests and procedures at the laboratory and the radiology department might be required. In addition, samples or patients themselves have to be transported, physicians from other units may need to come for medical consultations, and medical reports have to be written, sent, and interpreted. Accordingly, the cooperation between organizational units as well as the medical staff constitutes a crucial task with repetitive, but non-trivial character. In this context, healthcare processes of different complexity and duration can be identified. There are organizational procedures like order entry and result reporting, but also complex and long-running treatment processes like chemotherapy for in- or outpatients.

Physicians have to decide which interventions are necessary or not–under the perspective of costs and invasiveness–or which are even dangerous due to possible side-effects or interactions. Many procedures need preparatory measures of various complexity. Before a surgery may take place, for example, a patient has to undergo numerous preliminary examinations, each of them requiring additional preparations. While some of them are known in advance, others may have to be scheduled dynamically, depending on the individual patient and her state of health, i.e., *looseness* of the overall patient treatment process is a reality.

In general, the tasks of a healthcare process may have to be performed in certain orders, sometimes with complex temporal constraints to be considered [156, 157]. After an injection with contrast medium was given to a patient, for example, some other tests cannot be performed within a certain period of time. In contemporary healthcare environments, physicians still have to coordinate the tasks related to their patients manually, taking into account all the constraints existing in this context. In this context, changing a schedule is not trivial and requires time-consuming communication. For other procedures, medical staff from various departments have to collaborate; i.e., coherent series of appointments have to be arranged and for each activity appropriate information has to be provided. As a drawback, each organizational unit involved in the treatment process of a patient concentrates on the function it has to perform. Thus, the process is subdivided into function- or organization-oriented views, and optimization stops at the border of the department. For all these reasons several problems result. First, patients have to wait, because resources (e.g., physicians, rooms, or technical equipment) are not available due to insufficient coordination. Second, medical procedures cannot be performed as planned, if information is missing, preparations are omitted, or a preceding procedure is postponed, canceled, or requires latency time. Depending procedures might then have to be rescheduled resulting in time-consuming phone calls. Third, if urgently needed results are missing, medical tests or procedures may have to be performed repeatedly causing unnecessary costs and burdening patients.

For all these reasons, from both the patient and the hospital perspective, undesired effects occur: Hospital stays can take longer than required and costs or even invasiveness of patient treatment increase. In critical situations, missing information might lead to late or even wrong decisions. Investigations have shown that medical personnel are aware of these problems and that healthcare process support would be highly welcome by medical staff [223]. More and more it is being understood that the correlation between medicine, organization, and information is high, and that traditional organizational structures and healthcare information systems only offer sub-optimal support. This even applies more to hospital-wide and cross-hospital processes in health care networks [91].

The roles of physicians and nurses complicate the situation. Both are responsible for many patients and have to provide an optimal treatment process for each of them. Medical tasks are critical to patient care and even minor errors might have disastrous consequences. The working situation is further burdened by frequent context switches. Physicians often work at various sites of a hospital in different roles. In many cases, unforeseen events and emergency situations occur, patient status changes, or information necessary to react is missing. Additionally, the physician is confronted with a massive load of data to be structured, intellectually processed, and put into relation to the problems of the individual patient. Typically, physicians tend to make mistakes (e.g., wrong decisions, omission errors) under this data overload.

From the perspective of a patient, a concentration on his treatment process is highly desirable. Similarly, medical staff members wish to treat and help patients and not to spend their time on administrative tasks. From the perspective of healthcare providers, the huge potential of the improvement as well as (semi-)automation of healthcare processes has been identified: length of stay, number of procedures, and number of complications could be reduced. Hence, there is a growing interest in process orientation and quality management. Medical and organizational processes are being analyzed, and the role of medical guidelines describing diagnostic and treatment steps for given diagnoses is emphasized [141, 211, 263].

2.3   FLEXIBILITY NEEDS FOR HEALTHCARE PROCESSES

Providing appropriate support for the wide range of processes that can be found in healthcare environments (cf. Section 2.2) poses several challenges. Particularly, flexible process support can be characterized by four major flexibility needs, namely support for variability, looseness, adaptation, and evolution. In the following, a brief summary of each flexibility need is presented and illustrated by a healthcare process scenario.

2.3.1 Variability

Process variability is characteristic for the healthcare domain and requires healthcare processes to be handled differently—resulting in different *process variants*—depending on the given application context [121, 234]. Typically, process variants share the same core process whereas the concrete course of action fluctuates from variant to variant. Variability in the healthcare services provided, for example, often necessitates support for numerous process variants [121]. Moreover, process variants might exist due to differences in regulations found in different countries or healthcare organizations. Process variability might be further introduced due to different groups of patients, the kind of service provided, peculiarities of the respective service providers, or temporal differences regarding service delivery (e.g., daily changes). In general, the parameters causing process variability are mostly known *a priori*. Even though the concrete variant can often only be determined during process execution, the course of action for a particular context is well understood.

Example 2.1 *(Process variants for handling medical examinations). Consider the four process variants in Figure 2.1. The variants have several activities (e.g.,* Order Medical Examination, Perform Medical Examination, *and* Create Medical Report*) in common. In Figure 2.1, these common activities are gray-shaded. However, the variants also show differences, e.g., in respect to the kind of examination (i.e., standard vs. emergency medical examination), the way the examination is handled (e.g., scheduling an examination later by making an appointment with the examination unit or registering one for the same day), or the need of specific activities depending on the given application environment (e.g.,* Prepare Patient *or* Transport Patient*).*

2.3.2 Adaptation

In general, *process adaptation* represents the ability of a process-aware information system (PAIS) to adapt the process and its structure (i.e., the pre-specified process model) to emerging events. Respective events often lead to situations in which the PAIS does not adequately reflect the real-world process anymore. As a consequence, one or several process instances have to be adapted in order to realign the computerized processes with the real-world ones. Note that it is not always possible to predict all exceptional situations and the way they shall be handled during process execution. Even if this had been possible, one would obtain complex and spaghetti-like process models, which are difficult to comprehend and costly to maintain.

Drivers for adaptation. Process adaptations are triggered by different drivers. Adaptations might become necessary to cope with special situations during process execution, which have not been foreseen in the process model, e.g., situations that occur very rarely. Moreover, exceptions occurring in the real-world (e.g., an allergic reaction of a patient) or processing errors (e.g., a failed activity) often require deviations from the standard process.

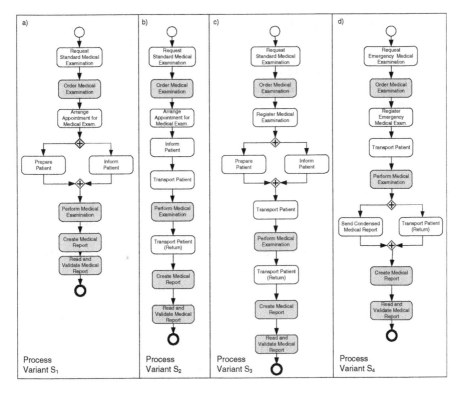

FIGURE 2.1 Examples of healthcare process variants.

Anticipation of adaptation. Many exceptions can be anticipated and, therefore, be planned upfront by capturing them in the process model. Generally, a deviation can only be planned if both the context of its occurrence and measures to handle it are known beforehand. However, it is hardly possible to foresee all exceptions that might occur during the execution of a particular healthcare process. Therefore, support for dealing with *unplanned exceptions* is additionally needed.

Example 2.2 *(Examination procedures in a hospital). A simple examina-tion procedure in a hospital comprises activities like* Enter Order, Schedule X-rays, Inform Patient, Transfer Patient, Perform X-rays, Create Report, *and* Validate Report. *Even for such a simple process, exceptional situations might occur, which require deviations from the prespecified process. For example, in case of an emergency, there is no time to follow the usual procedure. Instead the patient is immediately examined without making any appointment or preparing the examination facility. To cope with such a sit-uation, it should be possible to skip one or more activities. In exceptional situations it can further be required to perform additional (i.e., unplanned)* *activities for a particular patient (e.g., to carry out an additional preparation activity for the examination). In addition, changes in appointments, cancellations, and failures in the execution of activities (e.g., omitted preparations, loss of a sample, or incorrect collection of diagnostic material) might lead to deviations from the standard process (e.g., by redoing activities). If an appointment is canceled, for example, the patient treatment process (including the previously made appointment) will have to be aborted.*

In summary, in the medical domain, deviations from the standard procedure are rather the norm and have to be flexibly addressed by medical staff.

2.3.3 Evolution

Evolution represents the ability of the process implemented in a PAIS to change when the corresponding real-world process evolves. As healthcare processes evolve over time, it is not sufficient to implement them once and then to never touch the running PAIS again. In order to ensure that real-world healthcare processes and the PAIS remain aligned, these changes have to be propagated to the PAIS as well. Typically, such evolutionary changes are planned changes at the process type level, which are conducted to accommodate evolving needs.

Drivers for process evolution. In healthcare, process evolution is often driven by changes of medical knowledge, technological changes, and the emergence of new legal constraints. Another driver is organizational learning. All these drivers are external to the PAIS (cf. Figure 2.2). In healthcare, the evolution of real-world processes can be triggered by emerging medical knowledge (e.g., new evidence on the effectiveness of a treatment procedure) or changing patient behavior. Changes in the technological context might have far-reaching effects on the healthcare processes as well. For example, the increasing popularity of mobile devices is revolutionizing the way medical staff is interacting with its processes and, hence, the way the process shall be designed [223]. Changes might further be triggered by regulatory adaptations like, for example, the introduction of new laws or clinical practices. Finally, changes of healthcare processes might be a result of organizational learning and be triggered by emerging optimization opportunities or misalignments between real-world healthcare processes and the ones supported by a PAIS.

In addition to external triggers, changes of the processes implemented in a PAIS might become necessary due to developments inside the PAIS, i.e., there exist internal drivers for changes as well [73]. For example, design errors might cause problems during the execution of process instances in the PAIS (e.g., deadlocks or missing data). Moreover, technical problems like performance degradation (e.g., due to an increasing amount of data) may require changes in the PAIS. Finally, poor internal quality of process models (e.g., non-intention revealing naming of activities or redundant process model fragments) might require changes [327].

Extent of evolution. Process evolution may be incremental (i.e., only

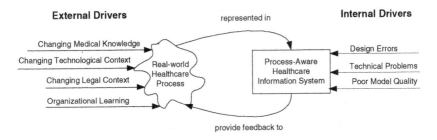

FIGURE 2.2 Drivers for process evolution.

requiring small changes of the implemented process) as for continuous process improvements, or be revolutionary (i.e., requiring radical changes) as in the context of process innovation or process reengineering.

Swiftness of evolution. Depending on the kind of evolutionary change, different requirements regarding the treatment of ongoing process instances exist [232, 237]. In some scenarios, it is sufficient to apply the changes only to those process instances that will be newly created and to complete the ongoing ones according to the old version of the process. This, in turn, would require *deferred evolution* and coexistence of different active versions of a process model within the PAIS. In many practical scenarios, however, *evolutionary changes* have an effect on ongoing process instances as well. For example, regulatory changes often have a retroactive impact and require ongoing process instances, if they have not progressed too far, to be adapted. Such *immediate evolution* is mostly relevant for long-running processes instances, i.e., process instances with a duration up to several weeks or months (e.g., cyclic chemo treatments).

Visibility of evolution. Evolutionary changes may either be changes of the observable process behavior or the internal structure of the PAIS. While changes of the observable behavior are always reflected by the PAIS support of the real-world processes, changes of the internal structure are kept inside the PAIS (e.g., to address poor internal process model quality). Adding activities to a process model (e.g., to add a lab test to a medical procedure for patients older than 60) constitutes an example of a change concerning the observable behavior. A typical change only affecting the internal structure of the PAIS includes the removal of process model redundancies by extracting common parts to sub-process models [327].

Example 2.3 *(Introduction of new medical devices). The introduction of new medical imaging devices in a hospital might have implications on the corresponding examination process. Assume that due to the high acquisition costs for the new device the hospital decides to use it for examining outpatients as well (in addition to inpatient examinations). This, in turn, implies changes in the registration procedure. These changes not only affect new patients, but ongoing examination processes (i.e., corresponding process instances) as well.*

*In this example, the evolution is triggered through economic concerns. Further-
more, the change is immediate, i.e., it affects ongoing examination processes
(i.e., process instances) as well.*

2.3.4 Looseness

Patient treatment processes, which are by nature knowledge-intensive, can
be characterized as non-repeatable (i.e., every process instance looks slightly
different), unpredictable (i.e., the exact course of action is unknown and is
situation-specific), and emergent (i.e., the exact course of action often emerges
during process execution when more specific information becomes available).
For processes of this category, only their goal is known *a priori* (e.g., treating
the rupture of a patient's cruciate ligament). In turn, the parameters determining the exact course of action are typically not known a priori or might
change during process execution. As a consequence, such knowledge-intensive
processes cannot be fully prespecified. In addition, it is not possible to establish a set of process variants for these processes, since the parameters causing
differences between process instances are not known a priori (unlike with variability). Instead, processes of this category require a *loose specification*.

Example 2.4 *(Patient treatment processes). Patient treatment in a hospital usually comprises activities related to patient intake, admission, diagnosis,
treatment, and discharge. Typically, treatment processes comprise dozens up
to hundreds of activities, and they are long-running (i.e., from a few days
to several months). Furthermore, the treatments of two different patients are
rarely identical. Instead the course of action often depends on the specific situation like, for example, the health status of the patient, allergies and chemical
intolerances, decisions made by the physician, examination results, and clinical indications. This situation may change during the treatment process, i.e.,
the course of action is unpredictable. Moreover, treatment processes typically
unfold during their execution, i.e., examination results yield information determining how to continue with the treatment. The overall treatment process
thereby emerges through the arrangement of simple, well-structured processes
(e.g., handling medical orders) often resulting in complex process structures.*

2.4 PROCESS VARIABILITY SUPPORT

As motivated in Section 2.3.1 and Example 2.1, respectively, a key flexibility
need in healthcare environments is to be able to cope with *process variability*.
In general, the reuse of a process model in different application contexts often
results in a large collection of related *process model variants* (*process variants* for short) belonging to the same *process family* [19]. In particular, the
process variants pursue the same or similar business objective and have certain activities (and their ordering constraints) in common, while at the same

time differences due to their use in different application contexts exist, e.g., certain activities might be only relevant for some of the process variants or different execution paths that need to be taken depending on the application environment.

To properly cope with process variability, a modeling approach for explicitly capturing variability in process models is needed, i.e., a family of related process variants shall be represented in a compact, reusable, and maintainable manner. Moreover, it should be possible to configure a process family to an individual process variant that fits best to the requirements of the given application context. This way, established practices and process knowledge of a healthcare organization can be reused, while still providing it with the flexibility to individualize its processes to the respective context. Thereby, the selection of the most suitable variant in such an application context is denoted as *process configuration*. For each *configuration option* (e.g., variation point) it must be decided which of the available alternatives shall be chosen. After making these choices, the finally *configured process model* can be transformed into an executable one by dropping those parts that are no longer required. The latter step is called *individualization*. Both the configuration and the individualization of a *configurable process model* constitute design time activities; i.e., they can be accomplished without need for any run-time knowledge.

Existing approaches providing process variability support split the design phase into two sub-phases—one during which the process family is designed, i.e., a *configurable reference process model* and its *configuration options* are specified, and one in which this configurable reference model is configured and individualized for obtaining specific process variants. A more concrete idea of the two phases of a behavior-based approach for capturing the behavior of all process variants in the same artifact (i.e., reference process model) is given in [309]. In this approach, which is denoted as *configurable nodes*, a reference process model merges a multitude of process variants into one configurable model capturing both the commonalities and the differences of the process variants. In respective reference process models, variation points are represented in terms of configurable nodes and execution paths. By configuring these, in turn, the behavior of the reference process model can be customized to the given application context, i.e., a concrete process variant fitting to this context can be derived.

In more detail, in a configurable reference process model, selected activities and control connectors (i.e., gateways) may be flagged as configurable. Such configurable nodes represent variation points of the reference process model and can be associated with a number of configuration alternatives. Furthermore, configuration constraints over the set of configurable nodes may be added to restrict possible combinations of configuration alternatives. By taking a configurable reference process model as input, and setting each of its configurable nodes to exactly one of the allowed alternatives, a particular process variant can be derived.

In principle, any activity or control connector of a reference process model may be flagged as configurable. In the reference process model depicted in Figure 2.3, for example, the configurable nodes are highlighted with thicker border. This reference process model describes a family of process variants for managing medical examinations, i.e., for handling medical orders and reporting related results (see Figure 2.1 for examples of process variants that may be derived from this configurable model). In detail, the depicted reference process model comprises five configurable activities and eight configurable control connectors. Its non-configurable nodes, in turn, represent the parts common to all process variants. For example, activity `Perform Medical Examination` denotes such a commonality since it is not configurable. Hence, this activity is contained in all process variants that may be configured out of the reference process model.

In detail, a configurable reference process model may comprise the following configurable elements:

a) **Configurable activities.** There exist three configuration alternatives for a configurable activity: included (ON), excluded (OFF), and conditional (OPT). The first two alternatives allow process engineers to decide at configuration time whether to keep an activity in the model of the process variant to be derived. The last alternative allows deferring this decision to the run-time, i.e., the execution of the activity may be dynamically skipped by users depending on the instance-specific context.

b) **Configurable control connectors.** There exist three different kinds of configurable control connectors: Configurable OR, Configurable XOR, and Configurable AND. A configurable control connector may only be configured to a connector being equally or less restrictive, i.e., the derived process model should be able to produce the same or fewer execution traces compared to the original reference process model. To be more precise, a Configurable OR may be configured to a regular OR, or be restricted to an XOR, AND, or just one outgoing/incoming branch. A Configurable XOR, in turn, may be set to a regular XOR or to just one outgoing/incoming branch. Finally, a Configurable AND may only be mapped to a regular AND, i.e., no particular configuration is allowed.

c) **Configuration requirements.** Configuration requirements define constraints over all the configuration alternatives that may be chosen for the configurable nodes of a reference process model. Only if these constraints are met, the resulting process variant is considered as being valid. Configuration guidelines, in turn, do not prescribe mandatory constraints, but only serve as a kind of recommendation guiding users during the configuration. Both configuration requirements and configuration guidelines can be expressed in terms of simple predicates. Graphically, they are depicted as post-it notes attached to one or several configurable nodes.

Example 2.5 *(Configurable reference process model for the handling of medical examinations). Consider the reference process model in Figure 2.3. It covers a family of process variants for handling medical examinations, including activities dealing with order handling, scheduling, transportation, and reporting. Examples of process variants that can be configured out of this reference process model are depicted in Figure 2.1. The gray-shaded activities in Figure 2.3 reflect the common parts of the producible process variants; i.e., these activities are contained in each process variant (see the variant examples in Figure 2.1). Process variability, in turn, is caused by varying factors like the kind of examination involved, the way examinations are scheduled, or the decision whether patient transportation is required.*

More precisely, emergency and standard medical examinations need to be distinguished from each other (Requirement 1). For standard medical examinations, either an appointment is scheduled or a simple registration is made (Requirement 2). (The latter means, the examination unit is informed about the later arrival of the patient, but does not appoint a date for the examination.) For emergency medical examinations, in turn, a specific registration is needed (Requirement 3). Furthermore, for a standard medical examination, activity Inform Patient *is always required (Requirement 4). Patient transportation, in turn, is mandatory for emergency medical examinations (Requirement 5), while for standard medical examinations this depends on other domain facts (Guideline 1). A condensed medical report has to be sent in the context of emergency medical examinations to enable quick feedback (Requirement 6). Finally, if the configurable activity* Transport Patient *is switched on, its counterpart (i.e., activity* Transport Patient (Return)*) has to be switched on as well (Requirement 7). Considering all requirements, there exist several activities that may be contained in some process variants, but which are not required for others (e.g.,* Prepare Patient *and* Inform Patient*).*

Overall, the configurable reference process model from Figure 2.3 comprises 5 configurable activities, 8 configurable connectors, 7 configuration requirements, and one configuration guideline. As discussed, configuration requirements constrain the alternatives that may be chosen for the configurable nodes of the reference process model.

Using such a reference process model, the desired process variants can be derived by setting the configuration alternatives of its configurable nodes accordingly (cf. Example 2.6).

Example 2.6 *(Configuring a reference process model). Consider the four process variants from Figure 2.1. The configuration settings needed for deriving the four variants from the given configurable reference process model (cf. Figure 2.3) are depicted in Figure 2.4. For each process variant, its configuration settings comply with the given configuration requirements, i.e., all four process variants are valid. Note that, in principle, it is not necessary to explicitly specify a configuration alternative for all configurable nodes since these settings can be partially derived from other configuration settings. In Figure 2.4,*

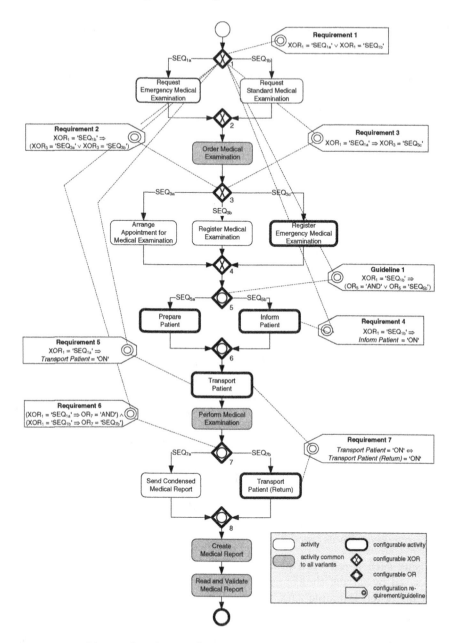

FIGURE 2.3 Example of a configurable reference process model.

for example, the configuration settings in gray color do not have to be explicitly specified when exploiting the knowledge on the configuration requirements defined in Figure 2.3.

	Settings of Configurable Connectors								Settings of Configurable Activities				
	XOR1	XOR2	XOR3	XOR4	OR5	OR6	OR7	OR8	Register Emergency Medical Examination	Prepare Patient	Inform Patient	Transport Patient	Transport Patient (Return)
Process variant S1	SEQ1b	SEQ1b	SEQ3a	SEQ3a	AND	AND	SEQ7b	SEQ7b	OFF	ON	ON	OFF	OFF
Process variant S2	SEQ1b	SEQ1b	SEQ3a	SEQ3a	SEQ5b	SEQ5b	SEQ7b	SEQ7b	OFF	OFF	ON	ON	ON
Process variant S3	SEQ1b	SEQ1b	SEQ3b	SEQ3b	AND	AND	SEQ7b	SEQ7b	OFF	ON	ON	ON	ON
Process variant S4	SEQ1a	SEQ1a	SEQ3c	SEQ3c	SEQ5b	SEQ5b	AND	AND	ON	OFF	OFF	ON	ON

FIGURE 2.4 Examples of configuration settings.

As alternative to configurable nodes, the Provop approach [121, 234] provides a structural configuration approach that allows adding, removing, or changing process behavior by adjusting the structure of a configurable process model accordingly (e.g., by adding or deleting activities).

Independent of the chosen approach, a particular challenge is to ensure that configured process variants are sound (i.e., correctly executable) and, hence, can be transformed to executable processes (see [120, 312] for corresponding techniques). Not that, when considering the large number of process variants that may be configured out of a reference process model, as well as the many syntactical and semantical constraints these process variants have to obey, this constitutes a nontrivial task. Finally, for the above-mentioned approaches, high-level configuration user interfaces for domain experts exist, e.g., questionnaire models, feature diagrams, and context-based configurators [119, 237, 245].

Altogether, enhancing process-aware healthcare information systems with configurable reference process models as well as the capability to derive sound process variants from them, will foster the reuse of process knowledge and increase process model quality in large process repositories

2.5 PROCESS ADAPTATION SUPPORT

As discussed in Section 2.3.2, in general, it is not possible to anticipate all exceptions in a healthcare environment and to capture their handling in a prespecified process model at design time. Hence, authorized process participants [330] should be allowed to situationally adapt single process instances running in the PAIS to cope with the non-anticipated exceptions and to realign the digital process running in the PAIS with the real-world case; e.g., by inserting, deleting, or moving activities for one specific process instance. Providing PAIS support for such instance-specific deviations from a prespecified process model, however, must not shift the responsibility for ensuring PAIS robustness to end-users. Instead, the PAIS must provide comprehensive support for the correct, secure, and robust handling of run-time exceptions through ad-hoc process instance changes.

To cope with unanticipated exceptions, authorized users shall be allowed to delete activities, to postpone their execution, to bring the execution of activities forward even though their preconditions have not yet been met, or to add activities not considered in the process model so far [233]. Generally, such behavioral changes of a process instance require structural adaptations of the corresponding process model, which shall solely be applied to that particular process instance. Examples of structural adaptations include the insertion, deletion, or movement of activities and process fragments respectively. While movements change activity positions, and thus the structure of a process model, insertions and deletions additionally modify the set of activities contained in a process model. In this context, adaptive process management technologies like ADEPT [73, 232, 236] provide high-level change operations, e.g., to move an activity or an entire process fragment within a process model. Usually, the change operations abstract from the concrete process model transformations to be conducted, i.e., instead of specifying a set of change primitives, the user applies one or more high-level change operations to realize the desired process model adaptation. ADEPT associates pre- and post-conditions with the high-level change operations in order to guarantee model correctness after each adaptation, i.e., to ensure correctness by construction [73]. A comprehensive set of change patterns, which are useful for structurally adapting processes models and, hence, process model behavior can be found in [328].

Example 2.7 *(Structural adaptations of a process model). Figure 2.5 depicts a simple example of a structural process model adaptation referring to a very simplified patient treatment process. As illustrated in Figure 2.5a, usually, the treatment process starts with the admission of the patient to the hospital. After having registered the patient, he is treated by a physician. Finally, an invoice for the treatment provided is created. Assuming that a particular patient is in a critical condition, it might become necessary to deviate from the prespecified process model to handle this exception; the treatment of the patient might have to start right away, performing the necessary steps for his registration at a later stage. To capture this behavior in the model of the respective process instance, activity* Treat Patient *has to be arranged in parallel with activity* Register Patient *(cf. Figure 2.5b), i.e., the unanticipated exception is handled by restructuring the model driving the execution of the respective process instance.*

To correctly deal with ad-hoc changes, process instance states need to be

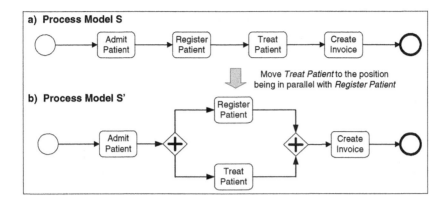

FIGURE 2.5   Example of a structural process adaptation.

taken into account as well. Generally, the applicability of a particular ad-hoc change depends on the state of the respective process instance. Example 2.8 illustrates this.

Example 2.8 *(Ad-hoc changes of healthcare process instances). Consider process model S on the left-hand side of Figure 2.6a. Assume that S is transformed into a correct process model S' by adding two activities (i.e.,* Test for Allergies *and* Deliver Drug*) as well as a data dependency between them; i.e.,* Test for Allergies *writes data object* Allergy Record*, which is then read by* Deliver Drug*. Assume further that this structural model change shall be applied to the process instances depicted in Figure 2.6b and currently being executed according to process model S. Regarding instance I_1 the described change can be applied without any problem as its execution has not yet entered the change region (cf. Figure 2.6c). Changing instance I_2 in an uncontrolled manner, however, would result in an inconsistent process instance state; i.e., activity* Prepare Patient *would be running even though its predecessor, activity* Test for Allergies*, would not have been completed. As a consequence,* Deliver Drug *might be invoked accessing data element* Allergy Record *even though this data element might not have been previously written. Regarding instance I_3, the described change may be applied. However, when relinking the execution of I_3 to S', activity* Prepare Patient *needs to be disabled and corresponding work items be withdrawn from user worklists. Additionally, the newly inserted activity* Test for Allergies *has to be enabled.*

As illustrated by Example 2.8, structural changes of a process instance require adaptations of the process instance state (i.e., the states of the corresponding activities) as well. Generally, the respective state adaptations depend on the applied process model change (e.g., deleting a process fragment vs. adding one) as well as on the current state of the process instance. Depending on the position where an activity is inserted, for example, it might

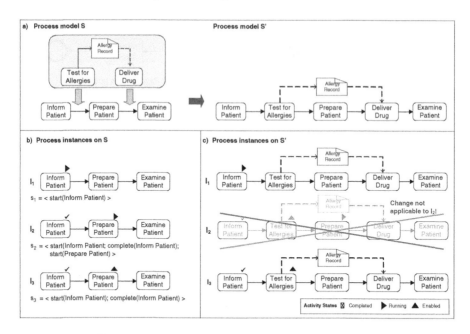

FIGURE 2.6 State-compliant adaptation of process instances.

become necessary to immediately enable the inserted activity or to disable other ones before continuing with the execution of the process instance. By contrast, when changing a not yet entered region of a process instance, no state adaptations become necessary.

In order to provide advanced user support, end-users should be supported in reusing knowledge about ad-hoc changes, which were previously applied to other process instances in a similar problem context. Accordingly, the changes must be recorded by the PAIS and be annotated with contextual information (e.g., reasons of the ad-hoc change). The latter, in turn, is needed to be able to present knowledge about those previous ad-hoc changes to the user being relevant in the current exceptional situation. For example, an MRT (Magnetic Resonance Tomography) must not be skipped for patients in general, but for those having cardiac pacemakers.

An approach that facilitates ad-hoc changes of process instances during run-time by supporting the retention and reuse of previously applied instance changes is presented in [329, 331]. In particular, this approach automates change retrieval by considering structured information about the current application context; e.g., the occurred exception and the current state of the process instance to be adapted. Further, if ad-hoc changes applied in a similar context can be retrieved in the given exceptional situations, but cannot be reused directly (e.g., in case the process instance has progressed beyond the point that the ad-hoc change can be directly applied), user support for adapting the respective change definition to the situation at hand is provided.

In summary, this section emphasized the need for structurally adapting the process model of single process instances during run-time in order to cope with unanticipated exceptions. We discussed fundamental issues that emerge due to ad hoc changes and showed how they can be addressed by adaptive PAIS. The section referred to high-level process adaptation patterns for defining ad-hoc changes at an abstract level (e.g., to move an activity). Additionally, it discussed the importance of considering the state of process instances as well as to adapt it when applying ad-hoc changes. In this context, we emphasized that a particular process instance only then might be dynamically changed, if the current instance state complies with the resulting process model (i.e., *state compliance*). We further discussed how users may be supported in reusing knowledge about previous ad-hoc changes applied in similar exceptional situations.

2.6   PROCESS EVOLUTION SUPPORT

As discussed in Section 2.3.3, any process-aware information system run in a healthcare environment should be able to cope with evolutionary process changes. This section presents fundamental techniques to cope with the evolution of healthcare processes as implemented in a PAIS at a technical level, i.e., to realize respective process changes within the PAIS. The basic assumption is that the healthcare processes are represented by prespecified process models in the PAIS, and changes of the real-world healthcare process require the corresponding process models to evolve accordingly at the implementation level. A major challenge in this context concerns the handling of long-running process instances that were created based on the old process model, but are now required to comply with a new specification (i.e., a new model version) and, therefore, shall be migrated to it [235, 243]. As thousands of active process instances might be affected, accomplishing such a migration correctly and efficiently becomes crucial [242].

2.6.1   Deferred Process Evolution

When evolving a process model S to a new process model version S' at the process type level, the PAIS must properly deal with corresponding process instances, i.e., process instances that were started and partially executed on S, but have not been completed yet. The easiest way to properly complete these running process instances is to continue their execution based on the original process model S, whereas new process instances may be created and executed based on the new model version S'—this approach is denoted as *deferred process model evolution* in [237]. In particular, it requires support for version control as well as for the coexistence of process instances belonging to different process model versions of a particular process type.

2.6.2 Immediate Process Evolution and Instance Migration

While the coexistence of process instances running on different process model versions is sufficient to support deferred evolution, long-running process instances often require immediate evolution, i.e., these process instances shall be migrated on-the-fly to the new process model version if possible. Example 2.9 illustrates this need.

Example 2.9 *(Need for immediate process model evolution and process instance migration). Consider a patient treatment process and assume that due to newly emerging legal requirements patients have to be informed about certain risks before a specific surgery may take place. Assume further that this change is also relevant for patients whose treatment process was already started. If the respective treatment process is supported by a PAIS, stopping all ongoing process instances (i.e., treatments), aborting them, and restarting them does not constitute a viable option. As a large number of treatment processes might be concurrently running, applying this change manually to the instances of ongoing treatment processes in the PAIS is hardly a realistic option. Instead, PAIS support is needed to add this new activity to all patient treatment processes for which this is still feasible, e.g., for which the surgery has not been started or completed yet.*

As a particular challenge, *immediate process instance migrations* have to be accomplished in a controlled manner, i.e., none of the correctness properties (e.g., soundness) guaranteed through the verification of a process model at design time must be violated for any of the migrated process instances. If this cannot be guaranteed for a particular process instance, it must not be migrated, but remain running on the old process model version. To meet this goal, it first has to be ensured that the new process model version S' is correct; i.e., S' has to satisfy the syntactical and structural properties of the process modeling language (e.g., BPMN 2.0) used, and it further must constitute a sound (i.e., correctly executable) process model.

The problem here is the same as when applying an ad-hoc change to a single process instance at run-time (cf. Section 2.5); i.e., similar challenges exist as for ad-hoc changes. In particular, the state of the process instances to be migrated (i.e., their execution traces) must be taken into account when deciding on whether their execution may be relinked from a process model S to a new model version S' (i.e., whether the instances may migrate to S'). A widespread correctness notion used for deciding about whether or not a particular process instance may be dynamically migrated to a new process model version S' is *state compliance*—a process instance I is denoted as being *state compliant* with an updated process model S' and can therefore be migrated to it, if the execution trace of I, which records all execution events related to I, is producible on S' as well. Using this correctness notion in the context of process model evolution, it can be ensured that process instances whose state has progressed too far will not be migrated to the new process model version

S', i.e., they will remain running on the original process model version. Furthermore, when migrating a running process instance to a new process model version its state has to be automatically adapted. For example, an already enabled activity may have to be disabled when inserting an activity directly preceding it or a newly added activity may have to be immediately enabled if the preconditions for its execution are met.

Example 2.10 illustrates a process model evolution together with the controlled migration of related process instances. Note that this example is similar to the healthcare scenario discussed in the context of Example 2.8.

Example 2.10 *(Controlled process instance migration). Consider the evolution of process model S to S' as depicted at the top of Figure 2.7. Furthermore, consider the three process instances I_1, I_2, and I_3 now running on S. Only those process instances (i.e., I_1 and I_2) are migrated to the new process model S', which are state compliant with it: I_1 can be migrated to S' without need for any instance state adaptation. Furthermore, I_2 can be migrated to S' as well. However, in this case the newly inserted activity X becomes immediately enabled, whereas the already enabled activity B becomes disabled. Finally, process instance I_3 cannot be migrated to S', as it is not state compliant with this model. Hence, I_3 remains running on the original process model S.*

Note that the controlled evolution of process instances as illustrated in Example 2.10 requires support for the coexistence of process instances running on different versions of a particular process model, as well as the use of appropriate correctness notions for deciding whether or not process instances can be correctly executed on the new model version.

2.7   PROCESS LOOSENESS SUPPORT

As motivated in Section 2.3.4, in the healthcare domain, it is not always possible to fully prespecify the model of a healthcare process in advance, i.e., while parts of the respective process model are known at design time, others might be uncertain and can solely be specified during process execution. For example, the treatment of a particular patient depends on his actual physical data and the list of symptoms and medical problems reported during process execution. To cope with this uncertainty, decisions regarding the exact specification of selected parts of the process model may be deferred to the run-time, i.e., instead of requiring the process model to be fully specified prior to the creation and execution of corresponding process instances, parts of the model can remain unspecified. Process participants then may add information regarding the unspecified parts of the process model during process execution.

This section presents two *decision deferral patterns*, which can be also applied to healthcare processes, i.e., *Late Selection* and *Late Modeling and Composition*. As opposed to structural process adaptations (cf. Section 2.5), whose application is not restricted a priori to a particular process model part,

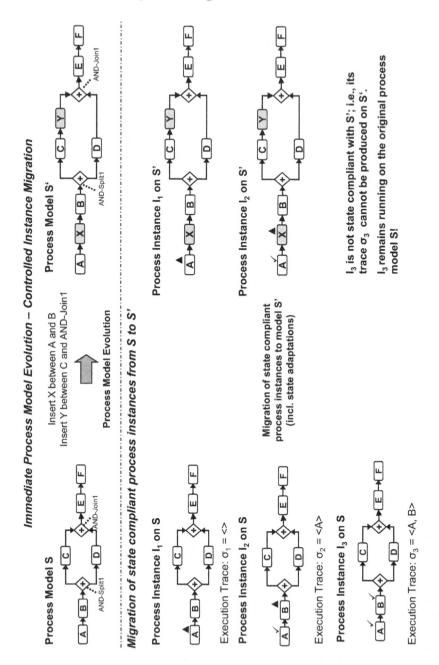

FIGURE 2.7 Process model evolution and process instance migration.

the decision deferral patterns define constraints concerning the parts of a process model that may be changed or expanded. In particular, the application of the patterns has to be anticipated at design time, which is accomplished by defining regions in the process model where potential changes may be performed during run-time (decision deferral patterns are therefore also denoted as *patterns for changes in predefined regions* in [328]).

A *loosely specified process* is therefore defined by a process model, which is not fully prespecified, but keeps some parts unspecified at design time by deferring decisions to the run-time. The aforementioned patterns differ in the degree of freedom provided to the user and the planning approach employed when concretizing the loosely specified parts of the process model during run-time. Moreover, the scope of decision deferral (i.e., prespecified parts of the process model or entire process) has to be considered. Taken together, these dimensions determine the provided degree of looseness. The considered patterns are as follows:

Late selection of process fragments. This pattern allows deferring the selection of the implementation of a particular process activity to the run-time. At design time, solely a *placeholder activity* has to be provided. Its concrete implementation is then selected during run-time among a predefined set of alternative process fragments either based on defined rules or on user decisions (cf. Figure 2.8). However, the selection must be accomplished before the placeholder activity is enabled or when it becomes enabled. Finally, the fragment substituting the placeholder activity may either be an atomic activity or a sub-process.

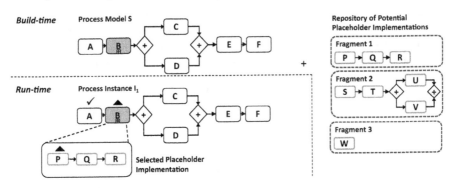

FIGURE 2.8 Late selection of process fragments.

Late modeling and composition of process fragments. This pattern offers more freedom compared to Late Selection. It allows for the on-the-fly modeling of selected parts of the process model at run-time, i.e., at design time, only a placeholder activity is provided, whose implementation is then provided during run-time (cf. Figure 2.9). Building blocks that may be used for late modeling and composition can either be all process fragments from a repository, a constraint-based subset of the fragments from the repository, or newly defined activities or process fragments. In this context, constraints may be defined, which have to be considered when modeling or composing an unspecified process part. Furthermore, late modeling can take place upon creation of the process instance, or when the placeholder activity becomes enabled or a particular state in the process is reached. Depending on the pattern variant users start late modeling with an empty template or take a predefined template as a starting point and adapt it as required.

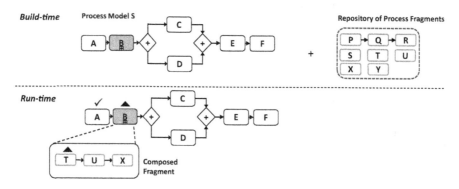

FIGURE 2.9 Late modeling of process fragments.

To give an idea of how decision deferral patterns can be implemented and applied in a healthcare context, with Worklets [1] we present a concrete approach realizing the Late Selection pattern. For this, each activity is associated with a set of sub-process fragments, which may be dynamically extended (i.e., additional fragments can be added on the fly)(cf. Figure 2.10). Again, the activities of a sub-process may be linked with a set of fragments. During run-time choices are made dynamically out of the set of subprocess fragments when activities become enabled. The selection of a suitable fragment is made using hierarchically organized selection rules–called ripple down rules. Users may adjust the automatic choice by adding selection rules. Once a fragment has been chosen, the placeholder activity is replaced by it.

Example 2.11 *(Late selection with Worklets). Figure 2.10 (adopted from [1]) illustrates the Worklet approach using a simplified example from the healthcare domain. The prespecified process model consists of the four activities* Admit Patient, Perform Triage, Treat Patient, *and* Discharge Patient. *Activity* Treat Patient *is linked with a set of 7 subprocesses. Depending on the actual physical condition of the patient and his list of symptoms, a suitable treatment is chosen during run-time. For this, the ripple down rules are evaluated once activity* Treat Patient *becomes enabled. The evaluation of the rules starts with the root node which always evaluates to true. As the next step, condition* Fever = True *is evaluated. If this condition holds subprocess* Treat Fever *is selected and activity* Treat Patient *is replaced by it. Otherwise, the evaluation continues with the next rule (i.e., condition* Wound = True).*

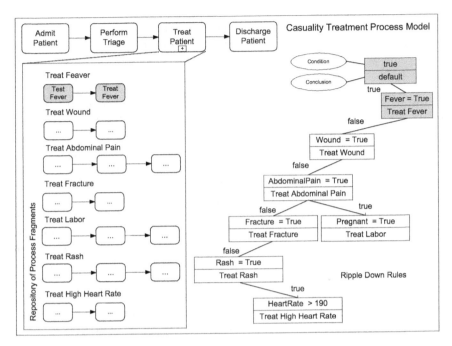

FIGURE 2.10 Late selection with Worklets.

A similar approach like Worklets, which is called Context-aware Process Injection (CaPI), is described in [193].

2.8 OTHER PROCESS FLEXIBILITY APPROACHES

For many years, the BPM community has recognized that a PAIS needs to be able to cope with real-world exceptions, uncertainty, and evolving processes [237]. To address the flexibility needs discussed in Section 2.3, besides the concepts and techniques presented in the previous sections, a variety of other process support paradigms, including *case handling, constraint-based processes*, and *data- and object-centric processes*, have been suggested and applied to healthcare scenarios.

2.8.1 Constraint-Based Processes

This sub-section introduces constraint-based approaches to process modeling and execution, which enable loosely specified processes as well [118, 313]. While prespecified process models define *how* things have to be done (i.e., in what order and under what conditions activities shall be executed), *constraint-based process models* focus on *what* should be done by describing the activities that may be performed and the constraints prohibiting undesired execution behavior.

Example 2.12 deals with a simplified medical guideline we adopted from [313]. It describes a constraint-based process of treating a patient admitted to the emergency room of a hospital suspected of having a fracture (cf. Figure 2.11).

Example 2.12 *(Fracture treatment process). Consider Figure 2.11. Before any treatment may be chosen, activity* Examine Patient *has to be performed by a physician (constraint* init*). If required, additional medical diagnosis is done by executing activity* Perform X-rays. *Depending on the presence and type of fracture, four different treatments exist:* Prescribe Sling, Prescribe Fixation, Perform Surgery, *and* Apply Cast. *Except for* Apply Cast *and* Prescribe Fixation, *which are mutually exclusive (constraint* not co-existent*), the treatments can be applied in any combination and each patient receives at least one of them (*1-of-4 *constraint). Activity* Perform X-rays *is not required if the specialist diagnoses the absence of a fracture when performing activity* Examine Patient. *If activity* Perform X-rays *is omitted, only the treatment* Prescribe Sling *may be applied. All other treatments require* Perform X-rays *as preceding activity in order to rule out the presence of a fracture, or to decide how to treat it (constraint* precedence*). Simple fractures can be treated just by performing activity* Apply Cast. *For unstable fractures, in turn, activity* Prescribe Fixation *may be preferred over activity* Apply Cast. *When performing activity* Perform Surgery, *the physician is further advised to (optionally) execute activity* Prescribe Rehabilitation *afterwards (optional constraint* response*). Moreover, the physician may execute activity* Prescribe Medication *(e.g., pain killers or anticoagulants) at any stage of the treatment. Note that activities* Examine Patient *and* Perform X-rays *may be also performed during treatment.*

Altogether, the process of treating a fracture comprises the activities Examine Patient, Perform X-rays, Prescribe Sling, Prescribe Fixation, Perform Surgery, Apply Cast, Prescribe Rehabilitation, *and* Prescribe Medication. *Moreover, constraints prohibit undesired execution behavior, e.g.:*

1) *Activity* Examine Patient *has to be executed first.*

2) *Each patient gets at least one out of four treatments (i.e.,* Prescribe Sling, Prescribe Fixation, Perform Surgery, *or* Apply Cast*).*

3) *Activities* Apply Cast *and* Prescribe Fixation *are mutually exclusive.*

- Perform X-rays *is a prerequisite for all treatments except* Prescribe Sling.

4) *If activity* Perform Surgery *is performed for a certain patient, the physician will be advised to execute activity* Prescribe Rehabilitation *afterwards.*

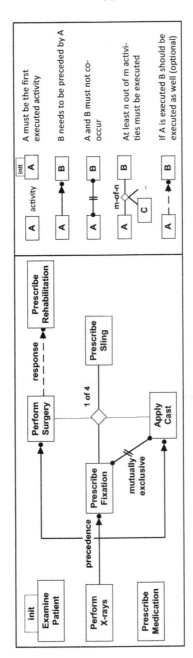

FIGURE 2.11 Example of a constraint-based process model.

Figure 2.11 depicts the loosely specified process model corresponding to Example 2.12 when using a constraint-based process modeling approach. The boxes represent activities and the relations between them are different kinds of constraints for executing these activities. The depicted model contains mandatory constraints (solid lines) as well as one optional constraint (dashed line). As opposed to fully prespecified process models that describe how things have to be done, constraint-based process models focus on the logic that governs the interplay of actions in the process by describing the activities that can be performed and those constraints prohibiting undesired behavior.

Note that in more complex cases, the physician in charge may have to choose from dozens or even hundreds of activities. While some of them may be executed any number of times and at any point in time during the treatment process, for others a number of constraints have to be obeyed; e.g., certain activities may have to be preceded or succeeded by other activities or may even exclude certain activities. Moreover, depending on the particular patient and his medical problems, certain activities might be contraindicated and should therefore not be chosen. The challenge is to provide PAIS support for such knowledge-intensive processes and to seamlessly integrate the described constraints within the physician's work practice. Generally, the structure of *knowledge-intensive processes* strongly depends on user decisions made during process execution; i.e., it dynamically evolves.

2.8.2 Object-Centric Processes

The process flexibility approaches presented in the previous sections are *activity-centric*, i.e., they focus on the coordinated execution of a set of business functions, represented by atomic process steps (i.e., activities), as well as the control and data flow between them. Typically, the primary drivers of *activity-centric processes* are the *events* related to activity completions. In turn, business data is rather "unknown" to the process engine of an activity-centric PAIS. The latter only maintains simple data elements needed for control flow routing and for assigning values to activity input parameters. In particular, business objects and their attributes are usually outside the control of an activity-centric PAIS [148].

In healthcare, however, one can also find processes not being activity-centric, but whose execution is driven by user decisions and patient data [58]. These processes are usually unstructured or semi-structured, and tend to be knowledge-intensive. In particular, they can not be straight-jacketed into a set of activities with prespecified precedence relations (as in the examples presented above). As a consequence, the activity-centric approaches presented so far do not adequately support these processes [148]. Moreover, the primary driver for the progress of a process is not the event related to activity completion, but the availability of certain values for data objects. When implementing such *user- and data-driven processes* in a PAIS, a tight integration of processes, data, and users becomes necessary [230].

There exists pioneering work targeting at user- and data-driven process management and enabling such a tight integration. As a first example, the case handling paradigm [115] needs to be mentioned. It focuses on the case (e.g., a patient treatment) and its flexible handling, whereby the progress of a case is determined by the values of its data objects, i.e., case execution is *data-driven.*

While case handling is appropriate for supporting simple process scenarios, it does not provide sufficient abstractions to deal with more complex and inter-dependent cases. Approaches focusing on *object-aware processes* offer more promising perspectives in this context; i.e., here the PAIS manages data by means of object types (e.g., medical report, medical examination) that comprise object attributes and relations to other object types. Accordingly, a business process coordinates the processing of several business objects of the same or different type among end-users enabling them to cooperate and communicate with each other. As shown in [147], object-aware processes provide a high degree of abstraction by enabling two levels of process granularity: *object behavior* and *object interactions.* Furthermore, object-aware process management supports *data-driven process execution, flexible choice of activity granularities,* and *integrated access to business processes and business data.* In [147] a framework realizing flexible object-aware process support based on a tight integration of processes, functions, data, and users is presented. In particular, the framework provides support for coordinating the execution of related processes and the interactions of their corresponding objects. In turn, the application of this framework to sophisticated healthcare scenarios is presented in [58].

2.9 SUMMARY

When efforts are taken to improve and automate healthcare processes through the introduction of a PAIS, it is of utterly importance that this does not lead to rigidity. Otherwise, the PAIS will not be accepted by clinical staff. Furthermore, variability in healthcare processes is deeply inherent to the medical domain, and unforeseen events are to some degree a "normal" phenomenon in current practice. PAISs should therefore enable a high degree of flexibility throughout the entire process life cycle.

To enable the required process flexibility in healthcare environments, several challenges need to be tackled: First, variability in healthcare processes, which is known prior to their implementation, should be captured and made known to the PAIS. Second, authorized process participants should be free to react in unplanned or exceptional situations by gaining complete initiative and by deviating from the prespecified process whenever required. Note that in the healthcare domain the process participants are usually trained to do so and, hence, enabling ad-hoc deviations from the prespecified process model forms a key part of process flexibility. In all these scenarios, the PAIS should be easy to handle, self-explaining, and—most important—its use should be not more cumbersome and time-consuming than simply handling the unplanned situation or exception by a telephone call to the right person. Third, process models may evolve over time due to environmental changes (eg , process redesign or new laws). Consequently, a PAIS should support process model evolution and provide appropriate techniques for dealing with already running process instances in this context. Flexibility features of a PAIS must neither affect its robustness nor the correct execution of the healthcare processes it implements. Fourth, to support knowledge-intensive processes, PAISs should enable the loose specification of process models at design time and their refinement during run-time, as well as data- and user-driven processes in cases where activity-centric approaches do not fit at all.

Existing approaches for the flexible support of prespecified or loosely specified processes have been already established in industrial practice for several years. Hence, they provide a rather high degree of maturity. By contrast, approaches enabling knowledge-intensive processes constitute cutting-edge research, but will become more mature and emerge in practical settings in a few years. While the conceptual and theoretical foundations of the different paradigms are well understood, there still exist numerous challenges regarding their practical use in healthcare environments. Amongst others, these challenges include proper end-user assistance, flexible support of mobile healthcare processes, and flexibility in cross-organizational processes (e.g., in the context of healthcare networks).

EXERCISES

2.1 *Ad-hoc changes.* Give examples of ad-hoc deviations that might become necessary for prespecified healthcare processes during their execution.

2.2 *Drivers of process adaptation and process evolution.* What are typical drivers of process adaptation and process evolution in a healthcare environment?

2.3 *Looseness.* Why is looseness a fundamental process flexibility need in healthcare, i.e., why is it not possible to always prespecify all parts of a healthcare process already at design time?

2.4 *Late selection versus late modeling.* Explain the differences between late selection and late modeling in the context of process looseness support.

2.5 *Process variability support.* Consider the configurable reference process model from Figure 2.3 and use it to derive two process variants different from the ones depicted in Figure 2.1. Which configuration settings have you made in this context?

2.6 *Process evolution versus process adaptation.* What are the commonalities between the migration of process instances to a new process model version (due to a process evolution) and an ad-hoc change of a single process instance? What are the major differences?

2.7 *Process evolution.* Why is a coexistence of process instances running either on an old process model version or new one needed for deferred as well as immediate process instance migration?

2.8 *Constraint-based process.* Discuss pros and cons of constraint-based (i.e., declarative) processes.

GLOSSARY

Ad-hoc process change: Refers to a dynamic process change being applied in an ad-hoc manner to a given process instance in the midst of its execution. Usually, ad-hoc process changes become necessary to handle unforeseen exceptions or situations not anticipated in the process model.

Configurable process model: A configurable process model may be configured and individualized for obtaining specific process variants.

Constraint-based process model: A constraint-based process model focuses on what should be done by describing the acitvities that may be performed and the constraints prohibiting undesired process behavior.

Individualization: After making configuration choices, the finally configured model is transformed into an executable one by dropping those parts that are no longer required. The latter step is called individualization.

Loosely specified process model: A process model, which is not fully prespecified, but keeps some parts unspecified at build-time by deferring decisions to run-time.

Process model evolution: Refers to the continuous adaptation of the model of a particular process to cope with evolving needs and environmental changes. Particularly for long-running processes, it then often becomes necessary to migrate already running process instances to the new process model version.

Process adaptation: Process adaptation represents the ability of a process-aware information system to adapt the process and its structure (i.e., the prespecified process model) to emerging events.

Process-aware information system: A process-aware information system (PAIS) enables enterprises to define their business processes based on explicit process models as well as to execute instances of the latter in a controlled manner.

Process evolution: Process evolution represents the ability of a process implemented in a PAIS to change when the corresponding real-world process evolves.

Process fragment: A connected region of a process model.

Process variant: Typically, process variants share the same core process whereas the concrete course of action fluctuates from process variant to process variant.

FURTHER READING

Reichert Manfred and Weber Barbara, *Enabling Flexibility in Process-Aware Information Systems - Challenges, Methods, Technologies*, Springer, 2012.

Casati Fabio, Ceri Stefano, Pernici Barbara, Pozzi Giuseppe, Workflow evolution, *Data and Knowledge Engineering*, 1998, vol. 24, n. 1, pp. 211–239

CHAPTER 3

Process Compliance

Stefanie Rinderle-Ma

University of Vienna, Vienna, Austria

CONTENTS

> And ceremony: let me comply
> with you in this garb
>
> — W. Shakespeare

THIS chapter describes how business process models have to comply with business level rules and policies (i.e., semantic constraints) stemming from real world applications. One very important goal is to ensure error-free executions at the semantic level, by equipping process management systems with control mechanisms for validating and ensuring the compliance with semantic constraints.

3.1 WHAT IS PROCESS COMPLIANCE?

(Business) process compliance refers to the following question: given a process P and a set of compliance constraints C, does P *comply* with the constraints in C? Comply means in this context that the model and all executions of P do not violate any of the constraints in C. In other words the model of P and all its possible executions adhere to the constraints in C. Take a treatment process and a constraint. Let the constraint define that before doing the surgery a patient has to be advised about the risk of the surgery. Then the treatment process would violate the constraint if in the model the step of advising the patient is not a predecessor of the step of doing the surgery.

This simple example refers to a constraint that can be checked based on the process model, i.e., the existence and order of steps. This is referred to as *design time compliance* (cf., for example, [250]). For design time compliance, patterns can be defined that reflect typical "ingredients" of compliance constraints over (business) processes. Ly et al. [169] collects constraint patterns based on the well-known patterns from Dwyer et al. [84] for design time compliance checking by classifying them into patterns that deal with the (co-) occurrence of activities in processes and the patterns on the order of activities. Examples for (co-) occurrence patterns are *existence/absence* of activities in a process. An example pattern for the order of activities is *activity X followed by activity Y*. Hence, for design time compliance, constraint artifacts are referred to as patterns (cf. Figure 3.1). There are several formalisms to express compliance constraints. A collection of formalisms is discussed in [90] and presented in Figure 3.1. Examples are logics such as Linear Temporal Logic (LTL) or SQL-like languages such as PQL. Some languages such as Compliance Rule Graphs (CRG) provide a process-oriented graphical abstraction based on underlying logic (here, First Order Logic).

Not all compliance constraints can be checked over a process during design time due to two reasons. The first reason is that compliance constraints might refer to data that is not available during design time, i.e., runtime data such as values of process data that are produced during process execution or actor assignments based on role resolution. The other reason is the availability of process model information. It cannot always be assumed that complete process models are at hand to conduct compliance checks. In turn, often the process execution data can be observed rather in terms of event streams [169]. Monitoring and verifying compliance constraints over process execution data is referred to as *runtime compliance* (cf. Figure 3.1).

Some words to be spent on the discussion of declarative and imperative process models: This distinction does not matter very much for runtime compliance as an event stream is observed instead of analyzing a process model. For design time, in a fully declarative setting the process model is expressed as constraints itself, resulting in a set of process model and compliance constraints. In practice, specifically with process modeling standards such as BPMN, imperative process models are often used, resulting in a mix with declarative compliance constraints (cf. Figure 3.1).

Two techniques for design and runtime compliance are model checking and pattern matching (cf. Figure 3.1). Pattern matching approaches aim at matching constraint patterns against process model (patterns) or event streams over process models. Model checking refers to producing all possible execution traces over a process model and to check whether a given constraint violates any of these traces. Conformance checking as one of the key tasks of process mining [307] can also be used for compliance checking. Specifically the compliance of completed process executions reflected in so called process logs can be assessed ex post. For this the logged traces are replayed on the process model and deviations are measured resulting in an overall assessment of the conformance of these logs with the model.

	Design time compliance	Runtime compliance
Process artifact	Process model	Events, event streams
Model paradigm	Imperative, declarative	Model (partly) not available
Constraint artifact	Patterns	(Anti-) patterns enriched with data values, time information, and resources
Constraint formalisms (selection)	LTL, CTL, CTL*, Event Calculus, Event-B, CRGs, TLA+, PDL, μ-calculus, PQL, APQL	
Techniques (selection)	Model checking, pattern matching	Model checking, pattern matching, data monitoring, conformance checking (ex post)

FIGURE 3.1 An overview on process compliance.

How can we use process compliance checking in the domain of health care? The questions is tried to be answered in the remainder of this chapter. In Section 3.2, challenges for compliance checking in the health care domain are collected. These challenges are discussed in detail in Sections 3.3 to 3.6. Section 3.3 presents how to model compliance constraints and how to conduct design time compliance checking based on a use case from skin cancer treatment. In Section 3.4 approaches for monitoring compliance constraints over health care processes are presented. Section 3.5 discusses data quality issues and Section 3.6 further important aspects such as interoperability.

3.2 COMPLIANCE FOR HEALTH CARE PROCESSES: CHALLENGES

Is process compliance relevant in the health care domain? We approach this question by conducting a literature review and summarizing the most important challenges with respect to process compliance in the health care domain.

In a first step a search on scholar.google.com was conducted using search string `allintitle: compliance medical process` (excluding patents and citations, accessed on 2016-09-26) resulting in 11 hits. From these hits three publications referring to process compliance and being published and available were selected. A second search using search string `allintitle:compliance process health care` resulted in 7 hits where 1 was extracted due to its focus on process compliance and its availability. In summary, the following publications were selected:

- EBMC^2-1 [26]: use case melanoma focusing on the European guideline on skin cancer treatment.

- EBMC^2-2 [82]: use case melanoma focusing on the European guideline on skin cancer treatment and log data from Medical University of Vienna, Austria.

- CHINO [278]: use case cross-organizational exchange of medical data between Italy and the UK.

- VeMoI [30]: use case stroke.

EBMC^2-2 [82] summarizes the main discovered challenges as "formalization and analysis of medical guidelines" and "comparing guideline-based treatment processes with empirical treatment processes".

Overall, the main utilized techniques and methods focus on:

1. Process modeling, i.e., describing health care processes using different formalisms, for example, BPMN [26, 278].

2. Describing medical knowledge by

    (a) modeling medical guidelines. Existing approaches comprise GLIF, Asbru, EON/SAGE, PROforma, GUIDE, PRODIGY [26], and BPMN [26, 278].

    (b) ontology-based approaches. They include medical ontologies such as SNOMED, standards for data exchange such as the HL7 model, and archetype-oriented approaches such as the Open-EHR initiative [26].

3. Quality of medical log data [26, 30].

4. Process mining techniques for discovering health care processes from log data [26].

5. Process simulation by generating and enriching log data [82].

6. Conformance checking. Checking conformance is applied to compare medical log data with guideline processes [26].

7. Compliance checking. The goal is to detect compliance violations by process models/log data when checked against compliance constraints [26].

8. Security and privacy concerning the usage of EHR across multiple organizations [278].

9. Interoperability and integration aspects [278].

10. Exchange formats for EHR [278, 30].

A more general search using search string `allintitle: compliance health care` (excluding patents and citations, accessed on 2016-09-26) resulted in 380 hits.

The results were divided into approaches that addresses compliance requirements and approaches that related to compliance checking. Compliance requirements seem to be an important subject to health care workers, health care services/programs/costs, health care providers, and patient behavior. Compliance requirements specific to diseases such as hypertension, asthma, diabetes, osteoporosis, and neonatology were found during literature search as well. Approaches related to compliance checking refer to regulatory compliance, privacy/assurance, and general as well as IT-supported compliance frameworks. Overall, computerized compliance was addressed by 12 articles.

Summarizing and aggregating the challenges collected in the literature review leads to the following overview results:

Challenges Ch1 – Ch5 for process compliance in the health care domain:

Ch1 Data quality and integration

Ch2 Extraction and modeling of requirements (medical guidelines)

Ch3 Extraction and modeling of process knowledge

Ch4 Comparison of medical processes (as is) with medical guidelines (to be)

Ch5 Provision of intelligible and helpful (user) feedback

Challenges Ch1 to Ch5 are described in mode retail in the following:

(Ch1) Data quality and integration: This challenge occurs due to heterogeneous data sources and heterogeneous requirements regarding the data collection processes [114]. As pointed out in [26], process-oriented log data is often not available in medical environments and does not fulfill any of the quality levels stated by the L^* model suggested by the process mining manifesto [308]. Examples for data that were encountered during the EBMC^2 project [26] were hand-written documents, csv data, and SQL data, all collected for different purposes. Another challenge is the ownership and privacy of data. In most cases, data must be at least anonymized and ownership must be clarified. Overall, aligning, cleaning, and integrating the data for compliance checking poses an enormous challenge. Ch1 is discussed further in Section 3.5.

(Ch2) Extraction and modeling of requirements: In general, as summarized in Figure 3.1, there are different formalisms to model compliance requirements into processable compliance constraints. A crucial prerequisite is to extract the knowledge to be modeled from the sources, demanding requirement extraction from unstructured data such as text. An example is the European skin cancer guideline [102] which describes the treatment of skin cancer patients in text, but should be modeled as constraint that is verifiable over a process model or process log data. In [26], the extraction and modeling was done manually – as it is often the case – in cooperation with domain experts. However, for a multitude of medical guidelines described in natural language or text, (semi-)automatic support for extraction and modeling would be of utmost interest. In addition, the question remains in which language medical guidelines should be modeled. There is a body of languages proposed by research on medical guidelines and clinical pathways such as GLIF or Asbru as well as the notations from the process modeling area such as BPMN. All of these languages are close to or are process modeling languages such that all of them appear to be usable options. Section 3.3 picks up Ch2.

(Ch3) Extraction and modeling of process knowledge: Process knowledge in the sense of as-is processes is mostly captured in existing reference models or as execution data (log data). In the latter case, process mining techniques [307] can be employed in order to derive the process models. The driving factor for the quality of the discovered models is again the data quality (see challenge Ch1). We comment on Ch3 in Section 3.5.

(Ch4) Comparison of as-is and to-be processes: We assume that the medical guidelines and/or reference process models reflect the to-be perspective which is to be matched against the real-world (as-is) processes or constraints. The latter is mostly reflected by the execution data of the medical processes (log data). Techniques to compare the log data with the medical guidelines or reference processes are conformance [307] and compliance checking [174]. Both techniques will be discussed in the context of the medical domain in Section 3.3.

(Ch5) Provision of intelligible and helpful feedback: It is not sufficient to just provide a diagnosis such as "treatment process X violates/does not violate" medical guideline Y. The reason is that often someone has to take some action due to a violation. Here the root cause for the violation is of utmost interest, perhaps even in connection with a strategy how to deal with the violation [26].

On top of these challenges, it can be seen that the constraints that are dealt with in medical process compliance can be divided in:

a. Functional constraints such as medical guidelines and standard operating procedures (SOP) that constrain the logic of the medical process and

b. Non-functional constraints such as privacy and security constraints.

3.3 CHECKING COMPLIANCE OF HEALTHCARE PROCESSES AT DESIGNTIME

Let us first look at a real-world example, i.e., the skin cancer treatment guideline described in [102] that is modeled and analyzed in [82]. Figure 3.2 (adapted from [82]) depicts the top level process model describing the essential steps (phases) of the treatment process. Note that all of these steps represent sub processes, i.e., they can be refined into more detailed process models. The process starts with examining the patient and conducting the surgery in parallel. This is followed by determining the therapy, followed by the aftercare. Depending on some decision, the entire process might be executed again.

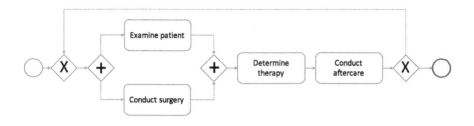

FIGURE 3.2 Process model (in BPMN) of the skin cancer treatment guideline at top level (all steps represent subprocesses).

Focusing on one of the phases, i.e., Conduct aftercare, the more detailed process model is depicted in Figure 3.3. The figure (adapted from [82]) shows that depending on the stage of a patient one or several appointments for different diagnosis activities are arranged. For patients with a stage in situ a Clinical examination will be scheduled. After the examination, the diagnosis is evaluated. Then either more examinations are required (loop back) or the patient leaves the Conduct aftercare sub process. Each of the appointment steps is again a subprocess that can be refined.

The reference process contains different constraints that must be fulfilled by any skin cancer treatment model to be implemented and by actual process executions. At first, let us for the sake of simplicity focus on constraint C1.

C1: After an appointment the diagnosis has to be evaluated.

C1 expresses a presence requirement on the diagnosis as well as an order requirement (diagnosis after examination). Typical compliance requirements would be to check C1 over a specific process model for skin cancer treatment in a hospital (design time), monitoring C1 during process execution (runtime), and checking for compliance/conformance of finished process executions (ex post). Each of these requirements will be discussed in one of the following sections. In this section, we focus on design time compliance.

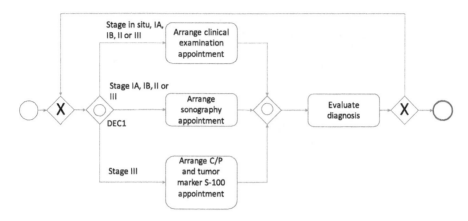

FIGURE 3.3 Reference process model R (in BPMN) for subprocess Conduct aftercare in the skin cancer treatment guideline (all appointment steps represent subprocesses).

Consider process model P modeled for skin cancer treatment in a given hospital (cf. Figure 3.4). Obviously, process model P differs from the reference model depicted in Figure 3.2. The question interesting with respect to compliance is whether or not P is in accordance with C1. First of all, the activities that C1 refers to, i.e., appointment and evaluate diagnosis, have to be matched against P. One challenge is that activity appointment is differentiated in the process model P by three appointment activities, i.e., clinical examination appointment, sonography appointment, and C/P and tumor marker S-100 appointment. As a consequence, C1 actually has to also be differentiated into three compliance constraints $C1_1$, $C1_2$, and $C1_3$ as follows:

$C1_1$: After clinical examination appointment
    the diagnosis has to be evaluated.
$C1_2$: After sonography examination appointment
    the diagnosis has to be evaluated.
$C1_3$: After C/P and tumor marker S-100 examination appointment
    the diagnosis has to be evaluated.

Often activity matching is employed to connect constraints and process models, however, an exact match is often difficult. Hence, using semantic concepts such as ontologies is often more helpful. An approach for activity instantiations in constraints as introduced in [171].

Back to the example, process model P ensures constraints $C1_1$ and $C1_2$, but does not ensure $C1_3$. The reason is that after conducting activity C/P and tumor marker S-100 appointment, the diagnosis is not evaluated as activity Evaluate diagnosis is not a successor of activity C/P and tumor marker S-100 appointment. Hence, overall, P does not ensure C, i.e., P is not compliant with C.

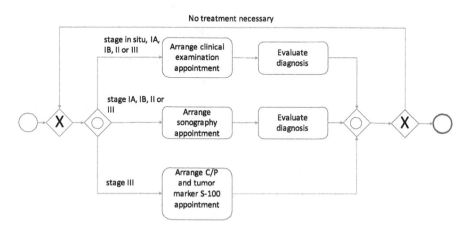

FIGURE 3.4 Process model P (in BPMN).

In addition to illustrating design time compliance (↦ Ch4) this example implicitly addresses Ch2 and Ch3 from a modeling point of view (extraction will be discussed in the sequel). For the example Business Process Modeling and Notation (BPMN) was chosen as a more process-oriented modeling language. Utilizing one of the existing compliance checking approaches requires the transformation of the constraint into the featured constraint language such as LTL, FOL, or EC. Constraint C1, for example, is represented in the different languages as illustrated in Figure 3.5. Note that Compliance Rule Graphs (CRG) offer a graphical notation (cf. Figure 3.5a) that is based on First Order Logic (FOL) (cf. Figure 3.5b), but could be also translated into Linear Temporal Logic. (LTL) (cf. Figure 3.5c) or Event Calculus (EC) (cf. Figure 3.5d). The FOL formula states that for all occurrences of an activity t of type Clinical examination appointment, there must be an activity of type Evaluated diagnosis for which t is a predecessor. The LTL formula states that always if an activity of type Clinical examination appointment occurs, eventually, an activity of type Evaluation diagnosis occurs. The EC formula first states the events that are relevant to the constraints, i.e., ClinicalExaminationAppointment() and EvaluateDiagnosis(). Then the EC formula defines that if the event ClinicalExaminationAppointment()

happens and is not followed by an `EvaluateDiagnosis()` event, an alert will be triggered. Note that for the EC formula not only the "checking part" of the constraint is defined, but also an action that is triggered if the constraint is violated, i.e., an alert.

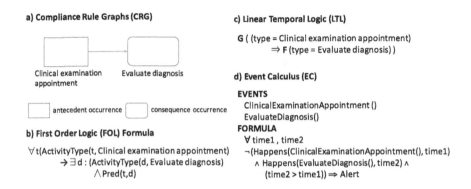

a) Compliance Rule Graphs (CRG)

Clinical examination appointment   Evaluate diagnosis

antecedent occurrence   consequence occurrence

b) First Order Logic (FOL) Formula

$\forall t (\text{ActivityType}(t, \text{Clinical examination appointment})$
$\rightarrow \exists d : (\text{ActivityType}(d, \text{Evaluate diagnosis})$
$\land \text{Pred}(t,d)$

c) Linear Temporal Logic (LTL)

$G \; (\; (\text{type} = \text{Clinical examination appointment})$
$\Rightarrow F \; (\text{type} = \text{Evaluate diagnosis}) \;)$

d) Event Calculus (EC)

EVENTS
ClinicalExaminationAppointment ()
EvaluateDiagnosis()

FORMULA
$\forall \; \text{time1} , \text{time2}$
$\lnot (\text{Happens}(\text{ClinicalExaminationAppointment}(), \text{time1})$
$\land \; \text{Happens}(\text{EvaluateDiagnosis}(), \text{time2}) \land$
$(\text{time2} > \text{time1})) \Rightarrow \text{Alert}$

FIGURE 3.5 Constraint C1 represented in different languages, i.e., CRG, FOL, LTL, and EC.

Further example constraints from the healthcare domain modeled as CRG and LTL formulae can be found in [237].

In the following, compliance checking is demonstrated based on the LTL Checker [174] that is realized as plugin in the process mining framework ProM[1], version 6.2. The LTL Checker takes constraints modeled in LTL as well as process execution logs as input and determines which of the constraints are violated / not violated and which of the instances cause the violation (incorrect) and which do not not (correct). In other words, both, the set of constraints and the set of instances is divided into two subsets.

At first, we simulated 100 instance executions of the reference process model depicted in Figure 3.3. A log entry for, for example, activity `Clinical Examination Appointment` looks as follows (in MXML format, http://www.processmining.org/logs/mxml):

```
<AuditTrailEntry>
    <WorkflowModelElement>ClinicalExaminationAppointment</WorkflowModelElement>
    <EventType>complete</EventType>
    <Timestamp>2016-10-11T15:27:41.364+01:00</Timestamp>
    <Originator>unknown</Originator>
</AuditTrailEntry>
```

Figure 3.6 summarizes the results of compliance checking. Specifically, constraint C1 is displayed ("always when A [i.e., ClinicalExaminationAppoint-

---

[1] www.promtools.org

ment] then eventually B [i.e., Evaluate Diagnosis]"). The result of the LTL checking is that all rules are satisfied and all 100 instances are correct.

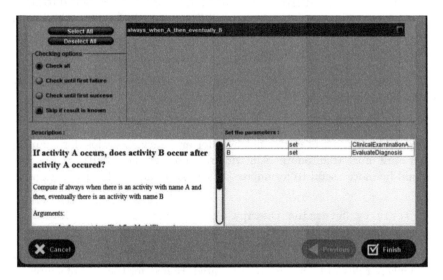

FIGURE 3.6 Checking compliance of reference process model (cf. Figure 3.3) with C1 using LTL Checker in ProM 6.2.

Let us now simulate 100 instances on process model P (cf. Figure 3.4) and check the resulting logs for compliance with $C1_3$. The result of the check is as follows: $C1_3$ is unsatisfied, hence there are no satisfied rules in this case. Out of the 100 instances, 64 are determined as correct, i.e., compliant with $C1_3$. Specifically, these are instances where activity **Arrange C/P and tumor marker S-100 appointment** was not executed and is hence not present in the log. $C1_3$ is violated for the other 36 instances where activity **Arrange C/P and tumor marker S-100 appointment** was executed and hence occurs in the corresponding trace. These instances are classified as incorrect.

3.4 MONITORING COMPLIANCE CONSTRAINTS OVER HEALTH CARE PROCESSES AT RUNTIME

Going from the model or design level to the execution level, it can be argued that P violates $C1_3$ since it enables an execution trace that does not reflect $C1_3$, i.e., the trace $\sigma_1 = $ <Start, Arrange C/P and tumor marker S-100 appointment, End>. As discussed in Section 3.1, at runtime not only control flow related information, but also additional information such as resources, time, or data values can be checked for compliance (cf. [169]). Runtime checking is also referred to as compliance monitoring ($\hookrightarrow$ Ch4).

3.4.1 Resource-Related Compliance Constraints

Assume that activity `Determine therapy` (cf. Figure 3.2) is assigned to an actor `Dr. Smith`. The corresponding compliance constraints is an authorization constraints and can be formulated as follows:

`C2: Does person Dr Smith activity Determine therapy?`

A corresponding check for the particular situation could utilize the following formula predefined in LTL Checker, ProM version 5.2):

`C2: <>( (person==Dr Smith ∧ activity==Determine therapy)`

Note that `C2` does of course not hold for arbitrary scenarios, for example, if there are more than one person with role `Doctor`. For arbitrary scenarios is would be more useful to formulate the check at the role level, for example, using:

`C2': Activity Determine therapy always done`
`    by a person having role = Doctor`

However, checking `C2'` requires the involvement of some organizational model where roles and persons are associated. Hence, for the sake of simplicity we abstain from introducing an organizational model here and stick with the checking `C2`.

Twenty-five process instances were simulated. For 23 instances, activity `Determine therapy` is conducted by `Dr Smith` and for 2 instances by `Dr Allen` (due to, for example, some unforeseen substitution). Applying LTL Checker, ProM 6.2. and corresponding to the simulation setting, 23 instances are determined as being correct and 2 as being incorrect. Those are the ones where `Dr Allen` substituted `Dr Smith` with working on `Determine therapy`. Note that the information on which person actually worked on a task is only available at runtime or ex post.

3.4.2 Time-Related Compliance Constraints

Take the following constraint C3 on arranging an appointment for sonography [169]:

`C3: For Stage IA patients an appointment for sonography`
`    has to be made within 12 months.`

Further on, consider the following trace σ_2 to be checked against C3:

`σ₂ = <Start(2015-01-01), Arrange sonography`
`appointment(2016-02-01), Evaluate diagnosis(...)>`

From a control flow point of view σ_2 does not violate C3. However, C3 is violated by σ_2 from a time perspective as activity `Arrange sonography appointment` is executed more than 12 months after starting the process (note that the time information is derived based on the time stamps in this case).

As a repetition: concerning data, time, and resources are typically not available until runtime, i.e., at runtime and ex post. For ex post validation, conformance checking techniques can be applied. The survey in [169]) elaborates that a number of approaches (in some cases supported by tools) exist that enable compliance monitoring. The main differences lie in the employed constraint modeling language ranging from Event Calculus to Linear Temporal Logic. Utilizing one of the existing approaches requires transformation to the supported constraint language. In the following one can see constraint C3 represented in Event Calculus (EC).

EVENTS
ArrangeSonographyAppointment()
EvaluateDiagnosis()

FORMULA
$\neg(\forall$ time1, time2
Happens(ArrangeSonographyAppointment(), time1) $\wedge$
Happens(EvaluateDiagnosis(), time2)$\wedge$
(time2 > time1) $\wedge$ (time2 <time1 + 12))
$\implies$ alert

In addition to demanding the presence of `Evaluate diagnosis` after the occurrence of `Arrange sonography appointment`, the time span between both activities must not exceed 12 months. The latter is reflected by introducing variables for the time.

3.4.3   Data-Aware Compliance Constraints

Process data captures the values of relevant data elements that are produced and consumed during executing process instances. If resource assignments are modeled as process data, we have already seen a data-related compliance constraint in Section 3.4.1. Process data often relevant in the context of health care processes are patient data such as age and treatment data such as dosage. Constraints on process data could be integrity constraints restricting, for example, the value range of a data element e.g., age values must not exceed 120 years. Note that the connection to the process is required in order to speak of a data-aware process constraint.

Ly et al. distinguish *unary* and *extended* data conditions. `age < 120` is a unary data condition as one data element value is compared to a value (in general: *data* $\odot$ *value*). Extended data conditions compare the values of multiple data objects, for example, temperature values measured by two different activities in the process. Further on, one can distinguish *activity* and *case* data constraints. Activity data constraints refer to data values produced or consumed by process activities. Case data refers to the process instance, for example, the name of the patient the instance is executed for. An example for activity data reformulated in [169] is "If the PainScore of patient p is greater than 7 and the status is uninitialized then the status must be changed to initialized and a timer event is generated to treat patient p within 1 h.".

One important type of data-aware constraints on business processes are decision rules at alternative branchings. Take the example process model in Figure 3.7. There is an alternative branching with a decision rule saying that if the pain score of a patient is greater than 7 a Pain treatment is conducted, otherwise the process directly proceeds to Determine therapy.

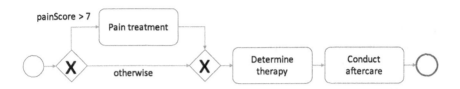

FIGURE 3.7 Process model with decision rule (in BPMN).

Here the process models directly implements decision rule

C4: If painScore >7 apply Pain treatment.

At design time the process model trivially fulfills C4. Still, it might be interesting to check whether the decision rule is really followed during process execution. The discussed approaches for process monitoring can be employed for this. Another possibility is to apply *decision mining* [247] which is actually more an ex post technique (as presented in Section 3.4.4), but still interesting. Decision mining derives decision rules that were applied to alternative branchings from event logs. Doing so the derived decision rules can be compared to the modeled ones. Let us assume that the result of decision mining would be that instead of C4, C4' holds with

C4': If painScore >6 apply Pain treatment.

This would be an interesting sense in terms of revisiting the originally foreseen constraint C4.

3.4.4 Ex-Post Compliance and Conformance Checks

Conformance checking is a technique to compare process logs against process models [307]. For this, the process models are typically represented as Petri nets and the logs are replayed on these Petri nets using a so called "token game". In detail, by replaying the logs it is determined whether tokens are missing that would be required to execute the process model or whether tokens are reflected by the logs that are not consumed when executing the process model. Both cases result in a penalty, i.e., a decrease in the optimal fitness value[2] of 1.0.

Consider the use case introduced in Figure 3.4, i.e., the reference model (reflected as Petri net) and a set of 100 process logs produced on process model P. Recall that compliance checking using LTL checker revealed that 36 of the instances were not compliant with the reference model, i.e., violated constraint $C1_3$. $C1_3$, in turn. is reflected in the reference model as each occurrence of activity `Arrange C/P and tumor marker S-100 appointment` is eventually followed by an execution of activity `Evaluate Diagnosis`. The analysis conducted by applying the plug in Replay Log on Petri Net for Conformance Analysis in ProM 6.2 reveals the non-conformance of 36 instances at activity `Evaluate Diagnosis` (and the conformance of 64 instances respectively). The fitness of the traces is determined as 0.86.

The example illustrates that conformance can be utilized to learn about the ex post compliance of process logs on process models. The process models, in turn, can reflect compliance constraints. If so, the conformance or compliance of the logs with these constraints can be analyzed by conformance checking as well.

3.5 DATA QUALITY IN HEALTHCARE

Literature names data quality as one of the major challenges for healthcare compliance (Ch1). The reasons are among others heterogeneous data sources where data was collected for different purposes and by different organizational entities, entailing different quality levels.

In general, for process compliance checking and in particular for process monitoring the ideal input is process log data. This data is event-oriented where events represent the execution of process tasks, e.g., conducting the surgery, equipped with a timestamp when the execution took place. The events are grouped along the instances their execution belongs to, and the instances are grouped based on the process type they have been created and executed on. In other words a process log L consists of event traces for each instance denoted by an instance id. Instances can be associated with a process type denoted by a process id. This minimally required information can be extended by information on the resource that has processed a task and the data that has been produced during task execution.

The process mining manifesto [308] introduces different quality levels for log data based on the so called L^* model:

* event logs of low quality, often manually collected, e.g., medical records on paper

---

[2] A set of process logs that totally conforms with a process model has a fitness value of 1.0.

** unsystematic, automatic collection by, for example, product management systems, embedded systems; untrustworthy, incomplete

*** unsystematic, automatic collection by, for example, ERP or CRM systems, trustworthy, incomplete

**** systematic, automatic collection by, for example, BPM or workflow systems, trustworthy, complete

***** systematic, automatic, and safe collection by, for example, BPM or workflow systems, trustworthy, complete, clear semantics

As the examples named by the L* model already indicate, medical records range on the lowest quality level (*). Often they are recorded by hand in an unsystematic manner. In the EBMC^2 project two main healthcare data sources were analyzed, i.e., the S4MDB and the GAP-DRG data [26]. S4MDB data is a database collecting information about three process tasks together with patient and medication parameters. This data set was not collected for process compliance checking originally and recorded by hand in an unsystematic manner, but can be considered as trustworthy and correct, hence ranging at quality level */**. The GAP-DRG data is also collected by hand, but in a systematic manner, and can be considered trustworthy and correct. Hence, we would put the GAP-DRG data at quality level **. What becomes obvious is that none of the sources was originally intended for process analysis and none of the sources was recorded automatically.

As discussed in the experience report from the skin cancer case [26] the quality of the data regarding the L* model was so low that the data had to be partly recollected. For this a tool was developed that enabled users to insert data in a way that they were used to (i.e., more database or table-oriented). The tool implemented a data model that enabled the direct production of process log data based on the data modeled presented in [26]. The data integration problem is omnipresent, i.e., not specific for the health care domain. Here, a body of research work has been provided, see, for example, the book on schema mapping and matching [23].

The other challenge with data extraction is deriving the knowledge about the guidelines in a structured way. Often guidelines are only available in unstructured form such as text. One way of eliciting constraints from unstructured data sources is manual extraction by experts. In the EBMC^2, for example, the skin cancer guideline process model was extracted by a modeling expert and discussed with medical experts afterwards. Manual extraction, however, can be time-consuming and tedious. It typically involves domain and modeling experts as the EBMC^2 experience shows as the domain experts have the domain knowledge and the modeling experts know how a structured result is supposed to look like. Overall, (semi-)automatic approaches suggesting candidates for constraints from unstructured data would be highly desirable.

3.6 SUMMARY AND FURTHER CHALLENGES

In summary, ensuring compliance of health care processes with constraints such as medical guidelines is of enormous importance. The challenges range from extracting and modeling the constraints as well as the process-related data from possibly various sources to checking compliance at design time, runtime, and ex post. For these checks during the process life cycle, different approaches have been proposed, mainly based on model checking and pattern matching. The approaches utilize different languages to define the constraints in a formal way such as LTL or EC. As compliance checking is relatively well understood there are still many open questions and challenges. A selection of these challenges are discussed in the following.

User feedback: So far compliance checking approaches mostly report back whether or not a compliance constraint is violated. In case of violation, certain approaches return a counter example, i.e., a process trace that violates the constraint. This might not very helpful for the end used who is in charge to deal with a compliance violation as first of all the understandability of the result is limited and secondly neither root cause for the violation nor a strategy of how to deal with it are typically provided [169]. Hence, there is a huge need for developing approaches for helpful user feedback in compliance checking.

Interoperability: Health care processes can be distributed among different (independent) organizations, for example, the hospital, the general practitioner, and some external lab. In these cases, the partner processes have to interact in order to provide the partner-spanning treatment. However, often, this interaction is not fully realized yet. This leads to two aspects:

1. Data exchange

2. Compliance checking in distributed process settings

Data exchange between different health care organizations has been addressed by defining exchange formats. Compare here, for example, the Health Level 7 (HL7)[3] organization and related standards as well as Electronic Health Records (EHR) [123]. This is a practically crucial challenge.

From a compliance perspective another challenging question is how to check compliance in distributed process settings. The difficulty here arises from two facts. First of all, in distributed process settings compliance constraints might not only be local, i.e., refer to partner processes isolated from each other, but also span multiple partners (global constraints) [92]. Hence, one has to deal with a mix of compliance constraints at different levels. Secondly, due to confidentiality reasons, in a distributed setting, the partners typically do not reveal details of their so called private processes, but only those parts that are involved in the interaction with the other partners (public processes). As a consequence, checking constraints over several partners becomes very difficult

---

[3]www.hl7.org

as not all process related information is available. Despite first approaches address these challenges (cf. [92]), more research work and case studies in the health care domain have to be conducted.

Compliance and change: Another challenges is the interplay between compliance and change. Health care processes might be subject to change [162]. At the same time these processes might be subject to imposed compliance constraints. Then it is crucial to ensure that the compliance of a process or process instance is not harmed by the process change. Consider, for example, a compliance constraint that demands for the presence of some activity in a process and due to an ad hoc change this activity is deleted. As a consequence, the constraint will be deleted after conducing the change. One option is to recheck all compliance constraints after conducting changes. The other option is to optimize the checks by determining which compliance constraints might be actually affected by the change and only check for those constraints [170].

EXERCISES

3.1 Consider the process model in Figure 3.2. Write down all compliant traces that can be produced based on the model. Provide one trace that is not compliant with the model.

3.2 Formulate the following constraint in LTL and EC: After the surgery no sonography must be conducted within 30 days.

3.3 Is the process model depicted in Figure 3.4 compliant with the following constraint For stage in situ patients, the diagnosis must be evaluated after conducting the activity Arrange clinical examination appointment?

3.4 Can the following constraint be checked/decided on based on the process model depicted in Figure 3.4: The diagnosis has to be made by a doctor?

GLOSSARY

Compliance: Given a process P and a constraint C, do the model of P and all executions of P NOT violate C, i.e., are P and its executions compliant with C?

Constraint: A constraint specifies a (business) rule, guideline, regulation, requirement, or law using a selected formalism such that it can be automatically checked for compliance over a process model or event traces.

FURTHER READING

Rinderle-Ma Stefanie, Ly Linh Thao, and Dadam Peter, Business process compliance, *EMISA Forum*, 28(2):24-29, 2008.

Linh Thao Ly, Rinderle-Ma Stefanie, Göser Kevin, and Dadam Peter, On enabling integrated process compliance with semantic constraints in process management systems - requirements, challenges, solutions, *Information Systems Frontiers*, 14(2):195–219, 2012.

Linh Thao Ly, Fabrizio Maria Maggi, Marco Montali, Stefanie Rinderle-Ma, Wil M. P. van der Aalst: Compliance monitoring in business processes: functionalities, application, and tool-support, *Information Systems*, 54:209–234, 2015.

CHAPTER 4

Modeling a Process for Managing Age-Related Macular Degeneration

Aitor Eguzkitza

Public University of Navarra, Pamplona, Spain

Jesús D. Trigo

Public University of Navarra, Institute of Smart Cities, Pamplona, Spain

Miguel Martínez-Espronceda

Public University of Navarra, Pamplona, Spain

Luis Serrano

Public University of Navarra, Institute of Smart Cities, Pamplona, Spain

José Andonegui

Department of Ophthalmology, Complejo Hospitalario de Navarra, Pamplona, Spain

CONTENTS

> A horse! a horse! my kingdom for a horse!
>
> ———————————————
>
> W. Shakespeare

THIS chapter applies a previously developed methodology to formalize the clinical process associated with Age-Related Macular Degeneration (AMD), reusing the existing electronic models when possible. Additionally, this chapter describes the implementation of the AMD monitoring service in a real healthcare scenario.

4.1 INTRODUCTION

Most health services in the world have hitherto been organized to treat acute episodes, whereas chronic conditions consume as much as 80% of national healthcare's budgets due to a suboptimal management of chronicity [103]. At this point, a paradigm shift is needed, otherwise the costs arising from chronic conditions will continue increasing unless health services adapt their care strategies from reactive to preventive.

At this point, the electronic healthcare, also known as e-health, takes on special relevance. The proliferation of Information and Communication Technologies (ICTs) and health devices connectable to data networks facilitates the exchange of relevant diagnostic information among health facilities. In this regard, the amalgam of papers and diagnostic tests in physical format has led to Electronic Health Records (EHR). This new context of electronic healthcare leads to reconsider traditional clinical practices toward more accurate diagnoses and a more efficient redistribution of resources, both material and human.

Although novel therapeutic strategies/mechanisms keep in constant evolution toward efficient healthcare strategies, most health services do not reconsider traditional clinical procedures because of the intense efforts required to remodel their static and vendor-specific electronic health information systems [77]. In this sense, the normalization of information and communications in medicine are considered strategic, as they facilitate the development of new e-health services that coordinate devices from different manufacturers. Those e-health services, in turn, will provide software tools that, relying on objective parameters, would facilitate an efficient management of healthcare resources [131, 271].

In this context, the advent of health information standards based on dual-model layered architectures, such as the EN/ISO 13606 or openEHR, has simplified the management of the clinical knowledge inside the EHR [267, 178]. This architecture defines two conceptual levels: on the one hand, a reference model that standardizes the way the information is handled inside the software, and, on the other hand, an archetype model that gathers knowledge about the clinical process to be managed.

The dual-model e-health standards guarantee standardization at different levels of interoperability to achieve a faithful exchange of health information. However, given the technical complexity of the standards, experts on clinical domain feel reluctant to actively engage in modeling their own clinical processes into model-driven information systems. To bridge this gap, the authors proposed a comprehensive methodology for formalizing clinical information in accordance with technical, syntactic, semantic, process/organizational, and presentation layers of interoperability [86]. As a proof of concept, the authors used such methodology in a previous effort to formalize a Diabetic Retinopathy (DR) screening service [86].

In spite of the ongoing advances in the field, there is still a clear need to make contributions to the existing corpus of electronic models, given the current scarcity of knowledge artifacts available so far. Such contributions would help in widening the range of healthcare scenarios to which the dual-model approach could be applied. Therefore, the main objective of this chapter is to formalize the clinical process of a real scenario of management of chronicity. The scenario chosen is a high resolution consultation for monitoring the intravitreal anti-vascular endothelial growth factor (anti-VEGF) therapy used to treat wet AMD in the Health Service of Navarre (Servicio Navarro de Salud – Osasunbidea, SNS-O). The rationale behind this selection is explained as follows. AMD is one of the most frequent causes of avoidable blindness in Europe. Although there are more frequent ophthalmic conditions (such as e.g., cataract), the chronicity of AMD often leads to severe and irreversible loss of vision when patients are not early treated [145, 222]. To avoid that scenario, the management of such chronic condition should entail the continued care of patients. However, given the traditional clinical procedures, there are not enough specialists in health services to handle the increasing workload arising from periodic revisions necessary to guarantee a suitable management of chronicity in ophthalmology. Moreover, due to the increasing life expectancy in developed countries, the occurrence of blindness or visual impairment will become even more common the coming years [254].

Additionally, the existing archetype corpus for ophthalmology and AMD is still scarce. As said before, there are two main standards supporting dual-model layered architectures, namely EN/ISO 13606 and openEHR. Both of them have repositories for electronic models. The former has recently launched the Clinical Information Model Manager (CIMM) [292], but to date, there is only one archetype defined (the entry blood pressure). Additionally, the Spanish National Health Service implemented a number of semantic resources to enable interoperability among the health services nationwide. However, it is a reduced set (10 compositions, 7 sections, 38 entries, 3 clusters, making a total of 58 EN/ISO 13606 archetypes) and none of them are related to ophthalmology [186]. On the other hand, openEHR launched the Clinical Knowledge Manager (CKM), which includes 499 archetypes, 78 templates, and 29 termsets [202]. Among them, only a few are related to ophthalmology (namely, Visual Acuity [VA], fundoscopic examination, visual field measurement, refraction, refraction details, and intraocular pressure [IOP]). In addition, the openEHR CKM includes a specific project to author ophthalmology models. To date, only the electronic models related to DR and developed by the authors are included.

Consequently, the objective of this chapter is twofold: first, the main objective is to apply the methodology proposed in [86] in order to model the clinical process associated to AMD in the SNS-O, reusing the existing electronic models when possible. Additionally, a secondary objective is to illustrate the implementation of the AMD monitoring service into the SNS-O.

This chapter is organized as follows: Section 4.2 provides readers with some medical background related to AMD and briefly presents the methodology already published by the authors [86]. In Section 4.3, the methodology is applied to the AMD scenario, resulting in a number of new electronic models. Section 4.4 shows the practical implementation of the AMD monitoring service in the SNS-O. Discussion is presented in Section 4.5 and final conclusions are drawn in Section 4.6.

4.2 BACKGROUND

4.2.1 Age-Related Macular Degeneration (AMD)

AMD is a degenerative process of the central retina that develops in elderly people. The macula covers the central area of the retina which actually is responsible for detecting high-acuity details of central vision. Therefore, when

TABLE 4.1   Classification of the severity of AMD according to the AREDS scale.

Category	Severity of AMD	Description
1	No AMD	No or a few small (<63 micrometers in diameter) drusen.
2	Early AMD	Many small drusen, a few intermediate-sized drusen (63–124 micrometers in diameter), or pigmentary changes on the macula
3	Intermediate AMD	Many intermediate drusen or at least one large drusen (>=125 micrometres), or geographic atrophy not involving the centre of fovea
4	Advanced or late AMD	Dry: drusen and geographic atrophy involving the foveal center. Wet: Choroidal neovascularisation or evidence for neovascular maculopathy

it gets damaged, the VA decreases drastically, especially in central areas of the Visual Field (VF).

The visual impairment due to AMD has devastating effects on the quality of life of patients. Consequently, daily activities such as reading, driving, watching television, recognizing faces or doing housework become great challenges for them [61, 122]. The severity of those consequences sets the AMD as the leading cause of blindness in people over 65 years. Indeed, its prevalence in people over 40 years in the United States is 6.5%, and more than one out of every 10 Americans over 80 has advanced symptoms of AMD at least in one eye [143]. Studies in other developed countries concluded that the increase of AMD depends on the age of patients [196]. Consequently, as AMD is a process strongly associated with age, the prevalence of AMD would increase in the coming years proportionally with the aging population.

4.2.1.1   Classification System

AMD is divided into two subtypes: atrophic (dry) and exudative (wet) [27]. The former is more frequent and it has not treatment yet, but its consequences are less visually debilitating for patients, whereas the latter occurs less frequently and is treatable, but its consequences are more severe for the vision. It is worth mentioning that the prevalence of wet AMD represents 10–15% of all cases of AMD, but accounts 90% of severe visual loss due to AMD [207].

One of the main classification systems for AMD was proposed by the Age-Related Eye Disease Study Group (AREDS) to define different categories according to progression of the disease [4, 251]. These categories established for AMD are further described in Table 4.1.

4.2.1.2 Strategy for Diagnosis and Follow-Up

The visual loss due to wet AMD progresses rapidly compared to dry AMD. As per wet AMD, a study of the natural progression showed that during 28 days elapsed between initial diagnosis and treatment, 44% of patients investigated had some degree of visual loss, and 16% lost more than 3 lines of distance VA [207]. Meanwhile, the appearance of geographic atrophy ranges from 2.5 to 5.9 years depending on the type of lesion [71]. Thus, to minimize the risk of visual loss, wet AMD has to be continuously monitored in short periods of time. Furthermore, the treatment is significantly more effective when applied at first stages of the disease, since the VA deterioration caused by delaying the therapy can become irreversible [190]. Nevertheless, the symptoms are imperceptible in the initial stages of AMD, so the population at risk, which usually consists on elderly patients, should be included into follow-up circuits guaranteeing the detection of the disease. Concerning those follow-up processes, the study of different viewpoints of the macula is required. Consequently, the tests of Non-Mydriatic Retinography (NMR), combined with either the diagnostic tests of fluorescein angiography or Optical Coherence Tomography (OCT) are involved in monitoring the progression of wet AMD [100].

4.2.1.3 Therapeutic Recommendation

Once the diagnosis of wet AMD has been confirmed, the progression of subretinal neovascularization which characterizes this condition can be retarded by repeated injections of anti-VEGF agents into the vitreous cavity [6]. Originally, all patients were treated equally by applying them monthly intravitreal injections. Actually, great results were achieved in terms of VA, but at the expense of a huge number of monitoring visits and invasive therapeutic procedures [39, 152, 246]. Therefore, considering that not all patients respond similarly to the same treatment, as we shall see later, more personalized treatment approaches are suggested in literature.

In that respect, in order to reduce the number of unnecessary treatments and clinical encounters, some authors recommend, after the three first monthly injections, including an evaluation for further treatment as part of the therapy. Consequently, the treatment could be adapted for patients not responding to the injections, and so the anti-VEGF agents are used only when they are effective [100, 116, 227]. In the same way, by reducing unnecessary interventions, the adverse complications resulting from intravitreal injections are minimized too.

Infectious endophthalmitis is regarded to be the most adverse postoperative complication of anti-VEGF intraocular injections, due to its vision-threatening potential [198]. Thus, when the intervention is considered necessary, it must undergo in compliance with procedure guidelines specially designed to guarantee the safety of patients. In this sense, the choices made according to the location where the procedure takes place, the strategy for ventilation, the sterilization of surgical equipment and barriers used to prevent the infection, the method employed to apply anesthesia, the preparation of antiseptics, the use of post-injection antibiotics, and the anti-VEGF agents used are critical to reduce the risk of infection to the greatest extent possible [89, 172].

Taking into consideration the pharmaceutical agents used for intravitreal injection, ranibizumab (LucentisR, Genentech/Roche, Inc., South San Francisco, CA) is the most cost-effective among treatments for neovascular AMD approved by the United States Food and Drug Administration agency [40]. However, bevacizumab (AvastinR, Genentech/Roche, Inc., South San Francisco, CA) has to be considered as an alternative to ranibizumab, since both are anti-VEGF compounds whose effectiveness has been proved for AMD before ranibizumab was licensed [38]. Indeed, the use of bevacizumab was approved in the USA in 2005 and in Europe in 2006 as a systemic anticancer therapy, but it is still being debated whether it is safe enough for intravitreal injections. In that respect, compared to bevacizumab, ranibizumab presents decreased risks of ocular inflammation and venous thrombotic events [341]. Even so, latest publications and guidelines support the safety of using bevacizumab within AMD, since the effectiveness is similar to ranibizumab but at lower cost [6, 25, 341]. Aflibercept (EyleaR, Regeneron Pharmaceuticals Inc., Tarrytown, NY) is another alternative and is also used, since it is as effective as bevacizumab or ranibizumab. Other medications such as pegaptanib sodium (MacugenR, Eyetech, Inc., Cedar Knolls, NJ), or alternative treatments such as antioxidant and vitamin supplement intake, Photodynamic Therapy (PDT), and thermal laser photocoagulation surgery are no longer used for the treatment of AMD.

4.2.2 Methodology to Formalize Clinical Practice into Information Systems

In a previous work, the authors proposed a methodology for formalizing clinical practice into information systems [86]. This methodology goes one step further than merely computerizing the domain knowledge using the two-level modeling approach. On top of that, it proposes using standardized terminology services, modeling computerized medical guidelines, managing workflow pathways of the clinical process, and formalizing the specifications for the User Interface (UI), i.e., how information is presented to users.

That would guarantee a suitable level of quality for the electronic models designed with the aim of ensuring continuity of care in patient-centered clinical processes that require tight coordination among multidisciplinary care providers. Considering all this, the modeling strategy proposed is comprised of three main phases (Figure 4.1). The details of the methodology were published in [86], but a brief summary is given below:

- Definition of the project: In this first phase, a work team is convened to analyze available information resources and define requirements to

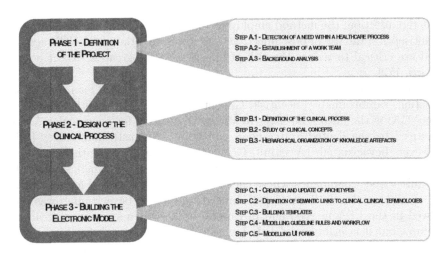

FIGURE 4.1 Methodology proposed for modeling the clinical knowledge into electronic models.

redesign a clinical procedure in response to deficiencies detected in daily clinical practice for a particular healthcare scenario.

- Design of the clinical process: At this phase, the methodology proposed must satisfy the requirements of the project described previously. The clinical process is defined as a combination of activities, decisions, and conditions that constitute the clinical pathways in the healthcare service. Those pathways are completed with the clinical concepts identified and then organized hierarchically according to the healthcare scenario chosen.

- Building the electronic model: At the third phase, all information necessary to build the electronic model has been already documented. Consequently, it is time to formalize the different aspects of healthcare for the clinical process designed in the previous phases. This section, therefore, would guide domain experts in building the knowledge artifacts considered by the proposed methodology: archetypes, templates, terminology bindings, guideline rules, and UI form specifications.

4.3 MODELING A HIGH RESOLUTION CONSULTATION TO MONITOR THE TREATMENT OF WET AMD

As seen in Subsection 4.2.1, the treatment of wet AMD is particularly critical regarding the management of chronic conditions in ophthalmology. In fact, this condition may present visual loss from 28 days from the time of last assessment [207]. Thus, the consultation required to manage this clinical process must coordinate tightly the assessment of progression of the disease, with an immediate provision of the most suitable therapeutic interventions to minimize the risk of visual loss in each case.

In that respect, the integration of ICTs with interoperable diagnostic tests provides a new framework toward modeling patient-centered efficient and accurate healthcare processes. In this context, this section proposes the formalization of a service designed for periodic and long-term monitoring of the treatment of patients diagnosed with wet AMD in the ophthalmology department of the SNS-O. To do so, the methodology proposed in [86] and briefly summarized in Subsection 4.2.2 was followed.

4.3.1 Definition of the Project

On the basis of the above, patients diagnosed with wet AMD must follow a strict treatment of intraocular injections to avoid irreversible progression of the disease (see Subsection 4.2.1). Likewise, in view of optimizing the effectiveness of this clinical procedure, the response of the patient to each treatment can be analyzed so as to adjust the next therapeutic intervention accordingly.

In the case of the ophthalmology department of the SNS-O, patients included within the treatment circuit are regularly examined out for any signs of progression within AMD. Namely, they are convened monthly for a monitoring of the treatment that includes the periodic measurement of VA, and the examination of the macula using slit lamp biomicroscopy and a non-contact fundus lens, combined with OCT. However, due to the complexity of the aforementioned procedure for monitoring each response to therapy, as the volume of patients requiring treatment for wet AMD increases the healthcare resources available to carry out this clinical process may become insufficient to treat all patients within recommended intervals [8].

Consequently, a multidisciplinary group comprised of ophthalmologists expert in retina (belonging to the Complejo Hosptalario de Navarra and the Hospital Universitario de Bellvitge), and specialists in ICT engineering (from the Department of Electrical and Electronic Engineering of the Public University of Navarra) was convened to work toward efficiency in devising a clinical process aimed at providing the appropriate therapy to patients diagnosed with wet AMD. In that respect, the work team proposed a high resolution consultation – also known as "one-stop outpatient consultation" – geared to manage the treatment of wet AMD.

This approach would optimize the waiting time and cost-effectiveness of the clinical process by conducting all examinations, diagnostic decisions and consequent therapies along a single outpatient visit. Thus, the work team determined the following changes upon traditional proceedings to integrate the high resolution consultation strategy into the monitoring of the treatment of wet AMD:

- Rethink of the treatment: Considering that the clinical knowledge evolves continuously, the modeling must consider the emerging new therapeutic strategies: as seen in Subsection 4.2.1, traditionally, the treatment by repeated injections of antiangiogenic agents into the vitreous cavity was systematically applied to all patients diagnosed with wet AMD. Conversely, the guidelines in the ophthalmology department of the SNS-O include, after each treatment, a stage for monitoring the progression of the disease so as to adjust the therapy accordingly. Thereby, the number of treatments per patient is limited to the cases in which such treatment is effective, hence the suppression of unnecessary interventions leads to alleviate the waiting lists.

With regard to intravitreal injections of VEGF inhibitors, the alternative use of bevacizumab is considered since its effectiveness is similar to ranibizumab or aflibercept but at lower cost (see Subsection 4.2.1). This makes the treatment accessible to more patients, considering a limited health budget to meet the demand of a treatment administered regularly and restricted by the recommended periods.

The location of the treatment itself has been reconsidered. Whereas traditionally intraocular injections were carried out within an operating room, by setting up a dedicated procedure room compliant to guidelines for best practice that guarantee the safety of patients, this intervention can take place in the same office where ophthalmologists assess the patients [89]. This will accelerate considerably the workflow regarding the time elapsed from the examination of patients until their treatment. In addition the waiting list of the operating rooms reserved to intravitreal anti-VEGF injections will be alleviated, and thus, those would be allocated to other interventions.

- Redistribution of the workload: The integration of ICTs in healthcare provides clinicians with ubiquitous access to the clinical information registered within a clinical process. This new scenario facilitates the redistribution of the workload of traditional healthcare processes toward services that use the human and technical resources more efficiently. This will facilitate dealing with the scarcity of highly qualified professionals in healthcare services. The workload can be divided in simpler modules but requiring very specific skills, and then the clinical staff available can be trained accordingly so as to cover diverse roles specifically defined to manage the clinical process. In that respect, it is noteworthy that the management of the treatment of wet AMD is limited by the scarcity of specialists in retina. Thus, routine tasks that require less specialization such as the acquisition of diagnostic tests can be delegated to specifically trained nurses. In this way, the workload of ophthalmologists would be alleviated, so they can concentrate their efforts on specialized tasks such as analysis of clinical data, determine therapeutic decisions or conduct surgery.

- Allocation of specialized workspaces: According to the high resolution consultation, every clinical encounter (diagnostic tests, assessment and treatment) must be completed along a single outpatient visit. To that end, differentiated points of care would be specifically equipped with the technical and human resources necessary to carry out each of the clinical encounters concerned. In this way, instead of making successive reservations at a non-earmarked ophthalmologist's office, disease-specific workspaces would be allocated, for some hours a day, to manage the complete workflow.

The integration of all these proposals into the process of monitoring the treatment of patients diagnosed with wet AMD should accelerate the flow of patients through the clinical process, and hence alleviate the waiting lists in that service. It is estimated that whereas an ordinary consultation of ophthalmology in the SNS-O attends approximately 24 encounters per day including patients presenting different eye diseases, the high resolution consultation proposed would alleviate a patient every 10 minutes exclusively from the waiting lists of wet AMD (about 30 patients dispatched in 5 hours of operation).

4.3.2   Design of the Clinical Process

4.3.2.1   Step B.1: Definition of the Clinical Process

The high resolution consultation designed by the work team manages patients from different clinical processes which, after specific diagnostic tests and assessments, have been diagnosed with wet AMD. Therefore, the clinical process actually begins when, based on clinical information gathered during diagnosis, a retinologist determines whether the therapy of anti-VEGF intravitreal injections is suitable or not for a patient being assessed.

If so, the patients selected receive the first cycle of treatments directly on the ophthalmologist's office, which entails one monthly intravitreal injection for three months. Thereafter, the progression of AMD must be monitored periodically, so patients are convened once a month and the corresponding diagnostic tests are performed and electronically registered.

Finally, a retinologist from a remote workstation examines the results of those clinical tests, and determines, depending on the response of the patient to the last treatment, whether to repeat or not the anti-VEGF intravitreal injections. The treatment takes place directly in the office of the ophthalmologist expert in retina, and whether treated or not, a patient's review is scheduled for next month.

Therefore, as shown in Figure 4.2, the management of the treatment for wet AMD was defined into four clinical stages, plus an additional stage to contextualize new patients diagnosed with wet AMD. Each one of these stages is analyzed in detail along this section:

- BACKGROUND (Diagnosis of wet AMD): Patients, who during routine

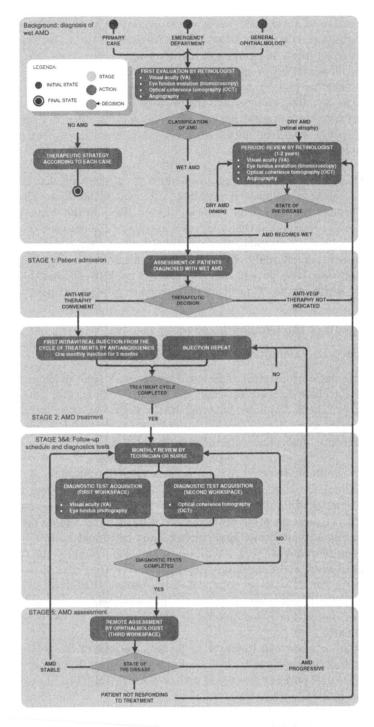

FIGURE 4.2 Activity diagram describing the workflow proposed for a high resolution consultation to monitor the treatment for wet AMD.

clinical encounters such as primary care services, eye emergency services, or general ophthalmology presented signs of possible AMD, are immediately referred for further examination to specialized consultation of a retinologist. During that consultation, the diagnostic tests of VA, eye fundus examination using slit lamp biomicroscopy and a non-contact fundus lens, OCT and angiography are undertaken. Besides, depending on each case, the retinologist can consider appropriate carrying out additional tests, such as direct eye fundus examination. Then, the retinologist examines those tests as a whole, and determines a diagnosis for the clinical findings that initially raised the suspicion of AMD. Once diagnosed, only patients presenting wet/exudative AMD are included in the healthcare process proposed, and thus receive treatment of intravitreal anti-VEGF injections. Nevertheless, patients with dry AMD could develop wet AMD in the future. Therefore, their condition is periodically reviewed (within periods of 1–2 years) to detect any sign of disease's progression leading to wet AMD. Finally, some of the patients examined could be affected any other condition beyond AMD, so an appropriate therapeutic strategy should be determined according to each case. This last scenario is out of the scope of the model proposed.

Actually, the high resolution consultation does not begin until the next stage, in which patients are enrolled for the treatment of wet AMD. For this reason, the process to establish the diagnosis of wet AMD was not included from the electronic model. Nevertheless, to avoid duplication of diagnostic tests, the decision on admission for the first cycle of treatments is mainly based on retrospective information from this stage. Therefore, the diagnostic tests resulting from the diagnosis of wet AMD are analyzed in the admission stage, to provide a context to each candidate for the intravitreal anti-VEGF therapy (Figure 4.2).

- STAGE 1 (Patient admission): The same ophthalmologist expert in retina entrusted of determining the diagnosis of AMD evaluates each patient to decide whether to enrol him/her into the long-term treatment for wet AMD. To that end, the retinologist must address two decisions before admitting a patient within the cycle of treatments proposed for wet AMD:

  − Diagnosis of wet AMD: As seen above, only patients assessed with wet/exudative AMD are included into the first cycle of treatments of intravitreal anti-VEGF injections. Thus, evaluation of new candidates for such treatment is triggered whenever the retinologist confirms the diagnosis of wet AMD during the review of a patient.

  − No contraindications for anti-VEGF therapy: Then, the ophthalmologist must determine the best therapy for each case, thus verifies whether patients fulfill the minimum requirements to receive the anti-VEGF injections. Thereby, patients presenting contraindications such as very low VA (values below 0.1 in decimal scale) or healed lesions resulting from previous treatments are excluded from the treatment.

Those patients chosen in accordance with those conditions are enrolled into the high resolution consultation service, and thus scheduled to receive the first cycle of intravitreal anti-VEGF injections described below.

- STAGE 2 (AMD treatment): The first cycle of treatments consists of monthly administration of an intravitreal antiangiogenic injection for three months. Once those treatments have been completed, an ophthalmologist must evaluate the response of patients to previous treatments right before determining each new retreatment. In this way, ophthalmologists are able to adjust the frequency of injections administered, or even interrupt the treatment according to the needs of each patient.

Whenever an ophthalmologist, as a result of the therapeutic assessment described along the last stage, determines the retreatment for a patient with wet AMD, the patient is called urgently to his office. There, the patient is informed about the procedure, then the ophthalmologist examines its eye fundus to prepare the intervention, and finally the intravitreal anti-VEGF injections are administered in-situ. However, there is an ongoing debate on the safest procedure for administering the intravitreal injections [89, 18]. In that respect, the following guidelines were established for the healthcare scenario of the SNS-O so as to ensure the safety of the intervention:

- Clinical setting for injection: Intravitreal injections may be safely performed in an office setting, with the added advantages of greater agility and flexibility compared to booking an operating room. Hence, most patients will receive by default, the injections directly at the same office used by the ophthalmologist for assessment.

- Prevention of infection: Both the clinicians responsible for the injection and the patient himself must wear surgical masks to avoid the microbe spread coming from their upper respiratory tract. The clinical personnel involved in the procedure must wear sterile gloves before any patient contact. The use of topical antibiotics is not considered necessary due to insufficient evidence in literature supporting this routine. To prevent contact between the needle/injection site and the eyelashes and eyelids, a speculum is used, or alternately, a nurse conducts a manual eyelid retraction while the ophthalmologist administers the injection.

- Topical anesthetics: Topical anesthetic drops are applied to reduce patient discomfort during the intervention.

- Antiseptic usage: Povidone-iodine (5–10%) is applied to the conjunctival surface at the intended injection site, avoiding eyelid contact on this area. This must be the last agent applied before injection so as to reduce the incidence of endophthalmitis. In addition, according to the guidelines in force at the ophthalmology department of the SNS-O, the application of povidone-iodine is also contemplated on eyelids, including the eyelashes and eyelid margins. In that respect, eyelid scrubbing or eyelid pressure should be avoided since, this routine increases the risk of liberating bacteria from the meibomian glands.

- Anti-VEGF agents administered: Ranibizumab, aflibercept and bevacizumab are injected indistinctly, as they present equivalent outcomes in the treatment of wet AMD (see Subsection 4.2.1).

- STAGE 3 (Follow-up schedule): The diagnostic tests aimed at the assessment of the response of patients to the treatment are then scheduled for the month following the last injection from the current treatment cycle. In this way, the ophthalmologists will have at their disposal the results of these tests just before proceeding with next treatment.

- STAGE 4 (Diagnostic tests): As seen in Subsection 4.2.1, the ophthalmologist must combine the assessment of the patient's latest measurements of VA, eye fundus photographies, and OCT studies so as to review the treatment of wet AMD. The measurement of VA must be conducted in the first place, in order to subsequently administer mydriatic agents to the patient. This is because, although mydriasis is recommended to conduct the OCT test, and it is beneficial for the acquisition of eye fundus images, it is contraindicated for the measurement of VA. Then, once the mydriatic effect is active, NMR and OCT tests could be carried out.

Based on these guidelines, three differentiated workspaces were proposed to distribute the patient flow due to the diagnostic tests involved on the high resolution consultation (see Figure 4.2):

- The first workspace: Point of care managed by a nurse specialized on VA testing and acquisition of non-mydriatic retinal photographs. It is worth mentioning that, at this workspace, the eye fundus evaluation using slit lamp biomicroscopy undertaken in traditional consultation of ophthalmology has been substituted by digital retinography. In this way, the eye fundus photographs will be ubiquitously available for their remote assessment. Therefore, the workspace must be equipped with a non-mydriatic fundus camera, and a Snellen chart for VA testing. Likewise, the illumination and dimensions of the room must be appropriate for such diagnostic tests. First of all, the nurse obtains the VA test in decimal scale. Then converts the results into a logarithm of the Minimum Angle of Resolution (logMAR) for easier comparison of values along subsequent consultations. Next, the nurse induces mydriasis to the eye or eyes affected by AMD so as to prepare the patient for the clinical imaging tests. Once pupils are dilated, the nurse acquires in-situ the non-mydriatic retinographies corresponding to the study of AMD, and orders a study of the macula for the OCT situated in the second workspace (described below).

Regarding the fundus photography, the same guidelines used for DR screening were considered adequate for the study of AMD. Thus, two funduscopic images are obtained, one centred from the papilla and the other from on the macula. Thereby, although the assessment of AMD is focused on the examination of the macula, the additional picture of papilla will be available for future studies, e.g., concerning DR. Finally, those images are uploaded to the Picture Archiving and Communication System (PACS), whereas the results of VA are registered into the EHR. In this way, diagnostic tests will remain remotely accessible for the ophthalmologist responsible for their assessment.

– The second workspace: This point of care is equipped by an OCT device. Therefore, a nurse or imaging technician specifically trained on the use of the OCT is in charge. The studies of AMD scheduled in the OCT consist of cross-sectional images of the retina nearby to the macula. Thus, in terms of the protocol used in the health-care service of the SNS-O in that respect, a scan containing ten OCT sections in parallel which covers the whole macula, plus an extra scan comprised of a high-resolution section centered on the macula are acquired. For the same reason as in the case of fundus photographs, all resulting OCT sections are uploaded to the PACS.

– The third workspace: It corresponds to the office of the retinologist in which the AMD monitoring was managed along with other eye diseases. Nevertheless, it is also the office from which the high resolution consultation is coordinated and monitored. Therefore, during the time slots reserved for the high resolution consultation, this workspace is dedicated exclusively to manage patients diagnosed with wet AMD. To that end, the office has been equipped with a workstation from which, the retinologist requests and assesses the diagnostic tests necessary for monitoring the progression of wet AMD. Those tests are acquired in the other two workspaces mentioned above, whereas the retinologist uses this office to evaluate the acquisitions remotely as it is described in next stage. Nonetheless, besides the treatment and the remote assessment, this workspace was prepared as well to host diagnostic examinations whenever required. Thus, patients presenting any adverse drug reaction such as the mydriatic agent, or other problems that require the specific expertise of a retinologist are called to this office for further examination. Likewise, if the retinologist, having assessed the results of all diagnostic tests available remotely, still requires additional information to make the adequate therapeutic decision, the corresponding patients are referred to his office for a face-to-face consultation. In light of this, the office was equipped with a slit-lamp with a non-contact lens given that the retinologist could consider necessary the direct examination of eye fundus.

- STAGE 5 (AMD assessment): Once the diagnostic tests contemplated in the high resolution consultation are completed, the ophthalmologist in charge of AMD assessment has remote access to all clinical information it requires to determine the most suitable therapeutic decision for the patient. First of all, the ophthalmologist must determine whether the condition is progressive, or on the contrary it has been stabilized due to previous treatments. In that respect, the progression of AMD is identified by the occurrence of at least one of the following criteria:

  - Loss of at least one line of VA, in comparison to the previous revision, associated with the presence of macular fluid indicative of activity on AMD. The macular fluid indicative of activity or progression on AMD is detected using the OCT, and can be either intraretinal or subretinal.

  - Persistence of macular fluid indicative of activity identified through the OCT.

  - Emerging new macular hemorrhage detected by digital retinography or fundus examination of the patient.

If the condition turns out to be stable, the retreatment is postponed and the next review of the patient is scheduled within a month. Nevertheless, if AMD is unstable, the effectiveness of anti-VEGF therapy must be guaranteed prior to decide the retreatment. In fact, patients not responding to the treatment may require a different therapy, hence the anti-VEGF treatment is permanently discontinued for the following cases:

  - There is established or suspicion of hypersensitivity to the anti-VEGF agents used on the therapy (ranibizumab, aflibercept, and bevacizumab).

  - VA decreased for three consecutive reviews below 0.1 in decimal scale.

  - Progressive deterioration of the morphology of the lesion, detected either by fundus examination or by OCT.

Finally, those patients with signs of progression but responding to previous treatments receive immediately a new intravitreal injection and next review is scheduled within a month.

4.3.2.2 Step B.2: Study of Clinical Concepts

At this point, the stages of the clinical process defined above were reviewed so as to identify the clinical concepts to be included in the electronic model. Nevertheless, the high resolution consultation proposed for monitoring patients receiving treatment for wet AMD is still in a pilot stage. This means that this healthcare approach will coexist with the traditional face-to-face consultation whilst the high resolution consultation is validated for the healthcare scenario of ophthalmology in the SNS-O. Hence, the EHR system must be prepared to handle indistinctly the information resulting from both strategies of consultation. In this sense, given that the high resolution consultation must cover the same procedures comprehended in traditional consultations held in an office of specialized care, the clinical concepts considered at this point should be valid for both models (Table 4.2). Nonetheless, the implementation of the new model has to be supported by objective parameters of efficiency and reliability with respect to the face-to-face consultation which to date is regarded as gold standard.

In consequence, besides the clinical concepts identified in the clinical process above, administrative and sociodemographic concepts for benchmarking both approaches were also considered. The inclusion of those non-clinical concepts in the modeling would enable the analysis of sociodemographic information (current age, sex, age at diagnosis, VA when the study began), the study of comparative administrative variables (time spent during each consultation, compliance with established time limits between revisions, need to repeat treatment, record of problems such endophthalmitis stemming from the treatment), and the consequent data mining of the studies from each of the two approaches (number of treatments received along the year of monitoring, patients with VA below 0.1, cases with no treatable damage). The outcomes of these parameters would be useful to take further steps toward validation of the high resolution consultation.

With consideration of all the above, the concepts listed in Table 4.2 were chosen to model a service that would gradually integrate in the SNS-O a high resolution consultation, into the current service monitoring the treatment of wet AMD. As seen in Table 4.2, the concepts identified at this point were reused, whenever possible, from those available either in the CKM or described in the model presented for DR screening [86].

4.3.2.3 Step B.3: Hierarchical Organization of Knowledge Artifacts

As in the modeling of the DR screening service [86], the clinical concepts identified in previous step were structured according to their occurrences into the clinical stages described along step B.1. Although this time, most concepts were reused from the archetypes modeled for the DR screening service. Thus, the organization of the concepts gained relevance with respect to the effort put into modeling. In that respect, the work team designed the diagram shown

TABLE 4.2   Clinical concepts identified as a result of studying each stage in the service proposed to monitor the treatment of AMD.

	Identified Concept name	Equivalent archetype	Archetype class	Stages
1	Reason for encounter	Found on CKM (usable as is)	Evaluation	1
2	Story/history	Found on CKM (usable as is)	Observation	1
3	Symptom/Sign	Found on CKM (usable as is)	Cluster	1
4	VA	Found on CKM, but has to be adapted	Observation	1, 4
5	Funduscopic Examination of eyes	Reused from DR screening service	Observation	1, 4, 5
6	Ophthalmic Tomography examination	No equivalences found (to be modeled from scratch)	Observation	1, 4, 5
7	Clinical synopsis	Found on CKM (usable as is)	Evaluation	1, 5
8	Problem/diagnosis	Found on CKM (usable as is)	Evaluation	1, 5
9	Classification of AMD	No equivalences found (to be modeled from scratch)	Cluster	1, 5
10	Contraindication	Found on CKM (usable as is)	Evaluation	1, 5
11	Recommendation	Found on CKM (usable as is)	Evaluation	1, 5
12	Enrollment in a long-term healthcare proc.	No equivalences found (to be modeled from scratch)	Evaluation	1, 5
13	Medication order	Found on CKM (usable as is)	Instruction	2
14	Medication action	Found on CKM (usable as is)	Action	2
15	Intravitreal injection details	Reused from DR screening service	Cluster	2
16	Adverse reaction	Found on CKM (usable as is)	Evaluation	2
17	Care plan (request)	Found on CKM (usable as is)	Instruction	3
18	Care plan	Found on CKM (usable as is)	Action	3
19	Referral request	Found on CKM (usable as is)	Instruction	3
20	Imaging examination request	Found on CKM (usable as is)	Instruction	3
21	Acquisition details on eye fundus images	Reused from DR screening service	Cluster	3, 4
22	Acquisition details on ophthalmic tomograph	No equivalences found (to be modeled from scratch)	Cluster	3, 4
23	Procedure	Found on CKM (usable as is)	Action	4
24	Medical device	Found on CKM (usable as is)	Cluster	4
25	Medical device details	Found on CKM (usable as is)	Cluster	4
26	Imaging examination	Found on CKM (usable as is)	Action	4
27	Anatomic location	Found on CKM (usable as is)	Cluster	4
28	Mydriasis application	Reused from DR screening service	Cluster	4
29	Medication amount	Found on CKM (usable as is)	Cluster	4
30	Diagnostic report request	Reused from DR screening service	Instruction	4, 5
31	Service request	Found on CKM (usable as is)	Instruction	4, 5
32	Healthcare procedure efficiency	No equivalences found (to be modeled from scratch)	Admin entry	5

in Figure 4.3 according to the specifications for establishing the hierarchy between knowledge artifacts.

4.3.3 Building the Electronic Model

4.3.3.1 Step C.1: Creation and Update of Archetypes

The high resolution consultation proposed to monitor the treatment for wet AMD consists of 32 different archetypes (excluding organizational section and composition type archetypes).

From those, 21 were obtained from the openEHR CKM and directly used on the model. Besides, the "Visual acuity" archetype was also included, in whose development we were actively engaged so as to meet the requirements of our electronic models. With regard to the remaining 10 archetypes not provided by CKM, only half were completely new, whereas the rest were reused from those previously modeled for the DR screening service (see Table 4.2) [86].

From the new archetypes proposed, "Healthcare procedure efficiency" is noteworthy. It introduces the admin entry class into the electronic model: a new type of entry-type archetype besides the care entry archetypes (observation, evaluation, instruction and action) seen up to now. This new type of archetype is used to capture administrative information in parallel to the clinical activity recorded by care entry archetypes.

In this regard, the "Healthcare procedure efficiency" archetype was designed to register objective parameters regarding the evaluation of efficiency for a specific healthcare activity, namely the encounter type, duration, healthcare resources expended, success of the encounter and so on.

Thereby, it constitutes a powerful tool to evaluate the efficiency for a specific healthcare activity, and hence a means of improving the management of healthcare resources. This archetype could be useful regarding the treatment of wet AMD, in terms of comparing the high resolution consultation with the traditional face-to-face approach.

4.3.3.2 Step C.2: Definition of Semantic Links to Clinical Terminologies

A total of 10 different termsets were used to extend the terminology of archetypes involved in the electronic model. Nevertheless, according to reusability of the knowledge artifacts, eight of the termsets initially designed for the DR screening service [86] proved to be applicable too in the clinical process monitoring the treatment for wet AMD. Furthermore, some of the termsets were reused along the clinical process corresponding to wet AMD (see Figure 4.3).

Consequently, only two new termsets had to be specifically created to adjust the electronic model to the new healthcare scenario proposed. Those new termsets were built on the basis of tables normalized in the Digital Communications (DICOM) standard, so as to increase their use in future healthcare scenarios.

All the aforementioned termsets and their use along the stages in the clinical process are described in Table 4.3.

4.3.3.3   Step C.3: Building Templates

The archetypes modeled in previous steps were structured into templates in the same way as described for the remote screening service for DR [86]. As a result of that modeling, 16 different templates were built: among those, 11 corresponded to templates designed to adapt the archetypes contained in each section identified in Figure 4.3 to the requirements of the service for monitoring the treatment of AMD. The remaining 5 templates were designed to manage the information corresponding to each one of the stages in which the healthcare was divided along the clinical process seen in Figure 4.3.

Among those templates corresponding to sections, 3 were reused along the clinical process: considering that there is some common ground between the first encounter for patient admission and the subsequent AMD assessments, the templates "Classification and treatment of AMD" and "Patient's enrollment in anti-VEGF therapy" were reused along the first and last stage. Likewise, the archetype "Next step in AMD monitoring service" was devised to manage the pathway among stages, so it was first used at the fourth stage to refer patients toward the office assessment once all diagnostic tests were acquired, but besides, turned out to be useful at the fifth stage to schedule the next review in a month, and then, arrange or postpone the anti-VEGF treatment.

In addition, the DR screening service modeled beforehand provided interesting patterns with regard to the current proposal for AMD. In this sense, 2 templates initially modeled for the DR screening were reused with the consequent time saving for modelers:

- Intraocular injection: Although originally used by the DR screening service, its template had to be enhanced since the intraocular injection is a critical activity on the treatment of wet AMD. Therefore, the corresponding template was redesigned in light of the service monitoring the treatment of AMD, and then, the model that describes the DR screening was retrospectively updated. Thus, at this point both models share the same template "Intraocular injection".

- Funduscopic test: This diagnostic test is required on both clinical processes, so its corresponding template "Acquisition and validation of NMR" resulted equally applicable in both models.

Many other templates used in the AMD monitoring service were slightly adapted from those originally built for the DR screening. For example, the

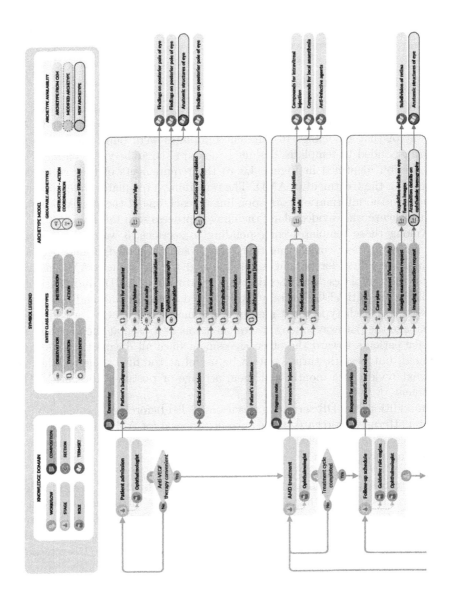

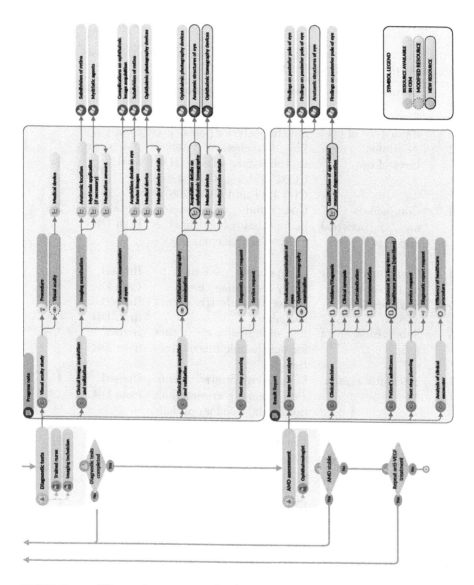

FIGURE 4.3 Hierarchy among the knowledge artifacts involved in the treatment of wet AMD.

TABLE 4.3 Termsets modeled to support the archetypes in the service proposed to monitor the treatment of AMD.

	Termset name	Description of termset	Availability	Stages
1	Findings on posterior pole of eye	Clinical findings identifiable in posterior pole of eye	Reused from DR	1, 5
2	Anatomic structures of eye	List of regions of interest in the study of eye (DICOM Tables: CID 4209, CID 4211 and CID 4266)	Newly created	1, 3, 4, 5
3	Compounds for intravitreal injection	Compounds administered in ophthalmology in the form of intraocular injection	Reused from DR	2
4	Compounds for local anaesthesia	Compounds available to apply local anaesthesia	Reused from DR	2
5	Anti-infective agents	List of anti-infective agents available	Reused from DR	2
6	Subdivision of retina	List of zones in eye retina for ophthalmic image positioning	Reused from DR	3, 4
7	Mydriatic agents	List of mydriatic agents and their corresponding doses validated for ophthalmologic use	Reused from DR	4
8	Complications on ophthalmic image acquisition	List of possible complications that may affect the quality of acquisitions (DICOM Table CID 4222)	Reused from DR	4
9	Ophthalmic photography devices	Lists the ophthalmic photography acquisition devices (DICOM Table CID 4202)	Reused from DR	4
10	Ophthalmic tomography devices	List of acquisition devices (DICOM Table CID 4210)	Newly created	4

templates "Patient's background leading to the diagnosis of AMD" and "Classification and treatment of AMD" enclose practically the same archetypes used in "Patient's background leading to suspicion of DR", but including some additional archetypes specific to the diagnosis of wet AMD.

Finally, the "Diagnostic tests in the DR screening service" and "Diagnostic tests for monitoring the treatment of wet AMD" share the same structure although the archetypes included must cover different diagnostic tests (see Figure 4.4).

4.3.3.4 Step C.4: Modeling Guideline Rules and Workflow

Six rules were designed to govern patients' flow through the clinical process:

- Anti-VEGF therapy convenient: From every patient diagnosed with wet AMD, only those which comply with this rule will access to the long-term treatment of wet AMD by intravitreal injections. Thus, this rule is activated when, after a consultation on specialized care, a retinologist determines whether the anti-VEGF therapy is convenient or not for the current patient. The archetype named "Enrollment in a long-term healthcare process" is used to register such decision.

    This rule checks the value chosen in the data element "admittance" of that archetype, and if the patient is inscribed in the therapy, activates the medication order to initiate the first cycle of anti-VEGF treatments comprised of three monthly intraocular injections.

- Treatment cycle completed: This rule verifies if every anti-VEGF injection ordered for a specific patient have been carried out, and, if true, automatically schedules the next consultation for patient review. Basically, it checks for every new contribution submitted to the EHR, if the pathway of the archetype "Medication action" has been registered as completed. If so, the rule queries the CPOE manager for all open orders for intravitreal injections related to a specific patient, and then tags as closed the corresponding one. At this point, in case of treatment discontinuation for whatever reason, the retinologist must intervene in consequence either by ordering again the missing interventions or by suspending definitively the treatment. Once all medication orders for intravitreal injection have been closed, this rule determines that the cycle of treatments is completed. As a result, the archetype "Care plan (request)" is instantiated, in which the diagnostic tests involved on reviewing the outcomes of the treatment for wet AMD are specified.

- Diagnostic tests completed: Similarly to the preceding one, this rule must guarantee the completion of every diagnostic test ordered for a specific patient before proceeding with the remote assessment. Except instead of medication orders for intravitreal injection, this rule must coordinate

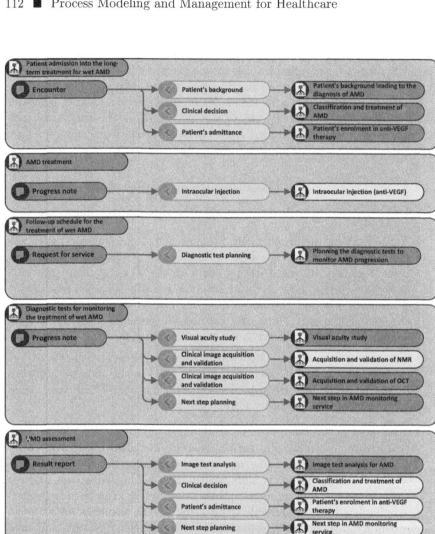

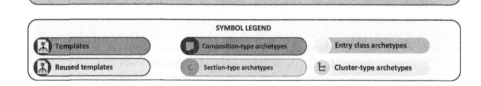

FIGURE 4.4 Structure of templates envisaged to register clinical encounters resulting from the high resolution consultation devised to monitor the treatment of wet AMD.

the lifecycle of every diagnostic test scheduled to review the effectiveness of the treatment of wet AMD (i.e., VA, NMR and OCT).

To that end, every new contribution of the archetype "Care plan" submitted to the EHR that corresponds to the "Service for monitoring the treatment of wet AMD" is reviewed. When the pathway of this archetype is set to "Care plan completed", it means that every diagnostic tests scheduled within the follow-up have been acquired. Consequently, the rule uses the archetype "Diagnostic report request" to request the remote assessment for the set of diagnostic tests acquired.

- AMD stable: Provided that the retinologist does not identifies signs of activity or progression on AMD since the last review (neither new haemorrhages nor worsening of VA), a new anti-VEGF injection would not be effective to treat such disease. In light of the above, this rule checks the therapeutic decision in the archetype "Recommendation", and if the therapeutic recommendation corresponds to "Do not treat", the rule will schedule the respective diagnostic tests to review the patient in a month. In this way, the progression of the disease is periodically monitored, whereas the treatment is postponed until applying the injections is really effective. At this point, the archetype "Service request" is instantiated to schedule the follow-up service for the treatment of wet AMD, where the diagnostic tests included in the monthly revision of wet AMD are planned (VA, NMR and OCT).

- Repeat anti-VEGF treatment: This rule orders a new intravitreal injection if the retinologist, as a result of the assessment of diagnostic tests, determines that the patient presents signs activity or progression on AMD. The criteria to repeat the treatment is the worsening of VA associated to macular fluid, identifying macular fluid, and emerging new hemorrhages within the macula. If any of these criteria are identified during the remote assessment of a patient, the retinologist would set the "Intravitreal anti-VEGF injection" as therapeutic recommendation for the archetype "Recommendation". Likewise, the rationale of the same archetype would be used to register the criteria used to reach that therapeutic decision. Finally, the retinologist must reconsider patient's enrollment in the intravitreal anti-VEGF therapy. Thus, the positive value of admittance registered in the archetype "Enrolment in a long-term healthcare process" for the healthcare process "Long-term therapy of anti-VEGF intravitreal injections" will trigger this rule. And whenever this rule is triggered, it will instantiate the "Medication order" archetype so as to schedule the anti-VEGF injection corresponding to the current month.

- Discontinuation of anti-VEGF therapy: Finally, if the minimum conditions of "Admittance" for the long-term therapy of anti-VEGF intravitreal injections are not fulfilled, directly the patient would not be included into the cycle of treatments (stage 1: anti-VEGF therapy not indicated). Moreover, if the patient is already included in the cycle of anti-VEGF injections, but the retinologist identifies contraindications to continue with the therapy during any of the periodic assessments, the patient's enrollment in the long-term treatment for wet AMD will be revoked (stage 4: patient not responding to treatment). Both scenarios above will trigger this rule, which in consequence excludes the patient from the treatment and then schedules the next consultation for AMD review at the retinologist's office. Thereby, these patients fall beyond the scope of our model, given that they have been excluded from the long-term therapy of anti-VEGF injections.

With consideration of the above, first of all, the rule verifies the latest contribution in the EHR of the archetype "Classification of age-related macular degeneration". In fact, only patients with the classification of "Exudative or wet AMD" are covered by the long-term therapy proposed, so other diagnoses will trigger this rule. Conversely, if the diagnosis of AMD corresponds to the abovementioned classification, then the rule must verify if there is any contraindication that could jeopardize effectiveness of intravitreal injections:

- Exclusion criteria for new patients: During the admission stage of the anti-VEGF therapy, those patients who show very low VA (below 0.1), healed lesions due to previous treatments (PDT, laser photocoagulation scars, or any vitreoretinal operative procedure), multimorbidity (coexistence of AMD with other alterations on the retina causative of visual impairment), or any known adverse reaction to anti-VEGF agents used in intravitreal injections will definitely trigger this rule.

- Exclusion criteria for permanent discontinuation of therapy: From the patients already receiving intravitreal anti-VEGF injections, those who at some point have presented hypersensitivity to the anti-VEGF agents used in the injections, those not responding to treatment (VA decreased for three consecutive reviews below 0.1 in decimal scale), and cases affected by a progressive deterioration of the morphology of the lesion will definitely trigger this rule.

In this regard, any contribution to the archetype "Contraindication" referring to intravitreal anti-VEGF injections will lead to withdraw the patient from therapy.

Thus, if any of the conditions above triggers the rule, it would be necessary to place on record the exclusion of the patient from the "Long-term therapy of anti-VEGF intravitreal injections". So that, the value of "Admittance" in the archetype "Enrollment in a long-term healthcare process" is set to false, and "Criteria" is established according to the value of "Evidence/Rationale" registered within the archetype "Contraindication". Finally, the "Service request" archetype is instantiated so as to schedule next patient's review at the retinologist's office.

4.3.3.5   Step C.5: Modeling UI Forms

When we considered designing UI forms for the DR screening service, we identified different solutions to the same end. However, each of the form definitions studied was exclusive to specific e-health implementations. The lack of agreement on UI specifications nowadays hinders the development of pervasive software tools for UI form modeling, which are in fact essential to implement this strategy. Therefore, for as long as no consensus is reached on this matter, we must stick with the UI form modeling tools available today.

On the one hand, the template designer of Ocean Informatics includes a form designer feature, which leverages the openEHR templates modeled to build customized UI forms. As an outcome, the template designer generates the C# code necessary to compile the resulting UI forms. However, the fact that the resulting code is provided in a given programming language limits the potential implementations on which these UI forms could be applied. Nonetheless standards-based open health computing platforms must interoperate with front-end applications functioning on heterogeneous electronic terminals, regardless if they are built upon diverse technologies.

Alternatively, the open source software tools provided by Cabolabs should be considered in this regard. Indeed, such tools have recently incorporated a library which parses the openEHR Operational Template (OPT) files and automatically generates the corresponding UI forms built upon HTML code. This avoided to define one by one the specific data fields necessary for representing the archetype paths defined within the openEHR templates. Moreover, although by default such library generates HTML code, given that the UI generation tool is provided in open source, it can be adapted to generate the UI views in other programming codes. However, the fully automated generation of views lacks of tools for customization of the UI to the needs of final user.

In this regard, the Marand EhrExplorer provides an excellent form builder which includes a dedicated web interface to model UI forms in an agile way. Once modeled, the resulting forms are saved into the EhrScape server as three complementary form resources: first, the form-layout, which arranges the information and data fields on the screen. Second, the form-description, which defines how the content of the form would be shown (language, data validation, data-types, etc.). And, third, the form-dependencies, which determine rules among the data elements within the form. The EhrScape server provides these form definition components in JSON format through REST interfaces. Thus, any front-end application connected to the EhrScape server can retrieve the form specifications modeled in a language-independent data format. Then, these form definitions would be transformed by each application into UI views on the programming language it corresponds.

Given the flexibility of this approach, the Marand EhrExplorer was chosen to build the UI forms for the AMD service. Consequently, 5 UI forms were created representing each one of the stages that comprise the AMD monitoring service proposed. This will enable to automatically generate the UI views to be displayed on front-end applications, based on the UI specifications detailed on the form-description files resulting from the UI modeling. However, given the lack of consensus on the definition of UI form specifications, the parsers available which transform the form specifications resulting from the Marand EhrExplorer into HTML views, will only work for front-end applications devised for the Marand EhrScape server. Therefore, specific UI generators must be implemented in order to reuse our UI form definitions into front-end applications compliant to other openEHR-compliant EHR implementations. For example, in the case of the open source applications proposed by Cabolabs, the UI generator from the openEHR-OPT project can be adapted to parse the UI form-description files instead of the OPTs used to define these UI forms. In this way, anyone could build their own HTML front-end applications based on the UI form definitions modeled herein.

4.4   IMPLEMENTATION OF THE SERVICE

Currently, both the high resolution consultation and traditional approach co-exist in the SNS-O toward monitoring patients receiving anti-VEGF therapy for wet AMD. This stems from the fact that the high resolution consultation proposed is still in a pilot stage. As such, before proceeding with an extensive implementation, it must prove its efficiency and reliability against traditional consultation.

As regards the traditional consultation model, except for the OCT acquisitions provided in printed form, the diagnostic tests involved in the study of AMD require the presence of the patient at the ophthalmologist's office (measurement of VA and eye fundus examination using slit lamp biomicroscopy). This facilitates the face-to-face assessment, in contrast to the high resolution consultation approach, which redistributes those diagnostic tests among specialized workspaces. Thus, in case of the latter approach, the evaluation of the acquisitions resulting of all those workspaces must be managed remotely. At this point, the need arises to share through the corporate network of the SNS-O, the studies acquired concerning the diagnosis and follow-up of AMD. Therefore, the proposal of a remote assessment service entails reconsidering the technical requirements of the current healthcare service, initially designed to accommodate the traditional consultation.

In that respect, the ICT infrastructure arranged in the SNS-O for the DR screening service described in [86] was reused to cover some of the technical requirements of the high resolution consultation. On the one hand, the workspace allocated for diagnostic test acquisition in DR screening was adapted to receive also patients affected by wet AMD. This workspace already included tonometry and pachymetry devices for IOP measurement, a non-mydriatic retinal camera, and a PC workstation to register findings identified during acquisitions. Thus, by installing a Snellen chart for VA measurement, this space covered every diagnostic test specified for the first workspace of the high resolution consultation (see Figure 4.5).

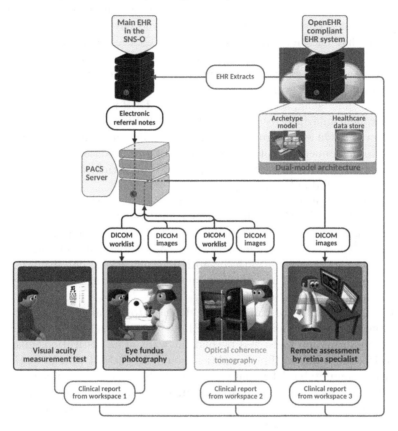

FIGURE 4.5 Flow of information through the service monitoring the treatment of wet AMD.

On the other hand, given that in principle, the OCT test was not considered for the DR screening, a new workspace was allocated in the SNS-O to host that test according to the specifications of the high resolution consultation. There, to connect such diagnostic device to the PACS server available in the healthcare service, the workstation and the server were configured in compliance with DICOM (see Figure 4.5).

Moreover, the workspace allocated for remote assessment (both for DR and AMD) was established into the office of an ophthalmologist expert in retina. In that office, the ophthalmologist uses a PC workstation, connected to the PACS and EHR servers, to evaluate remotely the diagnostic tests and then register the diagnostic reports (see Figure 4.5). Furthermore, given that some diagnostic tests are overlapped in the study of both DR and AMD, the whole set of tests contained in the PACS would be accessible regardless the process for which they were originally intended.

As proof of concept for the healthcare scenario modeled along this Chapter, the archetypes and templates built were loaded into an openEHR-compliant EHR. The same information systems used in the DR screening service were chosen to that end, namely the EHRServer and the EHRCommitter, both developed by Cabolabs [43, 44]. In this way, clinicians involved in both clinical processes can use the same EHR system to register clinical information specific to each healthcare scenario.

For the time being, the openEHR-compliant EHR is only used for research purposes, hence medical records must be recorded into the main EHR in the SNS-O as well. Once it is proved that the openEHR-compliant EHR is reliable enough to be connected to the main EHR, both information systems will be able to exchange EHR extracts. Consequently, the information among systems will be coordinated automatically.

Building on the electronic model described for the service monitoring the treatment of wet AMD, a solution was considered in order to standardize the information recorded through the web platform launched at the SNS-O to evaluate the telemedicine model for wet AMD follow-up. Originally, this platform was not compliant to the openEHR specifications, but given the clinical domain in common, it could be easily standardized using the knowledge artifacts modeled along this Chapter.

Standardization of the platform would enable to exchange medical records with other systems compliant to openEHR, hence extending the applicability of the information registered beyond the walls of an institution. Likewise, fine-grained data-mining functionalities would be enabled thanks to the semantically computable EHR data. This could be a proof of concept toward integration of many software tools and information systems found in health services, which being designed for very specific healthcare scenarios, usually end up being an information silo.

The challenge on this approach was to model, ex post, the use case scenario presented in the web platform. Therefore, instead of generating the UI views from the knowledge models, the modeling was reversed to avoid having to modify the UI views defined on the non-standardized web platform. In this case, an OPT was specifically designed to conform to the clinical concepts originally registered through the web platform. Most of the clinical concepts defined in the OPT have direct correspondence with the data fields represented on the UI forms. Conversely, other concepts defined in the OPT are not shown on the view. These must be inferred from the context, since the clinical practice is well-known for this healthcare scenario.

The aforementioned template was modeled in compliance with the Archetype Definition Language (ADL) 1.4 specifications, using the template designer developed by Ocean Informatics. Once finished, it was uploaded to the CKM under the name of "Consultation for AMD assessment", thus allowing the OPT to be available for everyone to download (steps 1 and 2 in Figure 4.6). Next, the methods provided by the project openEHR-OPT of Cabolabs were used to extract the paths pointing to every data element specified within the OPT [45] (step 3 in Figure 4.6). Each one of those paths was then assigned to equivalent data fields identified in the HTML file that depicts the UI form at the web platform. The data types (according to the openEHR reference model), default values, and other data constraints were also included into the HTML elements where necessary (step 4 in Figure 4.6).

Furthermore, the resulting HTML view was integrated with a controller as explained in the openEHR-skeleton example of how to create e-health apps [46]. This controller is responsible for validating the data entered in the form, creating EHR instances from these data, and committing them to the EHR. In this regard, the openEHR-OPT was used to validate the clinical data, and compose new EHR instances in conformance with the openEHR EHR information model [45]. Indeed, the openEHR compositions generated whenever the HTML form is submitted may be considered equivalent to a signed clinical document. In this way, although the resulting HTML form apparently presents no changes for end users, it would be prepared to exchange medical records with openEHR-compliant EHR systems (step 5 in Figure 4.6). To that end, the project EHRCommitter developed by Cabolabs was adapted to send the resulting versioned compositions to the EHRServer (last step in Figure 4.6).

4.5 DISCUSSION

The advent of model-driven information systems plus the methodology for modeling clinical knowledge proposed in [86] provided a direct way for clinical experts to be involved in the specification of the clinical models they work on.

Nevertheless, the novelty of this approach still requires modeling different healthcare scenarios to compete with specialized software tools used so far in healthcare. This is because the knowledge artifacts available for download are scarce, and there are even fewer peer-reviewed artifacts. In fact, healthcare modelers worldwide tend to define clinical concepts widely used in medicine, whereas more specific concepts are also necessary with regards to building electronic models for real healthcare scenarios. It is assumed that the more specific the clinical concepts are to a clinical specialty, the higher the likeliness that the corresponding knowledge artifacts either have not been modeled yet, or, at best, they are only available as draft proposals, i.e., they have not yet overcome the peer review procedure. This limits the use of the open-access clinical knowledge base available so far to very specific use cases, such as the case of ophthalmology.

Consequently, seeing no short-term prospects for leveraging the effort made in modeling healthcare, many clinicians will get discouraged from contributing with their expertise to open-access clinical knowledge repositories. In order to address this issue, the electronic models proposed along Section 4.3 of this

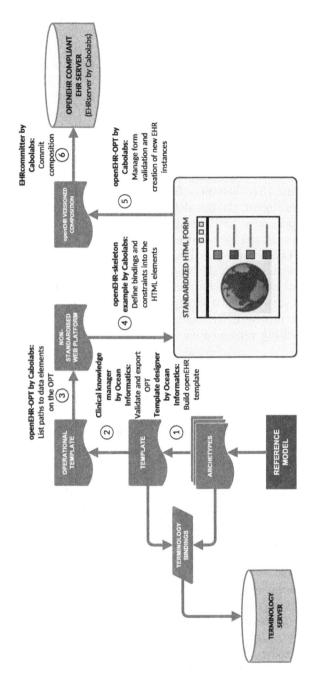

FIGURE 4.6 Adaptation of data registered through the non-standardized web platform into openEHR-compliant medical records.

chapter covered a real healthcare scenario in ophthalmology, more specifically, AMD. However, the task of modeling every possibility into each archetype involved in a complex clinical process (constraints, translations, terminology bindings, and maintenance regarding updates in the model) turned out to be a huge workload for a single research group. Therefore, each knowledge artifact proposed can be further improved if we analyze them separately. Nonetheless, the resulting electronic models were intended to provide comprehensive turn-key solutions for the three healthcare scenarios, i.e., any user interested in implementing our models can download and directly start using them. This should encourage clinicians interested in these specific implementations to contribute toward improving the specific components of these models. Therefore, it is expected the critical mass of clinicians involved in modeling the clinical knowledge to increase, and thus the quality of knowledge artifacts defined for ophthalmology. In subsequent revisions, the clinical processes proposed can be modeled even in more detail. For example, the electronic models proposed in this chapter were focused on assessment more than therapy. Thus, the stages corresponding to treatment can be extended in the future.

Finally, although in principle these models were built for the SNS-O, this work pursues the reusability of electronic resources that comprise these models, so they have been made available in the CKM. Consequently, any health-care institution managing AMD monitoring services can download the resources proposed (archetypes, templates, termsets, and rules) and tailor them to meet their specific requirements.

4.6 CONCLUSION

Previously, a methodology was proposed to model patient-centered clinical processes [86]. In this chapter, as proof of concept of such methodology, a service for monitoring the intravitreal anti-VEGF therapy used to treat wet AMD was formalized into electronic models.

During the definition of the domain knowledge for the electronic models provided along this chapter, a total of 32 archetypes were used for AMD monitoring, excluding organizational classes (section and composition). Of these, 25 were reused from the model built for DR screening, leaving 7 archetypes specifically created for AMD. This implies a high reusability of archetypes among related scenarios (circa 78%). Regarding non-repeated archetypes, 21 were used as is from the openEHR CKM, 2 were adapted to the needs of the healthcare scenario, and the remaining 9 were specially created from scratch for this chapter. These archetypes conformed to structure-specific clinical encounters within 16 different templates, of which 11 were devised to structure the aforementioned archetypes inside the sections in order to ease clinician readability. The remaining 5 templates were created to manage the compositions containing these section-type templates. Among all the clinical processes modeled, 6 guideline rules were designed to manage the navigation of patients through the healthcare service. Furthermore, 10 termsets were created to bind selectable data elements from the archetypes and templates to standard terminology services. Once modeled, these standardized representations for clinical knowledge were published in open-access repositories so that any healthcare service interested on implementing the same e-health services could download and adapt these resources to meet the needs of specific health services. In this way, although the clinical processes proposed were initially modeled for the SNS-O, these can be reproduced in a variety of healthcare scenarios, facilitating collaboration among healthcare facilities. Consequently, clinical information resulting from these e-health services would be managed electronically using model-driven health computing platforms. Besides the aforementioned elements, 5 UI forms were also defined; one for each composition-type template built. Nevertheless, these UI forms were not published given that their applicability was limited to the specific healthcare scenarios proposed for the SNS-O.

Additionally, specialized workspaces were set up in the ophthalmology department of the SNS-O, equipped with the technical and human resources necessary to implement the aforementioned e-health service. In the case of the high resolution consultation to monitor the treatment of wet AMD, a web platform was launched in compliance with openEHR specifications, to validate the therapeutic decisions made in the e-health service proposed.

As a general conclusion, this chapter shows how the creation of semantically enabled electronic models improves the management of electronic information in healthcare, the interoperability as well as the reuse of the resources.

EXERCISES

4.1 *Defining new projects.* Based on the proposal of wet AMD disease, define a service for following up patients with DR), describing the actors, their expertise as well as brief comments about their agreements (treatments, workload, workspaces, etc.).

Solution: The solution to this and the rest of the exercises can be found in [86].

4.2 *Designing clinical process I.* Taking as a proof of the concept your health system (public, private, regional, national, etc.), define and depict an activity DR screening service diagram showing the workflow of clinical stages. Use Figure 4.2 as an example and try to customize it for this new DR screening service.

4.3 *Designing clinical process II.* Based on your experience and the proposal of *Exercise 2*, describe the clinical concepts needed to be included into the electronic model of a new DR screening service. Use Table 4.2 as an example.

4.4 *Building an electronic model of clinical concepts (intended for techni-*

cians). Move from Figure 4.3 to a new hierarchy of information for a new DR screening service based on an openEHR archetype system.

4.5 *Implementing new chronic follow-up health services.* Using Figure 4.5 as basis, propose and depict a flow of information for a new DR screening service, including all elements required: diagnostic tests, health professionals involved, standards to transmit health information, health information servers, etc.

GLOSSARY

AMD: Age-Related Macular Degeneration (AMD) is a degenerative process of the central retina that develops in elderly people. The macula covers the central area of the retina which actually is responsible for detecting high-acuity details of central vision. Therefore, when it gets damaged, the Visual Acuity (VA) decreases drastically, especially in central areas of the Visual Field (VF).

Anti-vascular endothelial growth factor: Also known as anti-VEGF therapy or anti-VEGF medication, is the use of medications that block vascular endothelial growth factor.

Archetype: In openEHR, an archetype is the model (or pattern) for the capture of clinical information, that is, a machine readable specification of how to store patient data using the openEHR Reference Model. Archetypes are used to express reusable structured data-item definitions in the form of constraints on a reference model.

Dry AMD: In the dry (non-exudative) form, cellular debris called drusen accumulates between the retina and the choroid, causing atrophy and scarring to the retina.

Dual-model approach: The approach that some standards such a ISO/EN 13606 and openEHR use to model the knowledge. In openEHR, there two conceptual levels: on the one hand, a reference model that standardizes the way the information is handled inside the software, and, on the other hand, an archetype model that gathers knowledge about the clinical process to be managed.

Interoperability: The ability of two or more systems or components to exchange information and to use the information that has been exchanged.

openEHR Clinical Knowledge Manager: The Clinical Knowledge Manager is an international, online clinical knowledge resource. It is a system for collaborative development, management and publishing of clinical knowledge artifacts.

PACS: A Picture Archiving and Communication System (PACS) is a medical imaging technology which provides economical storage and convenient access to images from multiple modalities (source machine types).

Standardization: The use of common products, processes, procedures, and policies to facilitate attainment of business objectives.

Template: An openEHR Template is a specification that defines a tree of one or more archetypes, each constraining instances of various reference model types, such as Composition, Section, Entry subtypes and so on. Templates are used to create definitions of content such as a particular document or message, required for specific use cases, such as specific screen forms, message types or reports.

Terminology: Terminology is the study of terms and their use. Terms are words or compound words or multi-word expressions that in specific contexts are given specific meaning which may deviate from the meanings the same words have in other contexts and in everyday language.

User Interface: The user interface (UI), in the industrial design field of human-computer interaction, is the space where interactions between humans and machines occur, that is, how information is presented to users.

Wet AMD: In the wet (exudative) form of AMD, which is more severe, blood vessels grow up from the choroid (neovascularization) behind the retina which can leak exudate and fluid and also cause hemorrhaging.

CHAPTER 5

Scientific Workflows for Healthcare

Giuseppe Tradigo

Department of Computer Science, Modeling, Electronics and Systems Engineering, University of Calabria, Italy

Patrizia Vizza

Department of Surgical and Medical Science, University Magna Græcia of Catanzaro, Italy

Pietro Hiram Guzzi

Department of Surgical and Medical Science, University Magna Græcia of Catanzaro, Italy

Andrea Tagarelli

Department of Computer Science, Modeling, Electronics and Systems Engineering, University of Calabria, Italy

Pierangelo Veltri

Department of Surgical and Medical Science, University Magna Græcia of Catanzaro, Italy

CONTENTS

> The sea will ebb and flow,
> heaven show his face

W. Shakespeare

S cientific workflows refer to business process engines that enable the composition and the execution of scientific applications. The introduction of scientific workflows in healthcare is a relatively novel field that is currently growing. This chapter presents some applications of scientific workflows in two main healthcare scenarios from a patient perspective, namely: (i) interactive patient data processing (Section 5.2), which shows examples of interactive patient data manipulation, (ii) offline patient data processing (Section 5.3), whose focus is on modules for the *a posteriori* processing of patient data.

5.1   INTRODUCTION

Clinical workflow management systems help in handling huge quantity of information in clinical healthcare structures. They are implemented following the design of models used to support physicians and healthcare operators while managing information useful for health related services. For instance, managing information flow regarding patients in cardiology emergency intervention unit, is necessary to: (i) optimize processes while scaling in terms of number of patients versus number of operators, and (ii) report data regarding research interesting topics. In this chapter we describe possible extensions and evolutions of Clinical Workflow Management Systems, by following clinical different division cases and, for each one, presenting application scenarios. Workflow management applied to different divisions are of great help for researchers and also for physicians working in healthcare and clinical data management. The chapter presents examples of different cases in the fields of: cardiology and hemodynamic, electrophysiology, magnetic resonance analysis, patient data sharing and computational epidemiology, genome-wide association studies (GWAS) and proteomics, early detection and remote data analysis.

Clinical activities related to life science generate huge constantly growing datasets, containing data from many different actors, such as: clinicians, biologists, biomedical engineers, bioinformaticians, patients, citizens. Interactions among these actors are based on the exchange of information such as disease protocols, treatments and rules for early disease detection. This huge quantity of data can be extremely valuable not only for medical activity assessment or performance verification, but also useful to researchers and social managers. In fact, the diffusion of health related knowledge is an important aim for many governments, which are investing money for sharing information about: therapeutic treatments (e.g., for chronic diseases), protocols, results, follow-up procedures and more. Similarly, open data protocols are increasing the necessity of having well-defined data process management to allow the extraction of information useful to study chronic diseases, as well as reducing costs [99].

Medical activities are often very specialized and require highly trained professionals and complex devices. This complexity is reflected in health structures, where each department is in charge of dealing with a homogeneous set of diseases and treatments. We refer to department activities as workflow modules describing a hierarchy of activities of each department in the whole health structure. Each department workflow is also a portion of the whole health structure, which makes the information (e.g., patients, documents) flow through the various departments, from the admission towards the patient's discharge or the follow-up (e.g., age-related pathologies). Workflow management for different data sources in surgical operative units can be done by managing patients data and surgical operative units. For instance, it is possible to use a unique workflow system that may collect: (i) patient registration; (ii) day planning of surgical intervention; (iii) patient management during the follow-up and data analysis. Workflow module management may report abut clinical activities, geographical distribution, the mean time needed for the execution of a surgical intervention, the number of patients for each medical doctor for administrative management, etc. [48].

In this chapter, data flow in health structures is presented with workflow examples and applications. These modules can be used in clinical practice, each of which solves a specialized problem and is a real-world use case. Once the input and the output of these modules is clear, they can be used in a global workflow describing the activities of a Health Structure and take advantage of all of the benefits of the workflow theory seen in the previous chapters of the book. The following sections show workflow modules for the analysis and management of clinical and health care data.

5.2 INTERACTIVE PATIENT DATA PROCESSING

This section reports examples of modules for processing flows of data related to patients in an interactive way. For interactive data processing, we refer to workflow data management where information flow is obtained by means of signals coming directly from patients under study (e.g., surgical interventions). In the following, we present tools supporting clinicians during angioplastic surgery. Then, we report the development of a system for monitoring atrial fibrillation (AFib). Finally, we discuss a system for supporting neurologists during magnetic resonance.

5.2.1 Hemodynamics Clinical Data Processing

Vessels in humans are often subject to specific diseases that make difficult the flow of blood inside them. Such pathologies are often lethal without surgical intervention. The most used surgical intervention is known as angioplasty and consists in the placement of a stent, i.e., small tubes made of special materials inserted into the lumen of a vessel to keep the passageway open. Coronary stents are placed during a percutaneous coronary intervention, angioplasty. In order to avoid stent thrombosis, drug eluding stents, as well as bare metal ones, stent implantation should be perfectly deployed. Thus, the estimation of diameter and length of the coronary vessels as well as overlap of stents at the origin of large collateral branches, is critical. The *angioplastic clinical workflow* supporting these activities is composed by the following steps:

1. Intervention planning;

2. Surgery feasibility;

3. Acquisition of angiographic images from patients;

4. Estimation of the dimension of stent to be implanted;

5. Implantation of the stent.

The automatization of such a workflow results in a great support in surgery rooms. Currently, optimization techniques used by physicians to measure coronary stenoses, are included in software tools coming with angiographic equipment.

As an example of significant experiences, here we discuss *Cartesio* [130], an innovative software tool that might be used by physicians working in emodynamics surgery rooms. It helps in making a preimplant analysis for the estimation of the dimensions of the stent to be implanted. The tool interacts with virtually any angiographic equipment by acquiring its high-resolution video signal and offering a set of functions to play with images and to draw a virtual stent over the acquired video frames (see Figure 5.1). It allows the operator to calibrate the stent before implanting it. Measurements help physicians to evaluate the exact dimension of the stenosis and to define the physical parameters for the virtual stent in such a way that it will be compatible with the vessel structure. Each rendered measurement or stent preimplant analysis can be exported as a bitmap image on the file system or saved in an experiment repository on a relational database for future reference. The software uses a balloon catheter with radio-opaque iridium markers positioned at 10 mm from each other.

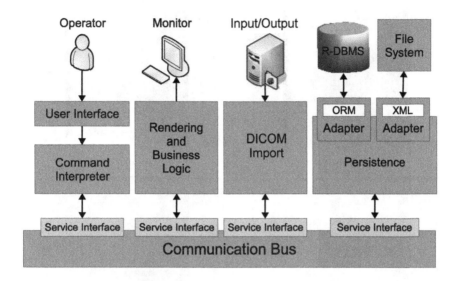

FIGURE 5.1 Block diagram of the Cartesio angiography workflow management tool.

Cartesio allows the operator to calibrate the images by making the operator click over two radio-opaque markers. After the angiographic images are calibrated the operator can use a software measurement tool to measure distances in millimeters instead of pixels. Furthermore, once the calibration is performed, all of the parameters of the virtual stent (i.e., diameter, length) can be expressed in millimeters. The physician obtains a precise preview of what will be implanted and, if desired, he can change some parameters or move the stent to better fit the disease. By using such a procedure, more conscious decisions can be taken before the real angioplastic surgery is performed.

A clinical advantage of the system is the visual analysis of radio-opaque markers to establish the stent length and the virtual reconstruction of coronary stent in the angiographic image allowing a further visual double-check analysis before the device is irreversibly implanted. The automation of the processes followed by a physician during the cardiac surgery activity is summarized by the following points:

1. Patient disease discovery phase: the doctor inserts a catheter through the femoral artery to the heart and acquires a set of video sequences showing different projections of vessels;

2. Disease evaluation phase: the physician analyzes the video sequences and

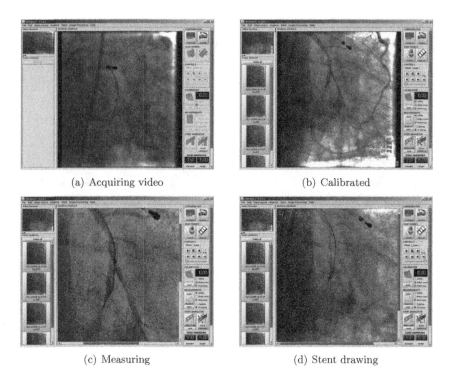

(a) Acquiring video   (b) Calibrated

(c) Measuring   (d) Stent drawing

FIGURE 5.2 Four interaction phases with the Cartesio tool.

frames in order to elaborate and possibly verify a clinical hypothesis on the disease;

3. Plan of action phase: the medical equipe decides what to do and how, evaluating potential problems and consequences and minimizing the decision time;

4. Intervention phase: implementation of surgery activities.

A calibration tool supports such phases and automatizes all the steps of image acquisitions, reconstruction of the stents. Data acquired during analysis can be stored as DICOM images and can be reused for case studies [179]. Figure 5.2 reports screenshots related to the acquisition, calibration, measuring and stent drawing and positioning simulation phases are depicted.

Cartesio is part of a *Distributed Electronic Patient Record*, in which the patient's personal data and family history are enriched with clinical files and DICOM images documenting exam results. The patient files are included during the coronarography planning and all files with biological data and DICOM images are included in the Electronic Patient Record for future reference.

The workflow management tools for cardiology intervention in hemodynamic room are very useful for managing information related to interactive patient data processing. Scientific data can also be obtained by analyzing the use of workflow management tools to perform much more efficient interventions by using DICOM measurement and calibration tools [75].

5.2.2 Electrophysiology Data Processing

Cardiac arrhythmias are disorders in terms of speed or rhythm in the heart's electrical system. Atrial fibrillation (AFib) is the most common sustained arrhythmia that is studied through Electrophysiologic study (EPS) procedures. These procedures consist of inducing a controlled fibrillation in surgical room to analyze electrical heart reactions or to decide for implanting medical devices. Nevertheless, they may generate undesired AFib, which may induce risk for patient and thus a critical issue for physicians. The unexpected AFib onset, aiming to identify signal patterns occurring in time interval preceding an event of spontaneous (i.e., not inducted) fibrillation, can be described by using a workflow management system. A workflow can be implemented in a software module able to profile signal patterns for the early identification of spontaneous fibrillations, such as in [15, 325].

The workflow module uses algorithms able to identify and predict AFib events by using intracardiac electrogram analysis. Literature reports that analysis of process and evaluation of HRAd (distal High Right Atrium) signals represents the best way to detect AFib events by just looking at a single HRAd recording [55]. The atrial fibrillation detection can be based on the workflow represented in Figure 5.3. It involves three main modules:

1. The preprocessing module, which is in charge of acquiring and preprocessing signals (e.g., noise reduction);

2. The feature extraction module, being in charge of identifying A-waves in HRAd signals;

3. The AFib prediction module, which evaluates A-waves and predicts AFib events.

The pre-processing step consists of two procedures: (*i*) acquiring the signal file and waveform generation and (*ii*) filtering the signal to remove baseline wandering, wideband noise and undesired components [187, 252].

Filtering process consists of [35]:

1. Band-passed filtering using a zero-phase second-order Butterworth filter;

2. Rectification calculating the absolute value of the output coming from the bandpass filter;

3. Low-pass filtering using a similar third-order Butterworth filter.

The aim of the Signal Features Extraction step is to extract A-waves from HRAd signals. A-wave detection starts from the identification of signal peaks

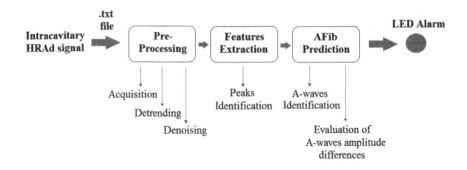

FIGURE 5.3 Workflow diagram of AFib prediction.

that exceed a fixed threshold. An implemented version of the workflow process can be found in [297].

The possibility of implementing the module helps in the definition of a common workflow for electrophysiology procedures able to formalize and predict atrial fibrillation events interactively during the surgery. This kind of tools is used diffusely in clinical procedures where patient's signal processing is performed in real-time.

5.2.3 Visual Stimuli Data Processing in Magnetic Resonance

This section presents the workflow analysis of patient behavior in Magnetic Resonance. Functional Magnetic Resonance Imaging (fMRI) uses signals derived from local changes in cerebral blood flow or metabolism in response to sensorimotor or cognitive stimuli.

To this end, special stimuli presentation devices are needed for both compatibility with the magnetic field and for monitoring behavioural responses. When comparing brain responses between patients and control groups, it is critical to consider task performance effects. If patients fail to reach a good level of performance, one can expect a decreased response of the task-related brain regions. On the other hand, such response may also enhance if an increased effort is required, in spite of a poor performance. This is particularly important to bear in mind when approaching studies of neural plasticity or recover of function after brain injury in humans [56].

It is highly desirable for fMRI users to have flexible and interactive tools for stimuli presentation. In principle, each parameter of an experimental design could be changed, depending on clinical characteristics of the subject groups. The clinical workflow management for processing information in magnetic resonance is used to represent connections among stimuli and brain functions. For instance Figure 5.4 represents an example of system architecture implementing a workflow management system relating external stimuli and magnetic resonance in an available software tool called StiMaRe [297]. The StiMaRe

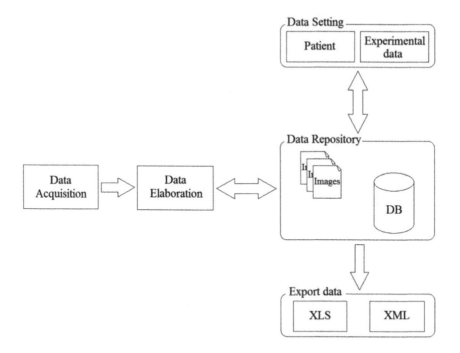

FIGURE 5.4 StiMaRe tool workflow.

tool is a software supporting the functional acquisitions in Magnetic Resonance. It has been designed and implemented following medical requirements, with the following main functionalities:

1. Defining new experiments;

2. Storing and retrieving experiments or sets of experiments;

3. Image stimuli projection to patient during fMRI analysis and response acquisition, subdivided into two subphases: a training one, where patient learns the correct sequence and a test phase, during which blind sequence is shown and patient's responses are acquired;

4. Storing patient results in an fMRI Electronic Patient Record.

Through the StiMaRe tool the operator can register the patients learning performances during the visualization of stimulus images. The clinical workflow follows the specifications of the associative learning technique described in [173, 208].

The workflow is organized as follows. First, the operator chooses the experiment parameters (i.e., number of phases, phases repetitions, patient data), timings and images to be shown. During the Magnetic Resonance test, the sequence of image couples are shown to the patient who will be asked to choose the image under which a known symbol is hidden. The right image is chosen by the patient and answers and answering times can be stored in a database.

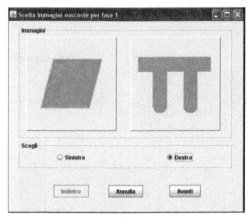

(a) Stimuli definition

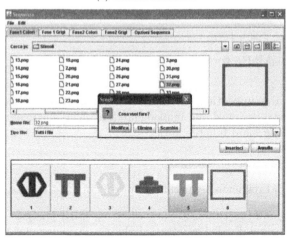

(b) Choose the stimuli order

FIGURE 5.5 Graphical user interface of an interactive tool using by patients during the magneting resonance.

Figure 5.5 shows an example of how workflow management is implemented for the patient interaction during magnetic resonance. The left part of the figure, shows the image stimuli selection phase, while the right part shows their presentation order.

A typical experimental workflow consists of two main phases:

Phase 1 (acquisition): Subjects are presented with a series of pairs of abstract objects that differ in color or shape, but not both (so that there is one relevant and one irrelevant dimension to the discrimination). On each trial subjects are required to predict which of the two objects is correct (reward). Over repeated trial blocks, subjects learn to choose the rewarded member of each pair.

Phase 2 (probe & transfer): stimuli are similar to phase 1, but the objects are changed so that the relevant dimension (color) is the same.

During the two phases, the patient is examined with fMRI and the workflow management tool collects statistical information about the patient responses, creating a scientific dataset that can be analyzed by the physician.

Implementing workflow modules that control magnetic resonance acquisition phases, allows to produce additional information regarding behaviour and properties that can be associated to images. This kind of real-time module hence can generate clinical as well as research data to study diseases and improve diagnosis processes [142].

5.3 OFFLINE PATIENT DATA PROCESSING

Offline patient data refers to information processed after the patient treatment procedure has finished. Datasets are typically created by physicians for *a posteriori* statistical analyses or epidemiological studies. We present examples of workflow modules for: (i) sharing electronic patient records among clinical structures, (ii) extracting spatial information from clinical datasets and analyzing it in geographical information systems, (iii) applying GWAS (Genome-Wide Association Studies) analyses in clinical workflows, and (iv) enhancing the information extracted from mass spectrometry data.

5.3.1 Sharing EPR Information for Clinical Protocol Studies

Sharing Electronic Patient Records (EPRs) among different hospitals is a key technology enabling both the improvement of document and information sharing as well as the improvement of patient status. A hierarchical network for information exchange may be used to share EPRs about specific pathologies or treatments among different health structures. Workflow implementation, as the one reported in the SIGMCC [49] system, enables the exchange of EPR meta data information hiding the complexity of heterogeneous patient records. The use of an XML-based distributed EPR repository enables nodes to share information among different health structures managing data by using personalized databases and systems. For instance, the XML schema in Figure 5.6 represents a meta-EPR for sharing patient data in the oncological domain. A hierarchical network (i.e., a peer-to-peer one) might map the workflow for clinical data processing among nodes (health structures), where physicians may perform queries and obtain results about patients or treatments. An XML repository can be used to store metadata extracted from heterogeneous EPRs. Health structure operators may formulate queries against an EPR schema from one of the nodes of the network (i.e., from a health structure).

The workflow can be composed by: (*i*) a data wrapper, which is in charge of extracting and organizing data from distributed EPR data sources in clinical structures; (*ii*) a module able to map information into metadata base (e.g., XML repository) storing subsets of EPRs; (*iii*) a query engine able to compose and distribute queries among nodes of the network; (*iv*) a security and update management module able to guarantee privacy and data updates (i.e., keeping updated information in the XML database). A workflow implementation instance can be used to retrieve information on clinical protocol applications and results (such as, follow-up information) improving cooperation among health structures.

Using a general purpose workflow avoids to use industrial standards in clinical applications solving the problem of sharing the results and feedbacks. Each health structure can provide one user interface (node) to submit queries against the network. Each node is in charge of collecting local data and distributing the query across the other nodes. Security data access mechanisms have to be defined in order to preserve patients data privacy. An example of instance of such a workflow-based module is implemented in [49], which has been tested at regional scale, proving an efficient and secure access to meta-EPRs.

5.3.2 Merging Geographic and Health Information

A common and frequent problem for a better understanding of clinical datasets is associating clinical features (e.g., diseases) with geographical and environmental data. Geographical software modules are able to associate information about disease diffusion with geographical layers containing land information. GIS (Geographical Information System) technologies can be applied to analyze clinical data containing health information about large populations. Often, clinical datasets already contain geographical data (i.e., zip codes, addresses) which can be used to geolocate clinical events (e.g., patients, diseases).

For instance, Geomedica [298] geocodes existing clinical data and extracts geographical coordinates which can then be mapped and analyzed/queried using both SQL-like languages and web-based graphical user interfaces. Geographical constraints can be collected in a QBE (Query-By-Example) mode to generate a query and to visualize data on a cartographic map. Figure 5.7 shows a workflow of relating GIS with clinical data.

Figure 5.8 shows the results of a query which has been previously generated by using the QBE form, and visualized in the Geomedica interface based on Google Maps APIs. Each data point represents an entry in a test dataset (e.g., individuals, buildings, health structures) which satisfies all of the alphanumeric and geographical constraints specified by the user. This result can then be stored in a geographical layer and used to query other layers for further investigation.

```
<?xml version="1.0" encoding="UTF-8" ?>
<xs:schema targetNamespace="MEPR" ...>
<xs:element name="MEPR">
 <xs:annotation>
   <xs:documentation>attribute name="IdHospital" attribute
   name="DateOfSource"</xs:documentation>
 </xs:annotation>
 <xs:complexType>
  <xs:sequence>
    <xs:element name="PersonalData">
    <xs:complexType>
     <xs:sequence>
         <xs:element name="Surname" type="xs:string" />
         <xs:element name="Name" type="xs:string" />
         <xs:element name="Sex">
         <xs:simpleType>
             ...
             <xs:pattern value="[MmFf]" />
             ...
         </xs:element>
         <xs:element name="DateOfBirth" type="xs:date" />
             ...
         <xs:element name="FiscalCode">
             ...
         <xs:element name="ResidentialData">
             ...
         <xs:element name="ClinicalData">
             ...
         <xs:element name="Diagnosis" maxOccurs="unbounded">
             ...
         <xs:restriction base="xs:string">
         <xs:pattern value="[1234]"/>
             ...
         <xs:element name="Mutation" type="xs:string" minOccurs="0"/>
             ...
         <xs:element name="TimeToTheProgression" ...minOccurs="0"/>
         <xs:element name="Metastasis" type="xs:string" minOccurs="0"/>
             ...
         </xs:complexType>
         </xs:element>
         <xs:element name="PerformanceStatus" type="xs:string"/>
         <xs:element name="LifeQuality" type="xs:string" minOccurs="0"/>
         <xs:element name="ConcomitantPathologies" ... minOccurs="0" />
         <xs:element name="Allergies" type="xs:string" minOccurs="0" />
         <xs:element name="FamilialAnamnesis" minOccurs="0">
             ...
         </xs:element>
         </xs:sequence>
    <xs:attribute name="IdHospital" type="xs:string" use="required" />
    <xs:attribute name="DateOfSource" type="xs:date" use="required" />
  </xs:complexType>
 </xs:element>
</xs:schema>
```

FIGURE 5.6 XML schema for health cancer domain.

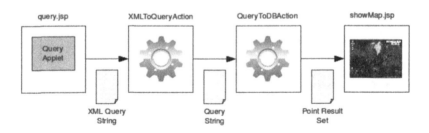

FIGURE 5.7 Workflow used to generate the query from the contraints specified in the *query-by-example* form.

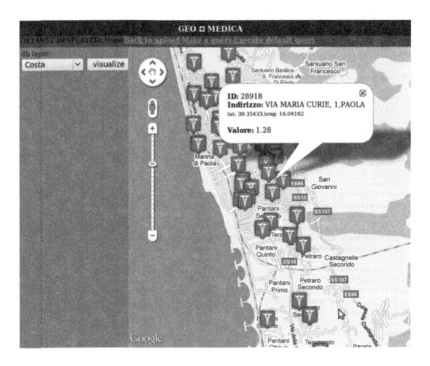

FIGURE 5.8 Example of a cartographic map showing the result set of a generated query.

Geographical Informations Systems integrated with clinical and environmental datasets can be used to implement workflow-based software tools that are able to monitor clinical information and also to add temporal and evolutionary information to the normal clinical data workflow. Researchers are particularly interested in such kind of workflows since new topics can be obtained by integrating apparently heterogeneous data regarding different populations and different geographical areas. For instance, recently, monitoring clinical-related phenomena regarding migrations highlighted the importance of relating population flows, epidemiological data, population data and geographical locations/areas [228].

5.3.3 Genome-Wide Association Studies for Precision Medicine

This section outlines an application of the use of novel workflow modules in Precision Medicine (PM) and its potential impact on clinical practice.

Personalized-based Medicine revisits current workflows in patients treatment and healthcare. The successful sequencing of the human genome [154], together with subsequent studies about the discovery of single nucleotide polymorphism (SNP) and genotyping efforts [101] showed that the human genome has a structure that is much more complex than the sequence of its nucleotides (i.e., primary sequence). One of the main discoveries is the linkage disequilibrium (LD) blocks which are separated by points of recombination throughout the entire genome. It has also been observed that it is possible to examine the DNA of an individual just by using a fraction of the million SNPs existing in the population, which has given a huge boost in genomics [249]. Genome-Wide Association Studies (GWAS) are a mature tool towards implementing PM, being able to link genetic features (e.g., particular gene variations and mutations) to phenotypical ones (e.g., diseases, analytes, life expectancy, BMI index, sex, race, age).

A major goal is to support physicians in finding the right drug for the right patient when they need it. This could also help patients affected by rare diseases for which it has been economically impracticable to find a cure so far. GWAS can be considered as the final step of a health workflow model in next generation clinical workflows. In fact, despite the availability of GWAS tools able to perform a number of analyses having a solid statistical foundation, there still is a lack of wide adoption among the clinical community. Some of the main challenges against the implementation of GWAS workflows in health care structures are: (*i*) difficult setup of the experiments, due to the statistical and mathematical knowledge required to deeply understand the models and to interpret the results and (*ii*) genetic datasets can be huge, thus requiring a long time for processing and analysis and also an adequate computational platform able to manage big data. GWAS studies often involve hundreds of thousands of genotyped markers for several thousands individuals. Novel genetic data acquisition instruments can also acquire entire genomes, making genome-wide analyses, for groups of patients or even populations, feasible. A GWAS tool, apart from the usual data management functionalities, can perform: (*i*) summary statistics, (*ii*) population stratification, (*iii*) association analyses, (*iv*) identity-by-descent estimation. The last one, for instance, is implemented in the widely adopted PLINK tool [224], where the authors show how this information can be used to detect and also to correct for population stratification, while identifying share chromosomal segments between distantly related patients. From the analysis of these segmental sharing patterns it is possible to map disease loci containing rare variants in population-based linkage analyses.

5.3.4 Mass Spectrometry Workflow for Peptide Discovery

Workflow representation can also be used for improving the identification of peptides (protein portions) in mass spectrometry analysis, such as in MS/MS ICAT analysis. The target is to increase the number of peptides identified and quantified in input samples.

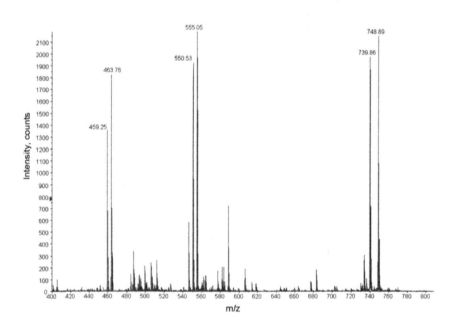

FIGURE 5.9 Mass spectrum of a biological sample; X axis contains mass/charge ratio, Y axis indicates intensities.

Figure 5.9 shows an example of a MS spectrum where [*m/z, intensity*] pairs are related to the presence of a biomolecule in the input sample, with mass-to-charge ratio m/z and abundance expressed by the *intensity* value [22, 129]. Typically, these biomolecules are peptides. In fact they are more suitable for MS/MS sequencing than a whole protein. The MS/MS process performs multiple MS analysis steps by generating a mass spectrum for fragments related to a subset of selected peaks identified in a previous step. This analysis is normally performed in data-dependent mode. During the chromatographic separation of peptides, the mass spectrometer automatically switches from full scan *MS mode* (detection of H/L pairs at a particular retention time), to *MS/MS mode* on the most abundant peaks.

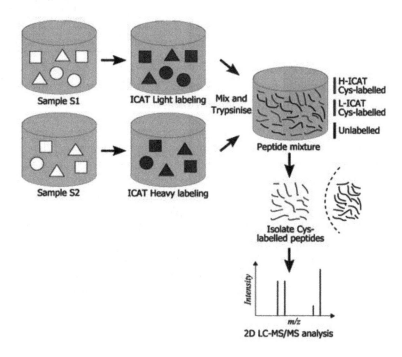

FIGURE 5.10 Workflow of a MS/MS peptides identification process.

Protein/peptide identification from MS/MS spectra consists in the computation of *qualitative* information and is performed by querying publicly available databases (e.g., the *SwissProt* database [29] queried by using *Mascot* [180]). Proteomics literature presents a large number of highly specialized repositories and tools for storing and handling large scale MS/MS proteomics datasets.

The protocol workflow, reported in Figure 5.10, marks two input protein mixtures (sample S_1 and sample S_2) with H and L labels, having identical chemical properties but different masses. Then, the labelled peptides are selectively captured by affinity chromatography. Identical peptides belonging

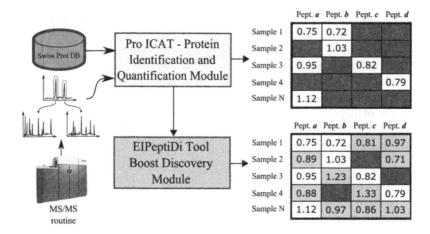

FIGURE 5.11 The workflow for MS analysis to identify proteins and its improvement by using the Eipeptidi tool.

to the same protein, but originated from different samples are detected at different m/z values because of the difference in mass, which corresponds to different flight times. After a database search, peptide sequence identification is performed to produce tables of proteins/peptides with their relative expression levels. Figure 5.11 shows an example of peptide identification process performed using the Applied Biosystems *ProICAT* software tool [295]. The table shown on the upper right of Figure 5.11 from [47] depicts a simplified result generated with *ProICAT* where values correspond to H/L ratios and vary from experiment to experiment. Workflow modules in MS/MS analysis can be used to optimize the data flow for the elaboration of clinical data. Scientific data can also be automatically extracted and used by researchers to perform statistical studies on populations or patient groups of interest.

5.3.5 Health Status Detection through Audio Signal Analysis

This section discusses the use of workflow modules for processing patients' data in a delayed and offline fashion, regarding the use of workflows to support clinicians in designing population-wide screenings for voice-related diseases.

The idea is to use an on-line system to support patients and clinicians while monitoring health related parameters. Web based systems can be used to monitor patients' health status, e.g., as a follow-up of surgical procedures. Analysis results, integrated with patients clinical information, can be used for early detection and parameters monitoring. Similarly, Hearing analysis can be realized by supporting patients in an on line analysis for acquisition and monitoring of patient signals. Offline analysis is performed to monitor patient status. Workflow based systems can be used to test hearing status and to give indication to medical doctors for tuning cures and strategy. Patients listen to a continuously increasing audio signal and give feedbacks acquired and measured by the system. The main modules for a workflow managing the audio analysis system are

1. Acquisition component, responsible for collecting clinical data from patients;

2. Screening component, implementing the hearing/voice health test;

3. Data analysis component;

4. Data management component;

5. Database component, which stores all the data and signals.

By using remote analysis it is possible to extract functional parameters from vocal signals and to measure the voice quality, e.g., the frequency of fundamental tone or the pitch, and to associate data features to the presence of anomalies.

Audio files can be used to check for anomalies. Among the others, the following phases can be performed on server-side: (i) pro-actively notify specialist physicians with acquisitions requiring attention, (ii) analyze novel acquired voice signals by extracting fundamental features from signal data (e.g., fundamental frequency or pitch, jitter, shimmer, noise level), (iii) store finished analyses in the database.

Pitch estimation can be calculated by using an *average magnitude difference function* (AMDF) and a *simple inverse filter tracking* (SIFT) [175]. In the first approach, the estimated fundamental frequency value (f_0) is obtained by filtering the signal by a proper *continuous wavelet transform* (CWT) and extracting its time periodicity with the AMDF method. The method is very sensitive to noise. A second approach uses an auto regressive (AR) model to describe the vocal signal applied to each data frame of a given length. The method is composed by the following steps: (i) estimation of the correct order p of the AR model by means of the singular valued decomposition (SVD); (ii) computation of the AR model parameters and the inverse filter (IF); (iii) estimation of the residual sequence by applying the signal to the IF; (iv) band-pass filtering in the range $50Hz - 1.5kHz$ and evaluation of the maximum of the autocorrelation sequence (AS) of the residuals in the frequency range $60 - 250Hz$. The computational complexity of the second method is rather high, nonetheless the procedure is very robust to noise and accurate. A measure of the dysphonic component of the voice spectrum related to the total signal energy is evaluated by using the Adaptive NNE (Normalized Noise Energy) index (ANNE). At lower ANNE values, the noise energy is larger and the signal becomes more noisy when ANNE is close to zero [175]. Voices affected by pathologies are characterized by a mean pitch lower than healthy ones. When a vocal signal analysis is not sufficient to recognize the pathology, an endoscopic analysis is necessary. Thanks to the usability and ubiquity of the web-based system, large screenings of patient populations are feasible.

The advantage of using offline and remote systems for signal analysis is the possibility for the physicians to create statistics and applying data mining models to perform population studies on vocal related pathologies. This also creates a powerful tool for post-surgery control and innovative follow-up procedures. Such a strategy can be used to support any signal analysis for health status.

5.4   SUMMARY AND FURTHER PERSPECTIVES

We discussed the role of workflows in information management systems for health structures and the problem of implementation and use of automatic system for workflow realization. Healthy structures can use a general purpose system to manage the data process through a unique web based system. Several modules can be used to manage information of interest for clinicians as well as researchers. For instance, it is possible to manage different clinical workflow modules by using an integration system that can manage information regarding clinical data. It can be used as a workflow shared source for any department that is in charge of managing different data and at the same time can customize clinical workflows.

This chapter presented different examples of workflow modules that can be used for different healthy related cases. Many of the proposed workflow models have been implemented in health systems and tested for research purpose at the University Hospital of Catanzaro. Nowadays the Management of Health Care structures is focusing on appropriateness of care measurement by using computer based methodologies to model the whole process of admission, permanent hospitalization period, resignation and controls of patients, considering both clinical and economic aspects. Moreover, we outlined the challenge of the introduction of the use of workflow system in healthcare structure. This challenge is very relevant for health structures (both public and private ones), which must optimize or improve services and monitor expenses in order to obtain refunds for the services offered to patients. Moreover, keeping expenses under control and making them more objective, could make the financial distribution of resources among structures (or operative units) much easier, thus helping decision makers for resource planning. Despite all the thus far introduced innovations, there is a substantial delay in the adoption of a global system due to the absence of comprehensive software tools for the management of a Health Structure as a whole. The definition of guidelines and laws for security, management and information distribution are not sufficient to guarantee the diffusion of digital information systems. Moreover, the results from these experiences seem to be that despite a big interest in single operative units, a support for the whole health structure is still far to be achieved.

EXERCISES

5.1 In a health structure cardiologists work both in a biology laboratory and in clinical structure. A clinical workflow module is used to manage patients in surgery room while biological samples are managed by an on line module connected with device related software (microscopy, NGS platform). Biological laboratory and health structure have different privacy related rules. Sketch an integrated workflow model able to allow to authorized cardiologists in using data coming from both workflow systems (surgery rooms and biological labs) to increase the capability of gathering new research results.

5.2 In a neurology department clinical data are related to results of magnetic resonance. There are different users all accessing to image systems managed by the magnetic resonance informatics system. Patients also perform signal analysis by acquiring data by using body sensors (e.g., EEG analysis). Sketch a workflow based system able to combine clinical information in an offline module extracting information from different diagnostic reports and eventually connecting signals results with magnetic resonance images.

5.3 Sketch a workflow module that can monitor and control patient parameters obtained by applying devices on patient while staying at home. Data should be acquired and transmitted to remote station and collected in a central database. Consider also the possibility of using different data loading center (i.e., different regional data center hospital) which are then used to feed a centralized information extraction module (as for instance the emergency management module)

GLOSSARY

ANNE: Adaptive Normalized Noise Energy.

Atrial fibrillation (AFib): Cardiac arrhythmias are disorders in terms of speed or rhythm in the heart's electrical system. Atrial fibrillation (AFib) is the most common sustained arrhythmia, affecting the atria of the cardiac muscle.

Chronic disease: Human health condition in which the disease is persistent or long-lasting.

DICOM: Digital Imaging and Communications in Medicine (DICOM) is a standard for distributing and viewing any kind of medical image regardless of the origin of the image itself.

Electrophysiology (cardiac): The science which studies the electrical activities of the heart.

EMR: Electronic Medical Record.

EPR: Electronic Patient Record.

fMRI: Functional Magnetic Resonance Imaging.

Follow-up procedure: Set of measures and procedures to monitor patient status over time.

GIS: Geographical Information System.

GWAS: Genome-Wide Association Study, able to find correlations among the phenotypes and the genotypes of a patient.

Hemodynamic: Part of cardiovascular physiology devoted to the study of the forces generated by the heart pump in the circulatory system.

HRA: High Right Atrium is a location inside the human heart.

ICAT LC-MS/MS: Isotope-Coded Affinity-Tag-based protein profiling with Liquid Chromatography and tandem Mass Spectrometry.

MRI: Magnetic Resonance Imaging.

Precision Medicine: An emerging approach for disease treatment and prevention that takes into account individual variability.

QBE: Query By Example.

RDBMS: Relational DataBase Management System: a DBMS implementing the relational data model.

XML: eXtensible markup Language.

FURTHER READING

Andrea Natale and Jalife José, eds. *Atrial fibrillation: from bench to bedside.* Springer Science & Business Media, 2008.

Slichter Charles P., *Principles of magnetic resonance.* Vol. 1. Springer Science & Business Media, 2013.

Craglia Massimo and Ravi Maheswaran, eds. *GIS in public health practice.* CRC Press, 2016.

Cedric Gondro, Van der Werf Julius, and Hayes Ben, eds. *Genome-wide association studies and genomic prediction.* Humana Press, 2013.

De Hoffmann Edmond and Stroobant Vincent, *Mass spectrometry: principles and applications.* John Wiley & Sons, 2007.

Kessel David O., Basic tools required to perform angioplasty and stenting procedures. In: *Handbook of Angioplasty and Stenting Procedures.* Springer London, 2010, pp. 1–11.

II

Advanced Topics

CHAPTER 6

Metrics for Processes in Healthcare

Jan Mendling

Vienna University of Economics and Business, Vienna, Austria

CONTENTS

> According to the measure of
> their states
>
> W. Shakespeare

THIS chapter is an introduction to the measurement of processes. Measurement is important since a precise understanding of the current situation in a quantitative way provides a solid foundation for taking action in terms of improving the process. First, the characteristics of processes in healthcare are discussed. Then, the measurement of specific aspects of a process are investigated: its structure, its understanding by stakeholders, its performance and its conformance. Finally, we describe connections between these different aspects of measurement.

6.1   CHARACTERISTICS OF PROCESSES IN HEALTHCARE

Processes in healthcare have specific characteristics in terms of their structure, performance and conformance. The BPM *context framework* proposed by vom Brocke et al. [326] help us describing some of their key characteristics. First, processes in healthcare are often described as being knowledge-intense. This means that healthcare personnel working in these processes require specific skills and insights to perform complex tasks. Second, process in healthcare are associated with a high level of interdependence. This means that an individual task in the healthcare process can be hardly isolated from the history of the previous tasks that have been performed. Third, processes in healthcare exhibit a diverging degree of repetitiveness. While some processes can be highly standardized like corrective laser eye surgery and executed in a highly repetitive way, there are highly complex and hardly repetitive conditions like multi-trauma. Fourth, even for the more repetitive healthcare processes, the level of variability tends to be rather medium to high. Various conditions of the patient have an impact on the permissible treatments and interventions. All these characteristics makes the management of healthcare processes a challenging, but also exciting task.

The characteristics of healthcare processes have an impact on their complexity, their understanding and also their challenges in terms of performance and conformance. In order to analyze and investigate the connections between them, we have to make them accessible to measurement (see [181]). *Measurement* refers to a process that assigns numbers to attributes of entities [94], i.e., processes in this context, in order to represent the amount or degree of those attributes possessed by the entities [296, p.19]. Measurement is essential for opening up abstract concepts to an empirical evaluation and is, therefore, a cornerstone of natural, social and engineering sciences. An attribute in this context can refer to a characteristic, a property or a feature of a process. Measurement serves the three purposes of *understanding, control* and *improvement*. The classical statement attributed to Galilei of "What is not measurable, make measurable" stresses the ability of a measurement to deliver understanding. The idea behind this phrase is that measurement makes things visible in a more precise way. Measurement also enables control in order to meet goals. According to DeMarco "you cannot control, what you cannot measure" [78]. Based on an understanding of relationships between attributes, one can predict whether goals will be met and which actions have to be taken. Finally, measurement is also essential for the improvement of processes. This observation is central to many management approaches including Taylor's scientific management [286] or Kaplan and Norton's balanced scorecard [138].

For measurements, it has to be clarified to which scale they conform. Stevens distinguishes nominal, ordinal, interval and ratio scales [277]. The values of a *nominal* scale can only be interpreted as being equal or unequal. Consider, for example, two healthcare process models that have the unique IDs 3 and 4. The *ordinal* scale represents the order relation between phenomena. This is for example the case for questionnaire items that ask to which degree a healthcare process is complex, and the answers are coded as 1 for trivial, 2 for rather simple, 3 for rather complex and 4 for incomprehensible. The *interval* scale can be linearly transformed without loss of information. Consider the duration of executing a healthcare process in minutes. This duration can be multiplied by 60 to get the duration in seconds. *Ratio* scales have a zero element that represents absence of a certain property. Count measurements belong to this category.

Measurements should be reliable and valid. *Validity* refers to the question whether conclusions based on a measurement are accurate and whether it captures what is intended to be measured. In particular for abstract concepts, the translation into a measurable operational definition or a metric provides plenty of room for mismatch (see [137, 150]). *Reliability* refers to the consistency of measurements over entities and time. While a scale can be reliable and not valid, an unreliable measurement cannot be valid. In this way, reliability establishes an upper bound on validity (see [269, p. 364]). Validity and reliability are both important for objective measurements like the duration of executing a process and for subjective measurements like customer experience during a certain healthcare treatment. Challenges of measurement stem from the fact that we are typically interested in abstract matters such as concepts like process standardization or process performance. In order to make them measurable, they have to be operationalized and it is often not easy to operationalize a broader concept by identifying quantitative measures that are associated with it.

In this chapter, we are specifically interested in measurements that are associated with important aspects of healthcare processes. We discuss measurement of such processes from four different angles. Section 6.2 discusses complexity of processes and how they can be measured using process models. Section 6.3 deals with the question of how different stakeholders can easily understand the process by the help of a process model. Section 6.4 investigates how the performance of a process can be measured based on the devil's quadrangle. Section 6.5 describes how the conformance can be measured.

6.2 MEASURING THE COMPLEXITY OF PROCESSES

The concept of *complexity* is in itself a complex one. In order to avoid a general discussion, we will focus here on the complexity as it is visible from a healthcare process model. The previous chapters have already introduced BPMN as the standard for modeling business processes both on a conceptual and technical level. Therefore, we will use BPMN models to illustrate the measurement of complexity.

Figure 6.1 shows the example of a surgery with anaesthesia process as reported in [107]. The process starts when the patient is brought into the operation room. Next, three teams are acting in parallel: the operation nurses prepare the operation room and lay out the instruments; the surgical team focuses on the lead time out using a checklist; and the anaesthesia team puts the patient on monitoring, induces the patient after the lead time out, and gives antibiotics prophylaxis if needed. Once all these activities have been conducted, the surgical team conducts the surgery and starts the lead sign out. Then, the anaesthesia team emerges the patient and transports the patient out of the operation room.

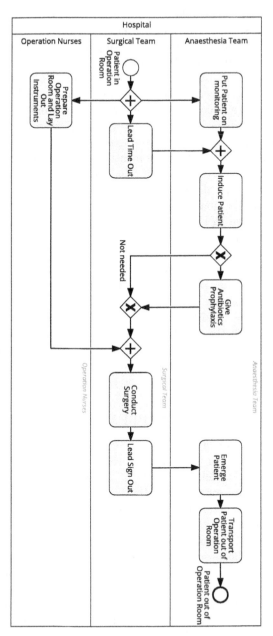

FIGURE 6.1 BPMN model of surgery with anaesthesia process.

Based on this BPMN model, we can distinguish various aspects that are connected with complexity of the control flow. In line with [181, 184], we group them into measurements for size, connection, modularity, gateway interplay and complex behavior:

- *Size measures* can be defined for all types of elements in the BPMN model including nodes, arcs, tasks, start-events, end-events, gateways, AND-splits, AND-joins, XOR-splits, XOR-joins, OR-splits, OR-joins. These measures are specific *counts* of the number of arcs and nodes. For our example process in Figure 6.1, we can easily determine these measures by counting the respective elements. For example, there are nine activities and five gateways in the model.

- *Connection measures* relate to various aspects of connections between nodes. *Density* is the ratio of the total number of arcs in a process model to the theoretically maximum number of connections. The *connectivity* is the ratio of the total number of arcs in a process model to the total number of its nodes. The *maximum degree* expresses the maximum sum of incoming and outgoing arcs of gateway nodes. For our example process in Figure 6.1, we can calculate the connectivity by dividing the number of arcs by the number of nodes. The result is $16/18 = 0.88$. The maximum gateway degree is four (one incoming and three outgoing arcs) for the first AND-split.

- *Modularity* defines in how far the process can be subdivided into two or more independent components [240]. Important for modularity are so-called cut-vertices. A *cut-vertex* is a node in the control flow that, if it is deleted, will leave two disconnected parts. In Figure 6.1, e.g., the first and the last AND-gateways are cut-vertices. The *separability* is the ratio of the number of cut-vertices divided by the total number of nodes in the process model. The *sequentiality* is the degree to which the model is constructed of pure sequences of tasks. *Structuredness* captures the extent to which a process model can be built by nesting blocks of matching split and join gateways [158]. *Depth* is the maximum nesting of structured blocks in a process model. The concept of the refined process structure tree provides the basis for calculating the most important metrics in this category [219, 320]. For our example process in Figure 6.1, there are several cut-vertices including the first and the last AND-gateways. These are cut-vertices, because when we delete them, we would separate the model into two disconnected parts. The process has a depth of two. When we determine the single-entry-single-exit components, we will find that the most deeply nested component is the XOR-block around "Give antibiotics prophylaxis", which is included in an AND-block, which is part of the overall start-to-end sequence.

- *Gateway interplay* refers to a potential mismatch of gateway. It is the

TABLE 6.1 Calculation of metrics for BPMN model of Figure 6.1.

Nodes	16	Separability	6/16
Arcs	18	Sequentiality	4/16
Tasks	9	Structuredness	1
Events	2	Depth	2
Gateways	5	CFC	1+2+0=3
Density	16/16*15	Cyclicity	0
Connectivity	16/18	Token Split	3
Maximum Degree	4		

sum of gateway pairs that do not match with each other, e.g., when an AND-split is followed up by an OR-join. *Control flow complexity* (CFC) [50], inspired by the cyclomatic complexity [106], captures the number of split gateways weighted with the combination of options to continue. For our example process in Figure 6.1, control flow complexity is low with 1 (AND-split with no choice) + 2 (2 XOR-Split options) = 3, because there are no OR-gateways in the model, which would contribute most to combinatorial complexity of potential execution sequences.

- *Complex behavior* refers to concurrency and repetition. *Cyclicity* captures the number of nodes in a cycle and relates it to the total number of nodes. *Token splits* gives the maximum number of paths in a process model that may be concurrently initiated through the use of AND-splits and OR-splits. For our example process in Figure 6.1, there is a cyclicity of zero, since no repetitions are possible. The token split captures the degree of concurrency. It is three, because the first AND-split produces three tokens.

Table 6.1 shows the calculation of the metrics for the BPMN model of Figure 6.1.

Complexity measures like the ones described have been found to be important factors of *model understanding* [240, 239]. Understanding is important, because good visualization of processes contributes to redesign success [144]. Beyond the complexity measures, there are also other model-related factors that contribute to understanding. Also user and task characteristcs play a role. For a comprehensive review, see Figl [96]. Not all of these factors are easily measurable, but they are equally relevant as the complexity measures. These factors include the following:

- *Modeling language*: The design of a modeling language has an influence on the understanding of individual models. This is apparent from research into modeling language deficiencies in relation to language semantics and notation. If a language contains elements that cannot be precisely associated with the domain of application, then persons using the models created in that language ambiguous [226]. Also, when the visual notation of the language has deficiencies, this will also have a negative impact on the usage of actual models [97]. BPMN as used in Figure 6.1 is a compact and well-designed language.

- *Text in model*: Also important is the way how the textual content of a process model is arranged in terms of grammar and terms. The grammar of activity, event and gateway labels is often recommended to follow a specific grammar, for instance verb-object for activities [164]. Deviating from this structure has a negative effect on understanding [182]. Also terms should be consistently used: usage of homonyms and synonyms is confusing for model users [218]. The example of Figure 6.1 shows labels that are formulated using the verb-object grammar like "Induce Patient" with the verb "to induce" first and the corresponding object "patient" followed.

- *Color highlighting*: Finally, the usage of color can help to make a process model easier to understanding. Meaningful highlighting supports the visual cognition processes of interpreting a given process model. Various works use color highlighting for showing the correspondence between different gateways [238] or the relevant regions for specific problem-solving tasks [214], both with a positive effect on model understanding. The model in Figure 6.1 uses modest coloring in order to increase the pop-out of the activities from the white background.

In the end, a process model should be designed in such a way that it can be readily understood. Guidelines like the *Seven Process Modeling Guidelines* [183] recommend to keep complexity moderate by complying with the following rules:

1. *Using as few elements as possible*: try to avoid too many elements and specifically try to avoid activities with the same text.

2. *Using as few connections as possible*: try to avoid gateways with more than three outgoing arcs, if possible.

3. *Using a clear start and end element*: make sure that the start and end conditions of the process are clear.

4. *Using modular structure as much as possible*: try to model the whole process with blocks of AND-gateways, XOR-gateways and OR-gateways.

5. *Avoiding complex elements like OR-joins*: the number of combinations to continue after an OR-split increases exponentially with the number of arcs.

6. *Following grammar rules like verb-object for activities*: this helps to make sure that it is clear what is the action and what the object.

7. *Decomposing models that have more than 50 elements*: introduce sub-processes to structure the model.

Our example in Figure 6.1 complies with all these seven guidelines. Also the complexity of information flow has been studied in the general area of software engineering. One of the classic metrics here is the *information flow metric* that is based on the data flow between different modules of a program [124] or between the activities of a process. Information can be passed between software modules in three ways: by a module invoking another one; by returning a result from the invoked module to the caller; and by exchanging information via a global data structure. The *fan-in* of a module M refers to the number of calls to the module plus the number of reads to global data structures. In a process model, this relates to the input variables of an activity plus its input messages. The *fan-out* captures calls to other modules and write operations to global data structures. For a process model, we have to consider the output variables and the outgoing messages. Based on these parameters, the information flow complexity (IFC) is calculated as

$$IFC(M) = LoC(M) \cdot (fan_{in} \cdot fan_{out})^2$$

The IFC metric can be used at design-time to predict which modules are likely to contain errors. The multiplication of fan-in and fan-out has been criticized in [94]. If a module has either no fan-in or fan-out the metric yields zero which is misleading.

There are also complexity measures that have been defined for organization models that are associated with process models [221]. The strongest drivers of such complexity are the *number of subjects and roles*. In a BPMN model, these can be associated with pools and lanes. Important is the *hierarchy* of the different roles or departments in the organization chart. The *maximum distance* captures the maximum of the shorts path between any two roles or subjects in the organization. Hierarchy is also partially visible in a BPMN model when lanes are nested with pools.

6.3 MEASURING THE UNDERSTANDING OF PROCESSES

The mentioned measures and factors have been shown to influence the understanding of process models. A timely literature survey summarizes corresponding research findings [96]. Gemino and Wand provide a framework for the measurement of understanding. It distinguishes the following aspects [104]:

- *Domain versus modeling knowledge*: It is important to recognize that understanding a process model requires two orthogonal knowledge components: modeling knowledge and domain knowledge. Modeling knowledge refers to all skills and competencies in relation to the creation and interpretation of a process model. In order to make sense of a BPMN model, one needs to know the symbols and their meaning. Still, this is not enough to truly understand a specific model. Consider the healthcare process of Figure 6.1: a basic knowledge of medical terms and phenomena is required to understand it. Model users can be novices and experts with respect to domain and modeling knowledge. There are some general insights into modeling expertise. Modeling experts are typically competent in abstracting and in goal-oriented information seeking in the context of a project [324].

- *Creation versus interpretation*: Understanding is an important matter and it is relevant both for the creation and for the interpretation of process models. During the creation, it is related to the organization of the model and its content, such that the modeler herself can understand it well to continue with the next step towards completing it. During the interpretation the focus is on a person different from the original modeler who wants to acquire some understanding of a process based on the model.

- *Product versus process*: Various aspects of a process model as a product can be measured such as the complexity measures discussed above. Also the processes of creating a model and reading a model can be analyzed. The process of process modeling has been analyzed using event data from modeling tools and process mining techniques. It builds on the the the assumption that a good modeling process results in a good model [59, 216]. Also the process of model reading has been investigated using eye-tracking technology. It demonstrates that a systematic inspection of the model leads to good understanding [214, 215].

- *Efficiency versus effectiveness*: Efficiency refers to the amount of resources spent for creating or interpreting a process model well, effectiveness states how good this created model or its interpretation is. Both criteria have been operationalized in various ways in process modeling experiments. Effectiveness is typically measured using a score that is associated with a particular task of creation or interpretation. Efficiency often puts this score in relation to the time spent for achieving this score. Important in this context is the actual performance in comparison to the perception of the effort needed. Cognitive effort is often measured with a self-assessment by the person working on the respective task.

There are some guidelines for the creation of a process model regarding the steps of domain knowledge acquisition. Often, the person creating a model has limited knowledge of the domain [80]. Different methods of discovery help to obtain the required domain knowledge systematically. First, existing documentation should be studied. If possible, event data can be used to automatically generate process models using process mining techniques. Then, observation of the process participants together with interviews should be conducted to clarify details. If possible, these steps can also be complemented with a work-

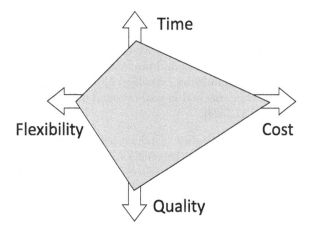

FIGURE 6.2 The devil's quadrangle.

shop of all involved process participants to obtain an integrated view of the process.

There are also some guidelines for facilitating understanding from existing models. Process models are specifically powerful to clarify the dependencies between different tasks. [299]. A challenge is sometimes that stakeholders have limited knowledge of modeling languages. Then, textual descriptions can be generated from BPMN models for these stakeholders [165].

6.4 MEASURING THE PERFORMANCE OF PROCESSES

The performance of a healthcare process can be assessed with respect to its desirable outcomes. In the ideal case, a process is fast, cheap, flexible and provides results of excellent quality. The fact that all these different dimensions of performance are difficult to achieve has motivated the description of the so-called devil's quadrangle [80] (see Figure 6.2). It states that time, cost, quality and flexibility are important dimensions of process performance. It also emphasizes that there are typically trade-offs between improving these criteria. For example, when a company makes a process cheaper, it often has to accept that the quality might decrease. Or, when a process is standardized in order to make it faster, it will be likely less flexible. For these reasons, the term devil's quadrangle was coined: it is hardly feasible to improve all dimensions at the same time.

There are various measurements that are associated with these performance dimensions [80]. The four dimensions time, cost, quality and flexibility can be operationalized in different ways. We discuss the measurement for each of them.

- *Time*: The time dimension is important for many processes. This is because being slow contributes to various types of cost, e.g., if it is associated with the time different process participants take to complete their tasks. There are various aspects that relate to time in a process. We refer to *cycle time* when we consider the overall duration of a process. In healthcare processes, time is often critical to avoid undesirable conditions. For example, measures like door-to-needle capture how quickly sproke patients are treated given a specific medical infrastructure in a city, a region or a country. The cycle time in this case includes all steps for making suitable treatment available for a patient. Cycle time can be split up into two components: processing time and waiting time. *Processing time* is the time spent for actually working on different tasks of the process. Often, its faction is rather small as compared to *waiting time*, which is the time the elapses between one task is finished and the next one starts. A share of waiting time can be explained by hand-offs between different steps, different systems, different persons and different organizational units [212].

- *Cost*: Various types of cost relate to processes. Those costs that are directly associated with the execution of a process are called *operational costs*. These include cost for the personnel working in the process and the materials used for providing the goods and services as output of the process. Processes require a specific infrastructure to be operational. In healthcare processes, these are for example machines and equipment, which are needed for conducting a surgery. These cost are often substantial and share the characteristics of *fixed costs*. This means that they are independent from the number of case that are processed.

- *Quality*: The dimension of quality is associated, among others, to the extent of errors, reworks, and variation in the process. These specific quality aspects relate to the *internal quality* of a process. In a healthcare setting, measures of quality include as number of complications, infection rates or survival rates of trauma cases. These measures are extremely important since quality issues will often have severe consequences for patients. Internal quality measures have a strong impact on external quality measures. *External quality* is often measured as the satisfaction of patients with a specific treatment.

- *Flexibility*: The dimension of process flexibility captures to which degree it is able to operate for a diverse set of cases. It has often been emphasized that healthcare processes intrinsically need flexibility since conditions of patients are complex and in certain ranges unique [231, 237]. We can distinguish flexibility at build time and at runtime. *Build-time* flexibility refers to the diversity of execution paths and the spectrum of tasks that process participants can handle. To a certain degree, build-time flexibility is visible from the number of decision points in a process model. Flexibility at *runtime* describes the ability to change the course of a case according to events and conditions observed during working on it. This is highly important for healthcare processes where important conditions like the stability of patient can change unexpectedly.

If a process does not meet its objectives in terms of time, cost, quality or flexibility, it is considered for process improvement. The understanding of process and its weaknesses in these four dimensions is typically the input of an improvement project together with redesign requirements, limitations, and catalysts [321].

6.5 MEASURING THE CONFORMANCE OF PROCESSES

The conformance of a process to a prescribed way of execution is an important concern in the healthcare domain. Treatments are defined in medical guidelines and the execution of healthcare processes is often accompanied with extensive documentation work in order to prove that decisions have been taken according to standards in an audit-proof way. We can distinguish three major perspectives of conformance in relation to healthcare processes: control flow, data, and resources.

- *Control flow conformance*: This perspective is concerned with the question if all required steps have been executed in the right order. Recent techniques of process mining support the automatic checking of conformance based on execution data of the process [307]. The idea is in essence to project the events that are observed during the execution of the process onto a normative process model. Often, the event recorded in healthcare information systems are on a more fine-granular level than the definition of the process such that they have to be abstracted [20] or enriched with semantic information [257].

- *Data conformance*: This perspective is concerned with the completeness of data that is consumed and produced during the process. Documentation of the medical treatment is important for legal reasons and for providing a basis for taking correct decisions in healthcare processes. Often, this is a burden for healthcare personnel that faces extensive workload and techniques have been defined to check whether documentation is complete and reasonable [244].

- *Resource conformance*: This perspective is concerned with question about who does what in the process. Several tasks in healthcare processes can only be executed by specifically qualified personnel. Furthermore, rules like four-eyes principle have to be complied with if, for example, complex conditions require a second opinion. Also the involvement of persons in a process can be analyzed using process mining techniques, e.g., to check compliance with four-eye principle [255].

6.6   CONNECTIONS BETWEEN MEASUREMENTS

The dimensions of measurement discussed in this chapter are closely connected in different directions. The structural complexity of a healthcare process can be a reason for making it difficult to understand by different stakeholders. If a process is difficult to understand, this can also make it more difficult to improve its performance and to secure its conformance. For these reasons, process standardization is often advocated as a means of improvement [338]. It has to be noted that certain conditions of healthcare processes are difficult to anticipate and therefore to explicitly integrate into the process design. The need for such flexibility should be carefully identified and lined off from standard behaviour. Those process redesign heuristics that aim to improve flexibility take this into account.

A full set of 29 redesign heuristics is included in [80]. Here, we focus on a few that are specifically interesting for the healthcare domain.

Contact reduction: The heuristic suggests to reduce the number of contacts with patient and third parties. This is specifically important in the healthcare domain where patients need to collect samples and examination data. Any additional contact delays the progress of the case and requires additional coordination effort.

Case-based work: Consider removing batch-processing and periodic activities from a business process. Several activities in a healthcare setting are batched, for instance the discussion of cases in a review team that meets on a regular basis. Often, also the standard cases are batched into these meetings, although there is no reason to delay them.

Numerical involvement: Minimize the number of departments, groups and persons involved in a business process. This is often difficult to achieve in a healthcare process since various specialists are required to contribute their expertise. However, this also increases the coordination effort and potentially leads to delays.

Activity automation: Consider automating activities. This is a good way of speeding up the process and reliefing healthcare personnel from cumbersome coordination tasks.

It is important to note that the redesign heuristics are heuristics. It is not guaranteed that applying them necessarily leads to the improvements that are expected. Therefore, every redesign initiative should be accompanied with measuring and monitoring the key performance indicators of the process. Experiments help to get timely insights into the viability of the redesign [332]. In this way, it can be ascertained that a redesign provides the desired performance improvement.

EXERCISES

6.1 *Measurement.* Why is it important that various aspects of a healthcare process are measures?

6.2 *Complexity.* What makes process complex? Describe the major dimensions of complexity.

6.3 *Complexity Measures.* Several complexity measures of a process model are discussed in this chapter. Please calculate them for the BPMN model of Figure 8.3.

6.4 *Performance.* What are the four dimensions that the devil's quadrangle captures? Why is it not called the Angel's quadrangle?

6.5 *Conformance.* What are important regulations for healthcare processes in your country? Can you identify rules in these regulations that relate to control flow, data and resources in a healthcare process?

6.6 *Connection.* Consider the redesign heuristic called Contact Reduction. If you rework a process model by applying this heuristic, how does this like impact the complexity of the process model?

GLOSSARY

Complexity: The extent to which a process model has many elements, many connections and complicated structured.

Conformance: The extent to which a process complies with rules and constraints.

Measurement: The process of assigning numbers to attributes of entities.

Performance: The extent to which a process requires little time and low cost and provides high quality and high flexibility.

Process Improvement: The set of management activities that lead to a change of a process with the expectation of improving its relevant performance indicators.

Understanding: The process of interpreting and making sense of a process model.

FURTHER READING

van der Aalst Wil M.P., *Process Mining - Data Science in Action.* Second Edition, Springer 2016.

Dumas Marlon, La Rosa Marcello, Mendling Jan, Reijers Hajo A., *Fundamentals of Business Process Management.* Springer 2013.

Mendling Jan, *Metrics for Process Models: Empirical Foundations of Verification, Error Prediction, and Guidelines for Correctness*, volume 6 of *Lecture Notes in Business Information Processing*. Springer, 2008.

CHAPTER 7

Healthcare Process Analysis

Robert Andrews

Queensland University of Technology, Brisbane, Australia

Suriadi Suriadi

Queensland University of Technology, Brisbane, Australia

Moe Wynn

Queensland University of Technology, Brisbane, Australia

Arthur H.M. ter Hofstede

Queensland University of Technology, Brisbane, Australia

CONTENTS

Here's to thy health

W. Shakespeare

T HIS chapter presents a variety of process mining analysis techniques that can be applied to healthcare processes and discusses, for each type of analysis, the data requirements, available tools and associated caveats.

7.1 INTRODUCTION

Healthcare plays a vital role in maintaining the well-being of any society and its individual members. Properly addressing the needs of a population as a whole and individuals within a population requires that a healthcare system have elements dealing with (i) population level concerns such as the environment, food and water, drug regulation, and control of communicable diseases (through, for instance, a vaccination program), and (ii) individual level healthcare services delivered in clinics, hospitals or even in the patient's own home. Were a healthcare system to be working perfectly, healthcare services would be accessed equitably by all members of the population, be delivered in a timely, safe, cost-effective and efficient manner with a focus on high quality care and patient outcomes. Studies show that health systems fall short of the ideal. For instance, access to healthcare services is far from equitable with divides along geographic, ethic, cultural and socioeconomic lines [279, 337]. Government spending on healthcare consumes a large proportion of gross domestic product (GDP: average 8.9% in OECD countries in 2013 [205]) with forecasts for spending on healthcare by government as a percentage of GDP in Australia to nearly double by 2050 [17]. Waiting times (for elective surgery), are often long [266] and medical errors resulting in harm to a patient ("adverse events") are frequent and negatively affect patient safety and outcomes [132, 333]. Continual improvement of services and service delivery then is a primary concern for organizations at all levels of healthcare systems.

Improvement is the desired outcome of an overall performance management strategy. Performance management has three main stages; selection of goals (improvement objectives), performance analysis and intervention actions (or improvement initiatives). The improvement initiatives are decided in the light of the analysis results and typically affect the activities being undertaken by the organization in such a way as to lead to the achievement of the improvement objectives. Determining whether improvement has occurred depends on having relevant performance indicators defined in advance of any improvement initiative being undertaken and analysis techniques that can quantify performance against the indicators. In healthcare settings, performance indicators have been defined as "measurable elements of practice performance for which there is evidence or consensus that they can be used to assess the quality, and hence change in quality, of care provided" [159]. Performance indicators are varied and applicable to population health, organizational, financial and clinical performance [70]. For instance, at the population health level, performance indicators include average life expectancy and the incidence of preventable diseases. At the organizational (e.g., hospital unit) level, performance indicators may include length of stay, unplanned re-admission rate and measures of patient satisfaction with the hospital experience. At the financial level, performance against budget is an indicator, while at the clinical level, performance indicators include mortality rate and hospital acquired infection rates [125].

In this article we are interested in analysis of healthcare processes, and in particular, operational processes, i.e., those processes that are patient facing or where the patient is the consumer of the product or service that is the output of the process. It seems reasonable to begin by considering some aspects of processes in general and healthcare processes in particular before considering what we mean by process analysis.

We define a process as a set of inter-related activities designed to achieve a goal. Other definitions include that in [248] as "the series of steps that a business executes to produce a product or service" or that in [60] as "a set of one or more linked procedures or activities which collectively realise a business objective or policy goal, [carried out] normally within the context of an organizational structure defining functional roles and relationships." Business processes can be seen individually as steps in a business cycle, or collectively, as the set of activities that create the value chain of an organization [69]. Any business process may be viewed as being either completely structured, unstructured, or somewhere in between (semi-structured) [167]. A structured process is one for which a well-defined process model exists which takes into account all process execution permutations and from which no process execution may deviate. On the other hand, an unstructured process is one for which only guidelines and goal states exist and every process execution may be different depending on the context in which it is executed and the knowledge and skills of the people involved. In [151], semi-structured processes lie somewhere in between and are characterized by not having a formal process model (but will usually having a process description), have many points where different continuation paths are possible and being largely driven by process context and human decision making.

Operational healthcare processes, e.g., those in hospital emergency departments, are best described as being semi-structured as they do not have a formal process model (but may have clinical guidelines and clinical care pathways), are complex and highly variable, patient-centric (with process executions being driven by context factors such as the patient's current physical state, availability of beds, availability of nursing staff, the experience of the treating physician, etc.) and are often multi-disciplinary [127], involving frequent interactions between clinicians, nursing staff, diagnostic support specialists and administrative personnel. Healthcare processes, especially those core patient-driven processes are also highly variable and "rife with exceptions" [284].

Notwithstanding the difficulty imposed by their flexibility and complexity, it is necessary that healthcare processes are able to be analyzed to determine actual process behaviors, evaluate process performance, verify their conformance to clinical guidelines, reveal opportunities for efficiency gains and cost reductions, etc.

7.2 BACKGROUND

Various quality and performance management methodologies have been developed over time and many have been implemented in health care settings. Such techniques include Program Evaluation and Review Technique (PERT) and the Critical Path Method (CPM) [168], Lean and Continuous Performance improvement (CPI) [275], Evidence Based Medicine [113] and Business Process Redesign [133]. Total Quality Management (TQM) has its roots in the manufacturing sector and aims to enhance organizational performance through ensuring the delivery of high quality products and services. In [189], the author reviews the reasons for the failure of TQM initiatives in healthcare settings reported in the literature (16 studies in 9 countries) and concludes that there are major impediments to successful implementation that relate to (i) the methodological requirement for the deep involvement of people at all levels of the organization (managers, physicians and patients), (ii) the fact that every patient is different and cannot be treated like manufactured products, and (iii) the difficulty in evaluating healthcare processes and outcomes to the intangibility of healthcare services.

Six Sigma is another performance management, quality improvement approach where the focus is on the minimisation of defects. Like TQM, Six Sigma is rooted in manufacturing. Motorola essentially invented the approach in the late 1980s as a means of dealing with increasing numbers of complaints from its field staff about warranty claims. The Six Sigma methodology, DMAIC (define, measure, analyse, improve, control) relies on statistical methods and implements control mechanisms to tie together quality, cost, process elements and people with the goals of aligning processes to critical customer requirements and reducing variance in the process output and thus improving quality [21, 285]. There are a number of key challenges and barriers to the implementation of Six Sigma in healthcare settings. First and foremost is the nature of healthcare processes, i.e., healthcare processes are driven by humans and the cause of variation are often difficult to identify and quantify. In manufacturing processes it is possible to eliminate most of the variation due to human decision making through automation, creating precise measures of variability [256]. Further, there is often a large up-front cost in training "Black Belt" champions [285]. Lastly, in the healthcare industry, it is often a struggle to identify processes which can be measured in terms of defects per million opportunities [155].

A workflow, as defined by the Workflow Management Coalition [160], is "the automation of a business process, in whole or part, during which documents, information or tasks are passed from one participant to another for action, according to a set of procedural rules". Workflow Management (WFM) [105] is a technology that supports (i) defining workflows and (ii) allowing for rapid change of workflows (re-design and re-implementation) as business needs change. Workflow specifications can be viewed from a number of different perspectives [315]. The *control-flow perspective* (or process defined in [80] as "the act of gathering information about an existing process and organizing it in terms of an "as-is" process model." Traditional BPM techniques for process discovery have been driven by analysts engaging with people from across the organization to share their knowledge and perceptions of what is happening within the organization and then developing workflow models of the process/es. This approach has many challenges including (i) getting the right people involved (difficult when processes span multiple, possibly geographically separated business units), (ii) dealing with *fragmented process knowledge* i.e., participants will have a general understanding of the whole process and detailed knowledge of their individual tasks (iii) being able to extract valid, unambiguous descriptions of what is actually happening, (iv) deciding whether analyst or domain expert is better placed to develop models, and (v) then being able to abstract models that truly reflect the "as-is" process (including variations). Discovery methods such as interview and workshop-based discovery require the analyst to rely on information provided by domain experts which may be incorrect, incomplete, unconsciously (or deliberately) biased. In healthcare, the situation is complicated through the complex and multi-disciplinary nature of processes within the healthcare system, delivery mechanisms where ad hoc decisions are necessitated to manage crisis situations on a day-to-day basis, and the different focus of clinicians and management regarding individual patient care and population-based health care system efficiency and effectiveness.

Business Process Analysis (BPA) software tools supporting process discovery also have issues including being too sophisticated and complex for most users, requiring large initial investment in terms of purchase, infrastructure and user training costs and being poorly integrated with BPM suites that execute processes thus reducing their value in process discovery and modeling.

The basis of a process improvement project is the development of models that are truly reflective of actual process behaviors and which support model-based performance analysis. As the use of information technology in supporting healthcare processes becomes more pervasive, so the amount of process-related data recorded in (hospital) information systems grows. Such process-related data includes the tasks that were performed, who performed the tasks and when. Consider, for example, a patient's transit through the emergency department. When the patient presents at the emergency department (ED), the hospital's patient record system is consulted to check for existing details of the patient. The date and time of the patient's arrival is recorded in the ED's system and triage is requested. The time and details of the member of medical staff who triaged the patient is recorded. When the patient is seen by a doctor, details of diagnostics tests ordered for the patient are also recorded (and sent to the various labs or diagnostic units) and, later, the results of the tests are entered by the various labs. Other clinical treatments and observations are recorded until, ultimately, the patient is admitted to hospital or discharged from the emergency department. In short, the entire history of the patient's presentation at the emergency department, along with his/her engagement with other hospital units (administrative, diagnostic, and therapeutic) is available.

Process mining [306], and its ever expanding range of tools and techniques for modeling and analysing process-related data, is an approach ideally suited for deriving objective, evidence-based insights as the basis for process improvements from this wealth of process-related data. Process mining can largely automate the process discovery and analysis phases of the BPM Lifecycle (with the caveat that relevant event data can be harvested from supporting information systems). Process mining affords the analysis of event data from a number of different perspectives [306] including the control-flow perspective (activities and their order of execution), the organizational perspective (work patterns, organization structures and social networks), the case perspective (insights into differences in process execution between cohorts of cases), the time perspective (providing insights into performance aspects such as bottlenecks, throughput times, waiting times, etc.), and the data perspective (data objects that act as inputs and outputs to activities).

7.3 PROCESS MINING FOR HEALTHCARE PROCESSES

Process mining, a relatively young branch of data science that sits between data mining and process modeling and analysis, aims to discover, monitor and improve processes by extracting knowledge from event logs readily available from information systems [306]. In the context of the BPM Lifecycle, process analysis and subsequent redesign hinge on the development of a process model that is properly reflective of actual execution behaviors, i.e., the so-called "as-is" process model, as a starting point. Process mining tools may be used to learn such a process model from records of historical process executions captured in event logs (*process discovery*). Process mining can further utilise the event log, as a representation of actual process executions, to check whether actual behavior conforms to an existing process model or clinical guidelines or best practice (*process conformance*). Further, a process model, either a discovered model or an existing model may be supplemented with information derived from the event log (*process enhancement*) to enrich the model with different perspectives each of which can be exploited through process mining. By including in the model, the role/resource responsible for completing each step in the process (the *organizational perspective*), organization mining [272] and social network analysis [314] can uncover information about workload, resource and role behavior (such as patterns of handover of work). By enriching the model with times that activities began and were completed, the *time perspective*, performance analysis [3, 220] can yield information such as the existence of process bottlenecks. Process mining tools can also exploit context information specific to each individual process execution, the *case perspective* to explain decision points and branches in process execution [247]. Other event attributes, such as activity frequencies and costs can be analysed to provide detailed process performance information. Analysing event logs that span different periods can reveal changes in process behavior over time (*concept drift*) [33]. Deviance mining [199], particularly relevant in environments where processes are flexible and show variability, can discover typical deviant execution paths and characterise each as according to whether they lead to better or poorer performance. Comparative process performance analysis can be applied to analyse process variants, or the behavior of different cohorts of cases to reveal performance differences [281]. Process visualization techniques overlay event information on the process model to facilitate several tasks common to data analysis including process overview, process animation, identification of outliers and comparison of different cohorts across multiple activities [319].

In this section we introduce elements of process mining that either have already been, or could be applied to process analysis in the healthcare domain. We discuss each element and provide examples from our own, and other researchers' practical experiences in applying the element to healthcare process analysis.

7.3.1 Preprocessing Hospital Data as an Event Log

An event log suitable for process mining contains data related to a *single process*. The event log consists of a set of cases (or traces) where each case consists of the sequence of events carried out in a single execution of a process (process instance). Cases within a log are uniquely identified by a case identifier. Irrespective of the type of process mining analysis undertaken, each event is minimally characterized by a case identifier which informs the case to which the event relates, and an "activity" label describing the related "action". Many process mining analyses, e.g., *process discovery*, require an attribute that allows ordering of events, e.g., a timestamp describing when the event occurred. Other types of analysis require that the log contains relevant supporting attributes. For instance, it is not possible to discover the social network of resources contributing to the process unless event data is enriched with resource information (see Table 7.1).

7.3.2 Data Quality

In process mining, as in other forms of data analysis, the validity and reliability of analysis results is highly dependent on the quality of the data used in the analysis (*garbage-in, garbage-out*). In process mining, the data is in the event log used as input by process mining tools. Various authors have provided methods for assessing the quality of an event log and its suitability for use in a process mining analysis. The Process Mining Manifesto [308] uses a star rating to assess log quality. Five-star rated log (excellent quality, trustworthy and complete) are characterised as being recorded automatically, systematically and reliably with all events and their attributes having clear semantics, while, at the other end of the scale, 1-star rated logs (poor quality)

TABLE 7.1 Exemplar event log of an ED admission process.

CaseID	Activity	Timestamp	Resource
1234567	ED_Arrive	2016-10-01 08:45:10	Reception
1234567	Triage_Request	2016-10-01 08:45:45	Reception
1234567	RN_Assign	2016-10-01 08:47:30	Reception
1234567	Triage_Start	2016-10-01 08:54:40	Triage_RN
1234567	Triage_Assessment	2016-10-01 08:59:20	Triage_RN
1234567	Dr_Seen	2016-10-01 09:12:00	FastTrack_Registrar
1234567	FBC_Order	2016-10-01 09:22:45	FastTrack_Registrar
...	...	...	...
1234567	ED_DischargeHome	2016-10-01 09:22:45	Reception
1239876	ED_Arrive	2016-10-01 08:52:45	Reception
...	...	...	...
1239876	ED_AdmitWard	2016-10-01 13:35:45	Reception

are characterized as having events that do not correspond to reality and may be incomplete (i.e., missing events). According to [308], logs with star rating of 3 or above are suitable for process mining analysis. In [31, 32] the authors outline a framework for classifying data quality issues in event logs in terms of the structural components of a log (case, event, attributes, timestamps, etc.) and whether the data associated with the component is missing, incorrect, imprecise or irrelevant. Recognizing and then dealing with data quality issues in event logs relies on knowing what sort of quality issues may exist in a given set of logs and is generally a tedious, and often, manual task. A patterns-based approach to recognising commonly occurring quality issues in event logs is described in [280]. Here the authors describe a collection of 11 event log imperfection patterns, distilled from their experiences in preparing event logs, that can be used to systematically identify the presence of the associated data quality issue in an event log. The authors show that the generality of the imperfection patterns arise from architectures and functionality commonly found in information systems (e.g., form-based systems, heterogeneous systems, styles of logging, etc.) and human fallibilities (keyboard/typing errors, recording events after they have occurred, etc.). As an example, the *Form-based Event Capture* pattern (illustrated in Figure 7.2) arises through the information system logging data fields on a form as activities and the timestamp for each activity as the time the user clicked "Save" on the form. The pattern manifests in the log as a set of activities each having the same timestamp thus either losing any sequencing of the activities or creating multiple activities when in fact only a single process step occurred (in this case the Triage Primary Survey). The authors then provide a set of remediation actions that can be applied to clean the log and thus avoid the negative impacts the presence of the patterns in the log would introduce into any process mining analysis. The authors further state that, as the patterns are agnostic of the purpose of the analysis, the patterns are generally relevant and the patterns and remedies thus form the basis of a systematic, (semi-)automated approach to cleaning event logs.

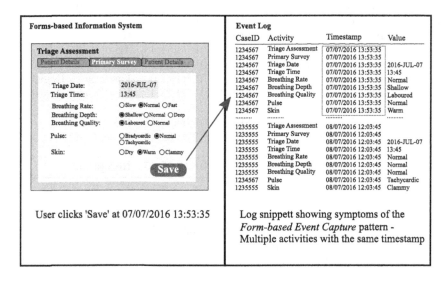

FIGURE 7.2 Example of the *Form-Based Event Capture* log imperfection pattern manifesting in an event log.

Recording of event data related to healthcare processes, including operational processes such as those found in hospitals, can introduce quality issues as a result of, among other causes, non-standard recording practices, heterogeneous systems leading to integrity and consistency issues i.e., data matching problems, recording of the same event in multiple systems and incompleteness of electronic records, i.e., reliance on paper-based records/charts. In [176] the authors point out that data science projects in hospitals often fail for reasons related to data quality. They propose the *healthcare reference model* as a data model that captures all the classes of data that can be made available for a process mining analysis and argue that such a model allows (i) analysts and stakeholders to reason about the questions it is possible to answer with the data available, and (ii) data managers to locate and extract data that is properly aligned with the questions of interest to analysts and stakeholders. The model could also be used as a template for process-aware (hospital) information system design to ensure process-related data is correctly logged.

7.3.3 Automated Discovery of Hospital Processes

To understand "how" processes within a healthcare services provider are actually conducted, Process Discovery techniques can be applied to reveal the control-flow perspective. In its most basic form, process discovery takes an event log as input, which is presented to a discovery algorithm which (automatically) generates a process model as output.

Data. Critical to the success of process discovery is the proper alignment of event data with the purpose of the analysis, i.e., with the questions of interest to the process stakeholders. The questions/data alignment issue must be considered prior to beginning the analysis and can be addressed by considering the following key questions:

1. What tools/techniques are applicable?

2. What data is required in order to answer the questions of interest?

3. What of this data is available/accessible (in electronic form)?

4. Is it feasible/possible to obtain the missing data (by for example digitizing existing paper-based records, altering electronic collection/logging to include the capture of the missing data elements, etc.)?

Conducting a study where data and questions are not properly aligned causes issues of reliability and accuracy of results. In such a situation, it may be necessary to revise the questions such that they are still meaningful but that the available data can be used for analysis, or if the gap is too great, to not proceed with the analysis.

Process discovery (for control-flow) requires that records in the event log contain at least three attributes: a case identifier (records that have the same case identifier are deemed to belong to the same process execution instance), an activity label (that identifies the process step), and at least one timestamp (that indicates when the activity occurred). The timestamp allows the sequence in which activities were carried out to be determined (thus revealing relationships between activities).

Some considerations when selecting event data in a hospital setting include:

1. Case identifier - Depending on the analysis, the case identifier may represent a patient or a presentation/admission (bearing in mind that any patient may have multiple presentations over time). Where data is extracted from heterogeneous systems, it is possible that information relating to a given "case" may have different identifiers in the different systems necessitating record linking/merging [93] to reconstruct the complete case.

2. Activities - Selecting a set of activities relevant for model development from the potentially detailed (hospital) information systems' logs is a non-trivial task. In [177] the authors describe a two-dimensional data spectrum (*event abstraction level* and *timestamp accuracy*) useful in classifying event data recorded by different hospital information systems. The authors note that Administration systems typically show a high level of abstraction (one event refers to a collection of individual tasks) while Medical Devices, such as x-ray machines show a low level

of abstraction (each recorded event refers to movement within a task, e.g., turning on, warming up, etc.). As process discovery algorithms are egalitarian in dealing with activities, it is good practice to select for modeling activities with similar levels of abstraction.

3. Timestamps - In [177], the timestamp accuracy dimension is further broken up according to the *granularity, directness of recording* and *correctness* of the timestamp value). An important consideration is what the logged timestamp for each event actually represents. For instance, events captured from Administration systems for admission/discharge will be recorded as the event occurs so the timestamp associated with the activity will represent when the activity actually occurred. Other events, such as medical staff updating a patient's electronic file from paper-based charts will record that an activity (such as an examination or an order for a blood test) was carried out for the patient, but the timestamp will represent when the activity was entered into the system rather than when the activity occurred. Such difference in the *directness of recording* will affect the apparent sequencing of events. Similarly, the *correctness* of the timestamp can affect the apparent event sequencing. Consider for instance a situation where dates are entered manually and the operator transposes day and month values. Lastly, the *granularity* of timestamps will affect activity sequencing. If the logged timestamp for some activities (such as those recorded by a medical device) are at the millisecond level and others are at only the day level, the representation level used for modeling will appear to make many events happen in parallel (if day level representation is used) or unreliably sequence those activities that have no time component of the timestamp (if millisecond level representation is used).

Tools and Applications. The Disco[1] tool is an easy-to-use, commercial tool that can quickly discover a process model from a given data set with adjustable level of granularity. An example of a patient flow model discovered using the event log of an Australian hospital is provided in Figure 7.3. While the Disco tool is easy to use, the model discovered is not "portable", in the sense that it cannot be exported and be used for analysis by tools external to Disco. Within the ProM[2] open-source framework, there are many more process discovery algorithms that have been implemented as plug-ins. For example, the Heuristic miner [334], Alpha miner [317], ILP Miner [318], and Inductive miner [161]. Each modeling tool will generate a model in some modeling language (e.g., Process Tree, Event-driven Process Chain, BPMN). Some of these techniques, such as the ILP Miner and Inductive Miner, are able to discover a process model expressed in the Petri net formalism, thus, allowing one to use the discovered models as input for other forms of process mining analysis

---

[1] http://fluxicon.com/disco
[2] http://www.processmining.org/prom/start

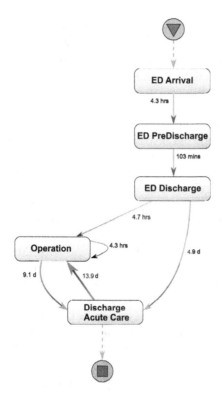

FIGURE 7.3 An example of a process model discovered by the Disco tool.

(such as conformance checking). The increasing interest in the possibilities of process mining is reflected in the growing number of commercially available tools with process mining capabilities including, but not limited to ARIS Business Process Analysis (Software AG), Celonis Process Mining (Celonis), Automated Process Discovery (Fujitsu), QPR ProcessAnalyzer (QPR), and LANA (LANA Labs).

Each tool will generate a process model in some format. The quality of the discovered model may be assessed in four dimensions: fitness (recall), precision, generalisation and complexity [306]. Fitness measures the degree to which the cases (traces) in a log can be parsed by the model. Precision (extent to which the discovered model "underfits" the event data) provides a measure of behavior additional to that found in the log that is permitted by the model. Generalization measures the ability of the model to correctly parse traces drawn from the process that were not seen by the modeling tool in discovering the model. Complexity is a measure of the size of the discovered model (in terms of numbers of nodes and connecting arcs). Models that show high fitness and precision and generalize well over previously unseen traces are particularly useful for subsequent model-based analysis. Models that are readable and understandable (related to complexity) are particularly useful in communicating process information among stakeholders.

Caveats. While there are many plug-ins and tools that can be used to discover a process model from an event log, it is often necessary to experiment with multiple plug-ins and/or tools to obtain a process model that is of the right fitness, precision, and accuracy. This is mainly due to the fact that different tools apply different process discovery algorithms that are often sensitive to the nature and complexity of the event logs used as input.

Further, it is generally true that process discovery algorithms apply their own heuristics, assumptions, and simplification in order to produce process models that are readable. This often comes at the cost of reduced accuracy in that certain behaviors may be abstracted out to reduce model complexity. For example, Figure 7.4 shows another discovered patient flow model of another hospital in Australia. The path between the activity "Medical Assign_Start" and "Arrive_Start" is currently shown due to its finer granularity view. However, depending on the process discovery algorithm used, such a path may be removed or ignored due to its low frequency (which is only "3"). Such a path, however, captures an interesting deviation in the way the emergency department runs. Thus, it may be advisable to attempt to discover process models using a variety of algorithms to get a more comprehensive view.

7.3.4 Checking Conformance to Clinical Guidelines

Healthcare processes often involve certain medical treatments or tests that are critical or recommended, either as best practices or clinically imperative. Therefore, a key question that one may ask in analyzing patient flows, for example, is to know whether a certain type of blood test is always performed for patients presenting with chest pain. To address such a question, one could apply the conformance check technique.

To conduct a conformance checking analysis, it is expected that one already has a normative model (e.g., a patient flow model) that captures all the necessary best practices or rules that clinicians should follow. Then, the conformance checking technique will attempt to replay events seen in the log over the process model to gauge the extent to which events seen in the log conform to the possible execution paths as captured by the normative model. Any sequence of execution that was seen in the log, but which is not allowed in the normative model, indicates deviation in the actual practices from the expected ones. Typically, a conformance check analysis will produce a "fitness" value (normally in the range of 0 to 1) that captures the level of agreement between the model and the events seen in the log.

Data. A key requirement to conduct a conformance check analysis is that the naming of the activities in an event log (that is going to be compared with its corresponding normative process model) can be matched with the names used in the process model. While the names do not have to be exactly the same

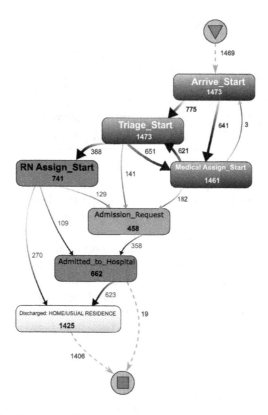

FIGURE 7.4 A discovered process model at a finer granularity view. Depending on process discovery algorithm used and their corresponding parameter settings, the path from the "Medical Assign_Start" to "Arrive_Start" may not be shown in other discovered process models due to its low frequency, and thus treated as noise.

syntactically, one should at least be able to map each activity name seen in the process model with exactly one activity name in the log.

Tools and Applications. A tool that is widely used to perform a conformance check analysis is the "Replay a Log on Petri net for Performance/Conformance" plug-in [2] that is available in the ProM toolkit. This tool expects a process model, expressed as a Petri net, as an input, in addition to its corresponding event log. The Disco tool does not have conformance checking functionality yet.

Another application of conformance checking is for process comparison. While there are other specifically created process comparison techniques (as detailed later in this section), conformance checking techniques can be used to gauge the extent to which a process A is similar to, or different from, another process B. For example, in our case study comparing the patient flows of four

TABLE 7.2   Results of the conformance checks of
the four patient flow models of Figure 7.5.

	Process Model (Petri net)			
Hospital log	H1	H2	H3	H4
Hospital 1 (H1)	0.918	0.756	0.745	0.749
Hospital 2 (H2)	0.651	0.831	0.836	0.748
Hospital 3 (H3)	0.586	0.784	0.847	0.726
Hospital 4 (H4)	0.611	0.725	0.770	0.871

hospitals in Australia [281], we first discovered the process models for all four hospitals (see Figure 7.5 (top), adapted from [281]). Then, we replayed each hospital's event log over the discovered process models of all four hospitals to obtain four different fitness scores.

Note that when we replayed a hospital log on its respective process model, the conformance check score actually reports on the fitness of the discovered process model (e.g., replaying Hospital 1 event log on Hospital 1 process model). However, when we replayed a hospital log on the process model of another hospital (e.g., replaying Hospital 1 event log on Hospital 2 process model), we obtained the similarity of the behaviors between the two hospitals. The higher the fitness score is, the more similar the behaviors are. For example, from Figure 7.5, we can see that the value reported when we replayed Hospital 1 log on Hospital 1 model is around 0.918, which means that the discovered process model of Hospital 1, using Hospital 1 event log, is quite fitting. At the same time, we can also see that the behaviors seen in Hospital 1 is most closely aligned to Hospital 2 as it has the highest conformance check value (0.756)

Caveats. The reporting of the conformance check value (also called the "fitness" value) using the "Replay a Log on Petri net for Performance/Conformance" plug-in actually reports on the overall alignment of events. In other words, it reports on the matching between the sequence of events seen in the log and the possible sequences of events as dictated by the corresponding normative model. One should be careful to note that a high fitness value *does not* mean that the majority of cases behave in exactly the expected manner (from start to the end of the processes). It is possible for a conformance check to return a high fitness value of, for example, 0.8, while *none of the cases fully fit the process model*. This is possible because we may see a sequence of, for example, "ABCDF" in an event log, while the corresponding model only allows "ABCFD" (note that the last two events are flipped). Thus, we can see that at the higher "case" level perspective, this trace does not fully fit the model, however, at the event log, the misalignment is minor. As a result, a high "fitness" value may still be reported.

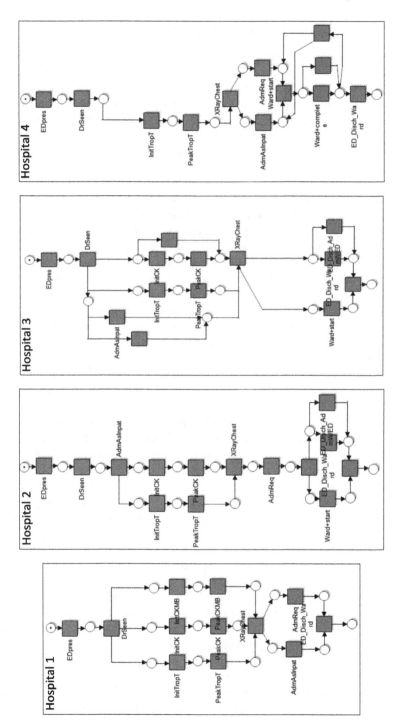

FIGURE 7.5 Four patient flow models from four hospitals in Australia.

7.3.5   Performance Analysis of Hospital Processes

Many performance related questions relate to time, capacity or resource usage/workload. Process mining provides a set of tools to answer performance-related questions, e.g., what is the average patient length of stay in a particular hospital's emergency department? How long do patients need to wait before they can be admitted to a hospital ward? Is there a capacity bottleneck in the hospital, or are resources under-utilized instead? How do the movements of patients across various wards affect the formation or dissolution of bottlenecks in patient flows?

Data. To facilitate answering time related performance questions using process mining techniques it is essential that event logs contain timestamp information that captures the different transaction types for work items conducted by resources. At a minimum, each work item should have one timestamp attribute capturing the occurrence of one transaction type (most commonly the "completion" time of a work item). More comprehensive analysis is possible where information about more transaction types is available for each work item. For instance, where only a single transaction type is available, e.g., "complete", it is possible to calculate only the elapsed time between the completion of two events. In the top part of Table 7.3, it can be seen that it took a total of 14 mins 10 sec for the patient's triage to be completed from the time his/her arrival in the ED was recorded. It is not really possible to answer the question "how long did it take to conduct triage for the case 1234567?" Where richer data is available, as in the bottom part of Table 7.3 adapted from [281], it can be seen that there was a waiting period of 8 mins 55 secs (between Request and Start) and that the actual duration of the triage step was 4 mins 40 sec (between Start and Complete). Supplementing the log with resource information allows performance questions relating to resource usage/workload to be addressed.

Tools and Applications. Figure 7.6 shows an example of how the Disco tool can be used to extract performance information in a relatively simple manner. In this figure, the median durations of any two activities (with temporal dependency) are projected into the respective paths of the process model discovered from a given event log. In Figure 7.6, the process model captures the patient flows discovered from an event log of an Australian hospital. Other performance information, such as average, maximum, minimum, and total duration of two activities, can also be displayed using Disco.

While Disco is quite a powerful tool (and we do recommend novice users to use this tool due to its ease-of-use), the richness of performance information that can be extracted is dependent on the completeness of the information contained in the event log being analyzed. For example, in Figure 7.6, we could not see the median working time for each activity in the model because the event log used only contained one transition timestamp: "complete". Without knowing when a task was assigned or started, Disco is unable to provide working time information for each activity.

TABLE 7.3   Exemplar ED event logs for performance analysis.

Event log with minimal transaction types - Complete only

CaseID	Activity	Timestamp	Resource
1234567	ED_Arrive	2016-10-01 08:45:10	Reception
1234567	Triage_Complete	2016-10-01 08:59:20	Triage_RN
...	...	...	...
1234567	ED_DischargeHome	2016-10-01 09:22:45	Reception

Event log with multiple transaction types

CaseID	Activity	Timestamp	Resource
1234567	ED_Arrive	2016-10-01 08:45:10	Reception
1234567	Triage_Request	2016-10-01 08:45:45	Reception
1234567	Triage_Start	2016-10-01 08:54:40	Triage_RN
1234567	Triage_Complete	2016-10-01 08:59:20	Triage_RN
...	...	...	...
1234567	ED_DischargeHome	2016-10-01 09:22:45	Reception

In this situation, other tools that incorporate more advanced algorithms can be used. For example, the *event interval analysis* [282] tool, available as a plug-in to the ProM toolkit, can be used to extract rich performance metrics even when the event log to be analyzed contains minimal timestamp information, e.g., only the completion timestamp for tasks is seen in the log. In addition to its ability to estimate the working time for various tasks (in the presence of only the completion timestamp information for each task), this tool also allows us to extract periods of time where resources (such as nurses) are likely to be idle, or where there are no available resources to serve patients. Another interesting capability of this tool is its ability to *estimate the workload* of resources, at any given point in time seen in the log being analyzed. Such information can then be used for further performance analysis, such as resources' efficiency analysis or capacity bottlenecks.

Another tool that can be used to analyse process performance is the *staged process flow* [200] tool, which is also available in the ProM toolkit as a plug-in. This tool allows one to analyze a process using the stage concept whereby a process is treated as a collection of a number of sequential stages. In combination with visualization schemes, this tool allows one to answer more complex performance questions, such as the evolution of process performance over time, the impact of the formation and dissolution of bottlenecks on process performance, and the impact of variations in demand and capacity on process performance.

Caveats. The lack of enough timestamps information for various timestamps affects the accuracy of the performance information extracted from the tool. For example, in Figure 7.6, the paths connecting two activities are annotated with the median time between the two activities. However, these time durations in fact also include both the working time as well as the waiting time of the second activities (that is, those activities to which the arrows of each path

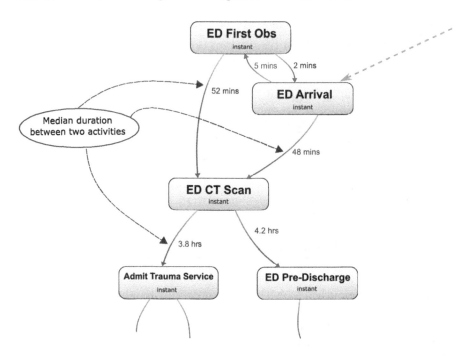

FIGURE 7.6 Using the Disco tool to project median duration between two activities.

are connected to). This is because there is information for only one transaction lifecycle type for each work item, thus, the time between the completion of any two activities should in fact be interpreted as the median of the maximum working times of the second activity (counting from the time the first activity is completed). Alternatively, assuming that the second activity is automated as its completion is instantaneous, the time duration can now be interpreted as the median of the maximum waiting time of the second activity. For example, the 48 mins time during between the activity "ED Arrival" and "ED CT Scan" can be interpreted as the median of the maximum working time of the "ED CT Scan" activity.

7.3.6 Comparative Analysis

Comparing processes to understand their similarities and differences is another typical process analysis that process mining supports. For example, one may wish to compare two patient flows: one that completed relatively quickly and another one that took a much longer time to complete. Such a comparison may be useful in gaining insights into how the differences in the flows identified impact patient flow performances.

Data. Events and cases in events logs used for comparative analysis purposes should be clearly labeled with their respective process variants (for example, one may add an extra attribute to each event in the log indicating the process variant to which the event belongs). Furthermore, for each process variant to be compared, the names and their corresponding interpretation need to be consistent to permit objective comparison to be made.

Tools and Example Applications. Process mining provides a number of tools that can be used to assist users in comparing processes, both in terms of process behavior and performance. For example, in one of our case studies, we employed the *configurable model visualization* tool, available in the cloud-based Apromore tool,[3] to highlight similarities and differences between two processes. This approach works by merging two process models into one and project, on top of this merged model, different colors on the activities and paths to indicate those that are unique to either one of the processes, and those that are similar across both processes. For example, Figure 7.7 shows a merged patient flow model of two different process variants discovered from the event log of an Australian hospital's emergency department. The red color in the figure shows those activities and paths that were unique for *emergency* patients and the "green" color for *semi-urgent* patients. Activities and paths that were shared by both cohorts are projected with purple color.

The *configurable model visualization*, while simple and powerful, is static and cannot effectively compare dynamic process dimensions, such as comparing the speed with which patients traverse through the various stages in an emergency department. To this end, the *log animation* plug-in, which is available both as a plug-in to the ProM toolkit ("Process Profiler 3D") and also in the Apromore tool, can be used. This tool allows one to replay all cases seen in an event log by projecting each case as a dot that moves along a merged process model, traversing activities and paths according to the sequence of events as seen in the log. Furthermore, each dot is colored according to the process variant to which it belongs, thus, allowing one to simultaneously see how cases from two or more processes progress similarly or differently over the same space (i.e., the merged process model). To ensure an effective comparison, the timestamps of all cases have been normalized in such a way that all cases start as if from the same point in time.

For example, Figure 7.8 shows a snapshot of a log animation comparing the patient flows of two patient cohorts. Given the same timestamp as the starting time for all cases, we can see how the cases from the "green" cohort progressed at a much faster rate than cases from the "red" cohort, as evidenced by the fact that most of the green cases have already moved on to the second half of the process, while many from the "red" cohort still remain in the first half of the process.

The two approaches discussed above compare process variants from a control flow perspective in that comparison is made with respect to process models. While they are useful, there are certain dimensions that may not be as

---

[3]www.apromore.org

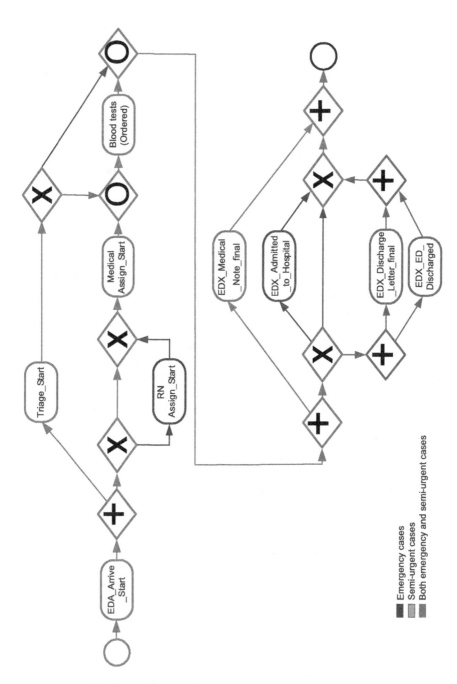

FIGURE 7.7 Configurable model visualization of two patient flows.

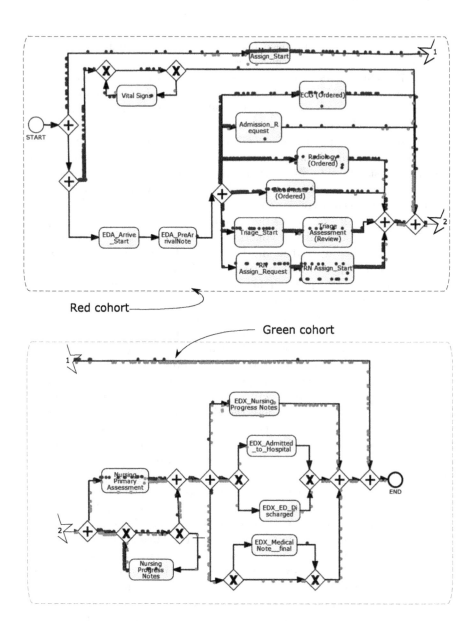

FIGURE 7.8 A snapshot of a log animation comparing two groups of patient flows of an Australian hospital.

obviously shown in such a visualization approach. For example, comparing both the performance as well as frequency of the occurrence of various activities simultaneously.

To this end, another approach has been developed. Though as yet only partially realized in software, the visualization approaches proposed by Pini et al. [217] include three different styles of visualizations referred to by the authors as the *general model*, the *superimposed model* and the *side-by-side comparison*. The general model shows the differences in performance (duration and frequency). The superimposed model compares process flows of different cohorts, from the perspective of one of the cohorts, such that correspondence of activities is visualized through alignment and superposition of an activity element. The side-by-side comparison is specifically concerned with the time perspective and exploits the process model's logical flow to describe temporal dependencies between activities through predecessor and successor nodes of a directed graph. An example of the general model is provided in Figure 7.9 from [217] whereby four different cohorts of patients, differentiated by the time period in which they arrived in the Emergency Department, are compared both in terms of frequency and duration of activities.

The general model approach has been implemented within the ProM toolkit as a plug-in named "Process Profiler 3D".[4] This plug-in requires an event log and its corresponding process model as inputs. Using this plug-in, we can choose how cases are to be split into various cohorts based on certain attribute values (such as time of arrival of patients at ED, injury severity code, triage category, or their combination). Once the event log is split accordingly, the plug-in will then extract various performance information for each cohort (such as waiting times between activities, frequency of activities, and duration of activities) and project it onto the given process model in a 3D space. One can also choose the display style of the performance information that is projected on the model. Detailed performance information can also be viewed as a pop-up table. An example of the output of this plug-in is provided in Figure 7.10.

Caveat. While these tools can be effectively used to help users in comparing processes, the main challenge in using them is on preparing the event logs that will be used as inputs. In particular, those event logs from processes to be compared need to use labels/names from the same domain. That is, the naming of the activities in the logs need to be consistent across all processes to be compared such that activities with the same semantics should share the same label. This is generally not an issue if one is to compare intra-organizational processes as the event logs for these processes would most likely come from the same information systems. However, this is a challenge if one were to compare inter-organizational processes. In such cases, log preprocessing is needed to ensure matching activity labels.

---

[4]http://www.promtools.org/prom6/packages/ProcessProfiler3D/

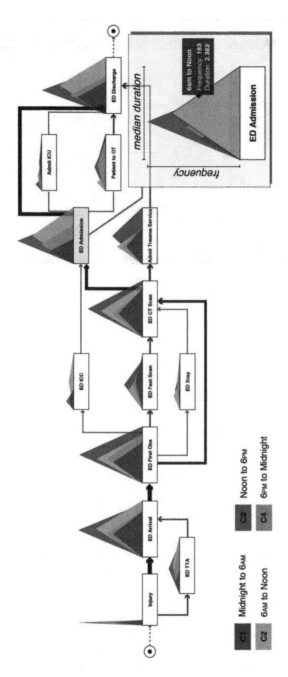

FIGURE 7.9 Visualization of behavior and performance differences between patient cohorts (based on arrival time at the Emergency Department of an Australian hospital).

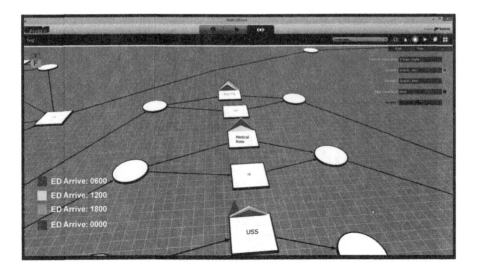

FIGURE 7.10 ProcessProfiler3D visualization of performance differences between patient cohorts (based on arrival time at the Emergency Department of an Australian hospital).

7.4 CHALLENGES AND OUTLOOK

In this short section we will discuss some challenges we see for process mining, particularly as they relate to the application of process mining in healthcare. While not an exhaustive list, we focus on challenges relating to data quality, tools and techniques, and the interpretation of analysis results by consumers in the healthcare domain to draw relevant and actionable insights.

As noted in our discussion of BPM, an accurate "as-is" process model is the foundation for reliable analysis, insights and process improvement/redesign. The discovery of high quality "as-is" process models using process mining techniques is dependent on the availability of high quality event data. While data quality is recognised as being critical to the success of a process mining analysis, and various authors have attempted to classify types of data quality issues found in event logs, currently no methods exist to quantify the extent to which an identified quality issue will compromise a process mining analysis. Similarly, no methods exist to determine *a priori* whether a given event log is suitable for a proposed process mining analysis, or with a particular analysis in mind, what should be the characteristics of the event log. To derive reliable and actionable insights, it is imperative that a high-quality log that aligns with the goals of a proposed analysis be available. A particular issue, prevalent in (but certainly not unique to) the healthcare domain, is the mix of directly recorded and after-the-fact recorded events in (hospital) logs. We have already discussed the problems in automated process discovery caused by having such a mix of activity timestamps. Here, an opportunity exists to exploit mobile devices, the so-called "Internet of Things" and technologies such as RFID to support passive, unobtrusive and real-time collection of process data, e.g., RFID tags to record movement of patients and medical staff through the hospital or the current location of medical equipment, specimens, etc. [34, 128, 213]. Such methods have the potential to improve data through ensuring the completeness and accuracy of logged process execution data.

The flexible, patient-centric and ad hoc nature of operational healthcare processes in which no two patients follow exactly the same process execution pathway are not dealt with well by current automated process discovery tools and often results in the discovery of so-called "spaghetti" process models [306] in which all of the process execution pathways are represented in a single model. The idea behind process discovery is for the discovered model to represent actual behavior at some relevant level of abstraction that is understandable by readers. Such "spaghetti" models are complex and difficult to read. To reduce model complexity it is necessary to preprocess event log data by applying filtering, grouping or outlier detection/removal techniques [68] to reduce the variability in the event log and subsequently, the complexity in the discovered model. Clearly, it would be beneficial for the process discovery techniques to be able to deal properly with "noisy" event log data.

In considering process performance analysis, we note that, despite the importance of context data in process mining being acknowledged [310], most process mining approaches still ignore context data. Consequently, while current techniques can be used to identify performance issues (such as bottlenecks), they are not able to reason about why such issues occur. Further, comparing the respective behaviors and performance for different process cohorts is a labour intensive and repetitive task as the majority of process mining approaches make use of one event log to carry out one type of analysis for one cohort (i.e., one event log to discover one process model or one event log to analyse the performance of one cohort), necessitating a cohort by cohort analysis and manual comparison of results (as shown in [281]). We note that there has been recently an attempt to conduct this form of comparative process mining in a more structured manner through the concept of ProcessCube [311]. Here too, only one type of analysis is applied to a specific cohort and the selection of ProcessCube cells applicable to that cohort needs to be done explicitly with subsequent comparison between different cohorts remaining a manual and ad hoc exercise.

The analysis of processes based on their performance and context always requires domain knowledge and human involvement [306]. Analysis techniques should enable these stakeholders to combine their domain knowledge with the analysis results to draw relevant and actionable insights. Our contention is this is best achieved using sophisticated visualization of analysis results in a form that integrates well with the process stakeholders' understanding of the process and which provides assistance to pinpoint significant insights.

Our vision is that addressing the challenges above will lead to process mining tools that are intuitive, interactive and facilitate guided exploration of analysis results hence realizing a shift from ad hoc, labor-intensive, and undependable analytics to targeted, (semi-)automated, and reliable analytics. Such development would make the techniques able to be more easily applied by healthcare domain experts with less reliance on specialist process analysts.

EXERCISES

7.1 *Data Quality.* Many hospitals' emergency departments rely heavily on paper-based charts for recording patients' observations, tests ordered by clinicians, prescribed treatments, medical and nursing notes, etc. Many such entries never get recorded (in machine-readable form) in Hospital Information Systems while others are often transcribed, from the paper chart to electronic records, some time after the entry was made in the chart (for instance, at the end of a doctor's shift). Other patient related information may be recorded in heterogeneous hospital systems, e.g. admission/discharge/billing, or even third-party systems, e.g., an independent pathology laboratory. From a process mining point of view, list the possible data quality issues that might manifest in an event log as a result of such data management practices.

7.2 *Analysis Results.* Like all other data analysis tools, process mining tools are generally data-quality unaware. That is, they will take input as provided, process the input and produce results generated by their respective algorithms. Discuss (i) the ways in which data quality issues impact on process mining analysis results, and (ii) the implications of not taking into account data quality issues when utilizing the results of process analysis as the basis for process improvement recommendations.

7.3 *e-Health Systems.* Recently, many hospitals are moving towards e-Health systems, a feature of which is real-time, electronic collection of patient related information. For instance, patient and equipment locations can be tracked using RFID tags, clinicians can carry tablet devices which provide real-time access to patient charts. Discuss the opportunities and challenges for process mining analyses and data-driven process improvement initiatives arising from the introduction of e-health systems.

GLOSSARY

Business Process Management Lifecycle: A six-phased (process identification, discovery, analysis, redesign, implementation, monitor, and control) framework around which a BPM initiative can be organized.

Comparative Analysis: Process of determining similarities and differences (structural and behavioral) between multiple processes, usually by analysis of respective process models.

Complexity: A process model quality metric based on the size of the model assessed in terms of numbers of nodes, arcs and gateways.

Configurable Process Model: A process model that represents multiple variants of a business process in a single, consolidated model and which (generally) allows users to isolate/highlight individual process variants.

Event Log: Collection of cases (instances/executions of a process) where each (event) record refers to a case, an activity and the point in time when the activity was conducted.

Event Transaction Types: Different phases in the life of an event: Start, complete, abort, schedule, assign, suspend, withdraw, etc.

Fitness: A process model quality metric that quantifies the degree to which a model can accurately reproduce behavior recorded in an event log.

Generalization: A process model quality metric that measures the ability of the model to correctly reproduce future behavior, i.e. process behavior not seen during process discovery.

Precision: A process model quality metric that quantifies the behavior allowed by the model but which is not found in the event log.

Process Conformance Checking: Comparison of an event log with a process model (for the same process) to check that actual execution of the process (as recorded in the event log) conforms with expected process execution (indicated by the model).

Process Discovery: The (automatic) construction of a model representing an organization's current ("as is") business process(es).

Process Mining: A branch of data science that automates process discovery and analysis by exploiting process-related data stored in event logs.

Replay: Method for conducting process conformance checking involving replaying each case in an event log against the process model, one event at a time, and reporting errors.

Working Time: For any event (activity/task) in a workflow, the period between the start and completion transaction types measured as the difference between start time and completion time.

CHAPTER 8

Exception Management in Healthcare Processes

Mor Peleg

University of Haifa, Haifa, Israel, and Stanford University, California, USA

Giuseppe Pozzi

Politecnico di Milano, Milano, Italy

CONTENTS

> But you will take exceptions to
> my boon
>
> ――――――――――――――――――――
>
> W. Shakespeare

T HIS chapter describes how abnormal events, also known as "exceptions", can be captured and properly managed within an healthcare process model. The chapter initially describes the different types of exceptions, their definition and their classification: then, the chapter provides the reader with some examples of exceptions in the healthcare domain. Next, the chapter describes a methodology (i.e., a set of steps, criteria and good practices to be followed at design time) helpful in defining exceptions and in executing them even if the deployed process engine doesn't come with an exception management unit. Finally, the chapter sketches out some conclusions.

8.1   INTRODUCTION

Process models are abstract formalizations of activities. Process models do not limit themselves to consider the schema, i.e., the structure of the process, the elementary work units (tasks) and the connections among them setting up the flow of execution. Process models have to consider additional aspects, and include some complementary models, which describe some related facets: e.g., the organization model; the information model; the transaction model; the exception model, to mention some of them.

The *organization* model [294] describes the organization itself where the process is executed. Typically, the organizational model describes some static properties of the agents (roles, authorizations, skills), as well as some dynamic properties of the agents (workload and availability times). Static properties do not change, or change very seldom: one agent continues to have the same role (e.g., "nurse" or "physician" or "general practitioner") for some time; his or her skills and authorizations to execute some tasks may remain unchanged for several years. Dynamic properties refer to the current/instantaneous workload (e.g., set of tasks assigned to that agent at the timestamp under consideration), or to availability times (e.g., daily shifts, illness related permits or holiday dates).

The *information* model [294] describes the data related to and managed by the process. The Workflow Management Coalition (WfMC) [294] identifies three different types of information belonging to the information model: worfklow control data (i.e., internal data managed by the execution engine, not visible outside the engine itself), workflow relevant data (i.e., data used by the engine to perform state transition for a process instance, and also know as process variables since every process instance comes with its own set of process variables), workflow application data (i.e., data managed by external applications, which can be invoked either directly by the process engine or by the executing agent).

The *transaction* model [111] describes how to group some tasks within one unique supertask [53] (or sublflow) and, in case of need, how to roll-back to a previously saved state or how to compensate the actions performed by the tasks within the supertask. One advantage of adopting a transaction model is that one compensating task can be defined to compensate the entire supertask, without having to manually define the compensation for every executed action.

The *exception* model [52, 210], finally, describes how to capture and properly manage abnormal events which occur during the execution of a process instance: such events, which must be suitably defined at process definition time, may cause the ·process instance to deviate from the "normal flow" of execution. Such a deviation is to be properly defined, so that the state of the process instance will remain under control.

These complementary models join the pure schema of the process and set up a full process model. Despite many efforts have been performed to achieve a common standard, currently some results have been achieved on the schema definition side (e.g., BPMN from OMG, XPDL from the Workflow Management Coalition), while remarkable results still are far away from being achieved on the side of organizational model, information model, transaction model, and exception model.

The chapter goes into details about the exception model and its deployment in an health-care process. In Section 8.2 we introduce some basic concepts about exceptions: their meaning, their classification according to the triggering (or initiating) event, and their formal definition by a suitable formal language. In Section 8.3 we introduce a methodology to be used when designing exceptions related to health-care processes: such methodology also has to enable exception management in those process engines which do not feature an exception management unit. Finally, in Section 8.4 we sketch out some final remarks.

8.2 BASICS OF EXCEPTIONS

An exception is an event which occurs during the execution of a case, i.e., of an instance of a process model. The occurrence of an exception is extremely relevant with respect to the semantics of the process: thus, neglecting an exception may lead to an unwanted situation, as well as to completely loose the control over the process. A good estimation evaluates that at least 5% to 10% of all the cases are affected by an exception [52]: in some application domains, exceptions occur more frequently, while in some other application domains exceptions occur less frequently.

Exceptions can be initially divided into two main categories: unexpected exceptions and expected exceptions [85]. *Unexpected* exceptions are more generic and, in most cases, occur outside the application domain: typical example of such unexpected exceptions are power failures, which force a computer system to shutdown immediately, or disk failures, which may cause loss of data. Such unexpected exceptions, however, can be properly managed by some techniques which are outside the application domain and outside the engine taking care of the case execution: e.g., UPS (uninterruptible power supply) units enable a computer system to continue running also in case of a power failure; RAID (Redundant Array of Inexpensive Disk) disks store replicated data so that a failure of one of the hard disks (while the remainders keep running) does not lead to any loss of data.

Expected exceptions are those exceptions which can, and actually must, be considered when designing a process model. Expected exceptions are strictly related to the application domain and come with a not negligible semantics, or the execution of the case can be no longer under control. Effects of expected exceptions may lead to changes within the normal flow of execution, thus deviating from the standard execution path. Exceptions carry along with them an extremely relevant semantics: thus, the execution of the case must proceed by suitably taking into consideration the semantics, the causes of the exception, as well all the current state of the case.

Expected exceptions are properly defined within the wider concept of process model. The process model, thus, does not only store tasks, their sequence of execution, criteria for task assignment to agents, process variables, etc.: the process model also has to store the description of those exceptional events that may occur during the execution of an instance of that process model.

8.2.1 Exception Definition

Exception definition can be performed in several ways. Most common ones are the ECA (Event-Condition-Action) paradigm and a set of graphical symbols to be suitably inserted in the graphical schema of the process model.

The ECA approach, such as the Chimera-Exception language of [52], requires to define the *event*, i.e., the event which starts the exception (namely, the triggering event), the *condition* which tests the real occurrence of the event and may involve several other aspects, and the *action* which is executed to manage the exception.

In the event detection mechanism, the triggering event, such as in [53], can be a *data* event, a *temporal* event, a *workflow* event, or an *external* event.

data event: A data event monitors when a process variable is touched: thus, a data event monitors (and captures the exception immediately as it occurs) if a process variable is inserted, deleted, or updated by the respective SQL commands `insert`, `delete`, `update`.

temporal event: A temporal event monitors if a given deadline is reached: a deadline can be a time timestamp (e.g., "Dec-25th-2016 at 12:00:00 a.m."), an interval (e.g., an amount of time elapsed since an anchor timestamp), or periodic (e.g., every Monday morning at 3:00:00 a.m.).

workflow event: A workflow event monitors if a task instance or a process instance (case) has been started or ended, so that some proper management actions can be activated, like informing the agent responsible of the case if that case has been successfully completed.

external event: An external event monitors if the workflow management system (WfMS, i.e., the process engine) receives signals from an external application, which previously registered into the WfMS itself. An external application may control any process variable relevant to the application domain, ranging from the level of water inside a basin to the heart rate monitored by an ECG machine. As soon as the external applications raises the signal, the WfMS receives it and captures the external event[1].

In the exception execution mechanism, the condition part of an ECA rule aims both at checking some particular features over process data, e.g., to verify if all the conditions really occurred, and at identifying the current state of execution of the case. In fact, the trigger may require different actions according to some process variables (and their values), and the condition part has to check all of these conditions. The identification of the context of the case is necessary due to the intrinsic nature of the trigger itself: in fact, the management of the trigger can be performed at any arbitrary stage of the execution of the process, and the trigger ignores both the case history and the current state of execution of the case. Thus, the only way of reconstructing the proper context, both of the case and of the trigger, is by suitably setting up some suitable conditions.

Again in the exception execution mechanism, the action part of an ECA rules states the proper action to be executed: the action will obviously be executed if all the elementary conditions of the condition part returned TRUE. If more actions are specified, all of them will be executed.

Exception definition is also permitted by graphical tools, such as in [117], or by suitable frameworks, such as in [110]: the process designer runs a graphical interface to obtain a graphical specification of the exception. Such a graphical specification is then compiled, verified, checked and finally translated to a rule-based language. The major advantage of such an approach is that the designer is not requested to have all the skills to define the trigger directly in the rule-based language.

8.2.2 Taxonomy of Expected Exceptions

Expected exceptions can be classified according to several dimensions. One dimension is the triggering event, thus leading to data exceptions, temporal exceptions, workflow exceptions, and external exceptions as we already described in Section 8.2. Moreover, other dimensions can be considered to better categorize exceptions. Some of these dimensions are more general, as they can occur in most applications domains: some other dimensions are more related to the healthcare application domain, and thus are to be considered in the context of the current book. Among more general dimensions we consider here synchronicity and scope; among healthcare related dimensions we consider here cause, triggering object, and severity.

Synchronicity is one of the more general dimensions [54]. In fact, an exception can be synchronous or asynchronous. Literally, synchronous means "by a

---

[1]The implementation is achieved by launching a server program on the same computer system where the WfMS runs: the servers waits for communications form the client, i.e., the external application, and as soon as the server receives one, it informs the WfMS.

shared time": that is, the exception is entitled to occur at specific given times during the execution of the case, only. In other words, the process model exactly knows during the flow of execution when the exception can occur: apart from those points, that exception can't occur –and it will not.

An exception which can occur only at the end of the task `GetPatientData` within the `Admission` process model is localized and synchronous. An exception which can occur either at the beginning of the execution of task `StorePatientData` or at the end of the execution of the task `GetPatientHabits` within the `Admission` process model is sparse and synchronous.

An exception which can occur at any arbitrary stage of execution within the `Admission` process model is asynchronous. The process model has no chance to know in advance when that asynchronous exception will occur: that is, the exception can occur during the execution of the task `GetPatientData`, or of the task `StorePatientData`, or of the task `GetPatientHabits`, or of any other task within the `Admission` process model.

Scope is another dimension, among the more general ones, according to which triggers can be classified [54]. An exception can be *process specific* if it affects all the instances (cases) of one process model, only. A process specific exception may affect one task only, thus being defined at the *task level*, a block of tasks, thus being defined at the *block level*, or the entire process model, thus being defined at the *process level*. As an example, an exception which is defined all over the `Admission` process model is classified as process level and it will affect all the cases of that process model, only.

Alternatively, exceptions can be *cross process*, thus affecting cases coming from several distinct process models. The scope of an exception is *limited cross process* if two or more process models are affected by that exception. The scope of an exception is *global cross process* if the exception can affect any process model. Typically, changes in the organizational model are global cross process exceptions: in fact, if an agent becomes unavailable, all the tasks which were assigned to that agent loose the executing agent, and the exception has to manage how to reassign those tasks.

Cause is one of the healthcare related dimensions to categorize expected exceptions [210]. Cause refers to the the reason by which the trigger has been fired, distinguishing the motivations that lead the system to capture the event.

A cause can be labelled as *human* or as *non-human*. Human cause may include error, malicious action, incomplete or suboptimal coordination or communication among agents, or non-compliance to the recommended protocol or process model or care pathway: also adverse effects or adverse reactions to drug are to be considered human cause, and their relevance as well as chance of occurrence are well know to healthcare experts. Non-human cause may include organizational reasons [112], resource unavailability, failure of a work item such as a lab test or an assisting device.

Triggering object is another dimension [210] typical of the healthcare related application domain. Triggering object denotes the *origin* of the triggering event and the *essence*. The origin can be *systemic* or *environmental*: a systemic source refers to a failure of a system component or of the process, including patient's side effects; an environmental source refers to an external source such as the result of a lab test which becomes available (and consequently some decisions can be taken or some therapies can be prescribed, accordingly). The essence of the triggering object can be *human* or *non-human*, thus recalling the distinction for the cause dimension from above.

Severity is one more dimension [210] typical of the healthcare related application domain. Severity refers to the potential effects of the exception on the normal operation of the systems. Severity distinguishes among: *ignorable*, when the normal operation of the system is not affected by the exception; *light*, when the exception does not cause any error but requires a continuous monitoring and supervision by a human; *true*, when the exception causes a malfunctioning of one or more major components of the system; and *hard*, when the exception does not permit the system to function any longer and any recovery from the crisis has failed.

Figure 8.1 provides a synthetic taxonomy of exception types and their classifications (as taken from [54, 210]).

8.2.3   Some Examples of Exceptions

We now show a typical example of an exception definition, disregarding the syntactical issues which are strictly related to the deployed exception programming language and to the WfMS. The trigger refers to an healthcare process model, namely `Admission`, which checks if the currently admitted patient has already been hospitalized: in case, the trigger notifies the agent who is responsible of the current case about previous admission(s). The trigger may have the following shape:

event	insert new admission
condition	exists a previous admission for the same patient
action	inform the case responsible that a previous admission exists for that patient

With respect to the taxonomy of Figure 8.1, the above exception is a *data* exception, because the event part of the trigger monitors the data event `insert values into Admission_Table`.

The exception definition language must be powerful enough as to enable the exception designer to properly consider and define all the exception types which could reasonably occur during the execution of a process model. For instance, if the patient's ECG is being recorded and monitored, an *asynchronous*

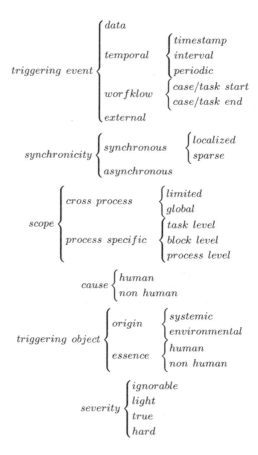

FIGURE 8.1 Overview of the taxonomy for expected exceptions.

exception is detected (and captured) when an electrode disconnects from the skin of the patient. Such an exception is an asynchronous one, because the event can occur at any time during the admission. As a consequence of the event, the action part of the trigger will set up an alarm, so that the nurse on duty will be asked to reconnect the electrode.

A cross procecss exception may occur when a nurse falls ill. That nurse is not on duty, and all the activities that were scheduled for execution by that nurse need to be reassigned [109]: the WfMS has thus to look for a replacing agent. That exception has a *scope* which is global and cross process: in fact, many process instances of different process model can require a new executing agent.

A human exception may occur when an admitted patient is administered a therapy: if the patient encounters some adverse reactions to the drug, that exception will show a *cause* to be human, because the exception is triggered by a human cause –even if not under voluntary circumstances.

An environmental exception may occur when a patient is admitted in an emergency room and some blood samples are taken and sent to the laboratory for tests. As soon as the lab test results are available, the nurse calls a physician. The *triggering object* is the availability of lab results: the exception is environmental, since an external source of information has produced the data.

Finally, many different levels of severity may occur for en exception. When the charge level of the internal battery of an assisting machine falls below a given threshold, the machine sets up an alarm. The *severity* of the alarm is light, since the assisting machine does not stop working: however, a continuous monitoring and supervision is required by a nurse until a replacement battery is applied.

It can be easily observed that the proposed taxonomy includes several dimensions, which do not exclude each other. In fact, the event "availability of some lab test results" is an external event (as for the triggering event), is asynchronous (as for the synchronicity) since the time when results will be available can't be foreseen, is process specific at the process level (as for the scope) since it affects only the cases of the process model which is waiting for the lab results, is non human (as for the cause) since no direct human involvement is required, is environmental (as for the triggering object) since it is generated by the environment, and may have an ignorable severity (as for the severity) since no particular change in the functions of the system applies.

8.3 DESIGN METHODOLOGY FOR EXCEPTIONS IN HEALTHCARE PROCESSES

A methodology is the set of techniques, criteria, and good practices to be followed at design time when facing a project or a problem. The design methodology refers to the proper methodology to be adopted when designing something: as an example, the process design methodology defines the steps to be followed when defining a process model [95]. If, as in the context of the current chapter, we aim at designing an exception, the exception design methodology refers to the steps to be followed in such a design [210]. Following the proper criteria, techniques, and good practices generally helps to guarantee that the achieved result is of high quality, compliant with the requirements, correctly documented, maintainable and –as much as possible– the less error-prone possible.

Before starting to consider exceptions and exception design, we must clearly recall the major differences between the formal flow of execution and the exceptional flow of execution. The normal flow of execution includes most of the semantics of the process, reads easily, is known to all the agents involved in process execution: on the contrary, the exceptional flow of execution reads hardly, can be started at any time during the execution of the main flow of the process, can be known to some agents, only. Moreover, an exception captures the abnormal flow of execution, and the semantics of an exception is corrective (changing the normal flow of execution) rather than additive (adding flow of execution).

While exception design is a very complex and delicate phase in the design of the entire business process model (just consider that the context of execution of an exception is not known at exception design time, because the exception can be started at any arbitrary stage during the execution of the business process), the major steps in the design phase of exceptions include *identification*, *modeling*, *mapping* to the deployed WfMS, and *execution*.

Exception *identification* requires that the process designer clearly identifies the boundaries of the exception itself. That is, the designer has to separate the aspects of the process model to be defined by the normal flow of execution from the aspects to be defined by the exceptional flow of execution. After the exception has been clearly separated by the remainder of the process model, the exception itself has been clearly identified.

The next step is that of *modeling* the exception: this step requires to consider the major and most relevant dimension of the exception, by choosing the most appropriate dimension among those of the taxonomy of Figure 8.1. Exception modeling includes exception elicitation, that is the cognitive task of thinking about which exceptions may occur: Table 8.1 and the table on guidelines for eliciting exceptions from [210, p. 743] help in modeling.

Since writing an exception from scratch is even harder, exception design can be performed either by difference, i.e., starting from a previously defined exception which preferably is of the same type of the one we are defining, or by looking into suitable catalogs of patterns [51] of exceptions: this latter approach requires to browse a catalog of patterns (a repository of exception templates), classified by type, and pick the pattern most suitable to the need of the applications currently being modeled. A pattern is an empty frame for exception definition, which needs to be tailored and customized to the specific need of the application domain. Generally, a catalog of patterns includes several templates for every category of exceptions: the user can then select the most appropriate one. Once the pattern has been selected, the user is requested to customize the pattern, in order to derive the full code of the exception: such a customization requires the user to enter the specific required details which are defined for the selected pattern. Specifically, since we are interested in browsing a catalog of patterns for exceptions, the patterns have to support a mechanism for detecting the exception, and, especially, for transferring responsibility and accountability for recovering from the exception to the appropriate actor [109, 110], if no automatic exception management is possible.

Catalogs of patterns generally come with some graphical interfaces, too: graphical interfaces provide the user with a schematic view of the trigger and also help to better customize the pattern. Since the application domain can require a trigger to span over more than one dimension, e.g., the major dimension of the trigger is the *triggering event* as in Figure 8.1, but some other dimensions are involved by the trigger such as *synchronicity*, *scope* and *severity*, the user has to first focus on the major dimension, only: then, within the patterns for that major dimension, the use may refine the search for the most appropriate pattern.

As an example, let us consider a trigger that has to monitor the late execution of the task `GetPatientHabits`, aimed at collecting the habits of the patient. By looking up at the taxonomy of Figure 8.1, we discover that the major dimension for the exception is that of triggering event, temporal event related to an interval, with a task start as anchor event. However, the exception we are going to define has other secondary dimensions, too: in fact, it is synchronous and localized, since the exception may occur within the business process model the task `GetPatientHabits` belongs to, and after some time from the starting of the task itself. The same exception has a scope which is process specific at the task level, according to the fact that the exception has to monitor the late execution of `GetPatientHabits` for a specific process model. Then, accordingly to the severity we may want to assign to the exception an ignorable or light level. Thus, the designer will look for the appropriate template starting from the major dimension of triggering level, that is triggering event, workflow event, task start: then, within the set of patterns returned by the first, high-level search, the designer will refine the choice of the most appropriate template by looking for the template which also covers the other secondary dimensions.

Once the designer has selected the most appropriate pattern aimed at checking a late execution, the design requires him or her to define the name of the task whose execution time has to be monitored, the duration beyond which the task is to be considered as a late one, and the action to be executed, would the late execution be detected. These customization's details enable the designer to customize the empty pattern, to adapt it, and to derive the full trigger to be then included into the full process model.

After modeling, the exception is defined in the exception definition language and ready to be executed on top of the WfMS, on condition that the deployed WfMS has a suitable exception execution engine. Unfortunately, very few WfMSs come with a fully fledged exception management unit, capable of understanding and executing the exception and its definition language: as a consequence, the process designer has to map (*mapping* phase) the exception into the process model by using the standard components provided by the activity graph of the deployed WfMS. Thus, the process designer has to move from the plain process model (formally, $\mathcal{P}$), which is not capable of managing any exception. Formally, we may describe such a plain process as

$$\mathcal{P} = < \mathcal{N}, \mathcal{A}, \mathcal{C} >$$

that is an N-uple with $\mathcal{N}$ nodes, $\mathcal{A}$ arcs, and $\mathcal{C}$ conditions coupled to every arc.

Then, the process designer derives an enriched process model by adding suitable fragments (set of tasks, arcs, and conditions). Such an enriched process model (formally, $\mathcal{P}^+$) has the behavior of the plain process model (i.e., $\mathcal{P}$) plus it is capable of capturing and managing the exceptions, due to the fragments which have been added. Formally, we may describe the enriched process model as

$$\mathcal{P}^+ = < \mathcal{N}, \mathcal{A}, \mathcal{C}, \mathcal{N}^+, \mathcal{A}^+, \mathcal{C}^+ >$$

that is an N-uple with $\mathcal{N}$ nodes, $\mathcal{A}$ arcs, and $\mathcal{C}$ conditions coupled to every arc coming from the plain process model $\mathcal{P}$, plus $\mathcal{N}^+$ nodes, $\mathcal{A}^+$ arcs, and $\mathcal{C}^+$ conditions coupled to the arcs $\mathcal{A}^+$, aimed at managing the mapped exception.

Mapping techniques to derive the enriched process model $\mathcal{P}^+$ are strictly related to the basic features of the exception (see Figure 8.1), and for every type of exception, the proper mapping technique can be defined [54] and properly implemented. It can be easily observed that adding some suitable fragments to the plain process model $\mathcal{P}$ to enrich its behavior increases the complexity of the resulting process model $\mathcal{P}^+$, and makes its readability and maintainability more challenging.

As an example, if we have to enrich the plain process model by verifying if the patient has previously been admitted, we can immediately identify that such an exception is local, synchronous, and refers to data with respect to the taxonomy of Figure 8.1. The exception can occur just within the Admission process model (i.e., it is local), at the end of the execution of the task GetPatientData (i.e., it is synchronous since its time of occurrence is known a priori, that is at the start or end of the execution of another task), and triggered by operations on data (i.e., some process variables are involved). The fragment to be included into the process model to manage such a local and synchronous exception is depicted in Figure 8.3: please, observe that the fragment is launched immediately after the task GetPatientData ends, since the exception is triggered at the end of the task GetPatientData. The action part of the trigger, i.e., those actions to be executed after the event has been captured and all the conditions specified by the trigger returned TRUE, must be properly assigned to the task(s) of the fragment itself.

If, instead, we have to enrich the plain process model so that it will monitor the late execution of a task, the exception is local, synchronous and temporal. The exception can occur just within the Admission process model (i.e., it is local), during the execution of that task whose late execution we want to monitor (i.e., it is synchronous since its time of occurrence is known a priori), and triggered by an interval temporal event (i.e., a specified amount of time elapsed since that task was started). Thus, we have to add a suitable fragment which is launched in parallel with the task to be monitored: this fragment runs as a "sentinel" task. Then, the first task to complete (the normal task, i.e., the one that is monitored, or the added fragment, i.e., the sentinel that monitors) will enable the process model to detect if the late execution occurred (see Figure 8.4). Such a trick requires to add a suitable fragment for every task whose late execution needs to be monitored: thus, if within a process model we have 10 tasks whose late executions must be monitored, the process designer has to add 10 times the respective sentinel tasks.

Finally, if we want to enrich the plain process model of Admission by a fragment which takes care of capturing an asynchronous event (i.e., an event whose time of occurrence can't be foreseen a *priori*), we need the exception monitoring fragment to be kept alive for the entire time of execution of that case: the resulting structure is that of Figure 8.5. Please, observe that the sentinel task (the one that monitors if the exception has occurred) is to be periodically invoked throughout the entire execution of the case: that is, the sentinel task can be terminated only as the case ends –or the exception may occur during the case execution and go undetected.

Exception *execution* is the final phase. This phase requires that the WfMS comes with the proper exception management unit. It should be clear that adding too many exceptions will return in a heavy workload for the engine itself, and consequently will reduce the overall performances of the system.

Moreover, if the WfMS does not come with an exception management unit, the mapping phase, which added the fragments into the activity graphs to manage exceptions, will produce a not negligible increase of the overall workload to the system, as well as increase in the metrics of the process model (see Chapter 6): this suggests to limit the number of exceptions within the process model. Obviously, exceptions are mandatory to properly model all the semantics of the process, and finding a good compromise between performance and modeling correctness is a very critical issue.

8.3.1   Some Examples of Exception Mapping

Let us assume that we have a very simple, streamline process model which manages admissions to an hospital. The plain process model, namely Admission, is depicted by the BPMN (Business Process Modeling Notation) graphical notation in Figure 8.2. The plain process model starts with the task `GetPatientData` collecting demographic data about the patient: next, the task `StorePatientData` stores collected data. The task `GetPatientHabits` collects the life habits of the patient: then, the task `GetBloodSamples` takes some blood samples. Finally, the last task, namely `Admit`, admits the patient to the hospital. All these tasks are executed by the `EmergencyRoom` swim lane, that is the only swim lane of the plain process model.

In order to keep the process model simple, no check is performed to verify if the patient has been previously admitted to the hospital, or to any other federated hospital. Since data from previous admissions are extremely relevant from a clinical point of view, the process model designer adds an exception which checks such a situation. As we already defined in Section 8.3, the exception is local and synchronous: in fact, the exception may occur within the `Admission` process model, and at the end of the task `GetPatientData`, only.

The trigger has already been described in a high level format in Section 8.2.3. When the task `GetPatientData` ends (i.e., the "insert new admission" command of the event part has been executed), if more data are available about the same patient (i.e., the "exists a previous admission for the same patient" of the condition part returns `TRUE`), then the process informs the agent responsible of the case (i.e., the "inform the case responsible that a previous admission exists for that patient" of the action part).

The mapping phase (see Section 8.3) requires the designer to add one fragment in the activity graph of the plain process model: such a fragment is depicted by Figure 8.3. After the task `GetPatientData` ends, the control flow is passed to the task `CheckPastAdmission` belonging to the `System` swim lane of the added fragment: the task checks if any previous admission is reported for the current patient. If no admission is reported, the control flow returns to the `EmergencyRoom` swim lane and the task `StorePatientData` is then scheduled for execution: instead, if any admission is reported, the task `NotifyPastAdmission` is executed, to inform the agent of the `EmergencyRoom` swim lane that data from previous admission(s) must be considered. The WfMS, by accessing the process model and the organizational model, may easily find all the proper information about the agent to be notified. The execution then continues with the task `StorePatientData`, belonging to the plain process model.

It can be easily observed that mapping such an exception by a fragment within the plain flow of execution required to add two tasks (`CheckPastAdmission` and `NotifyPastAdmission`, namely) and two routing tasks (the two diamonds with an X sign inside, denoting an XOR execution path).

Another example of exception mapping refers to the monitoring the late execution of a task. In fact, it may occur that, due to several reasons, the execution of a task requires an amount of time greater that the duration expected for the task itself. Such an abnormal situation is to be carefully monitored,

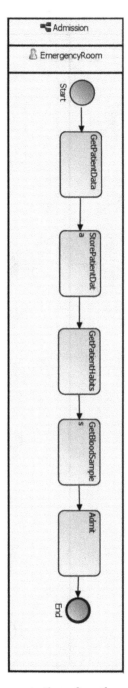

FIGURE 8.2 BPMN representation for the plain **Admission** process model.

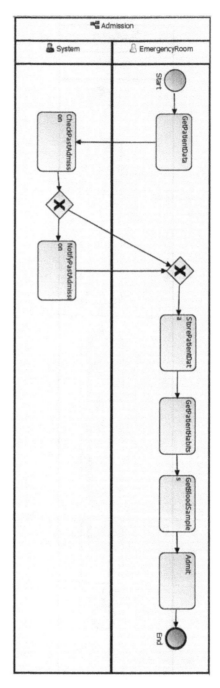

FIGURE 8.3 Example of a fragment inserted into the plain process model **Admission** to monitor if the patient has previously been admitted to the hospital.

especially in those domains where, when a critical situation is detected, the proper reaction is to be executed within some temporal constraints and deadlines.

Also for exceptions aimed at monitoring a late execution of a task, the mapping phase (see Section 8.3) requires the designer to add one fragment in the activity graph of the plain process model: such a fragment is depicted by Figure 8.4. After the task StorePatientData ends, the control flow is passed to the DelayChecker fork task, which starts the parallel executions of the task GetPatientHabits, which belongs to the plain process model, and of the task WaitForPossibleDelay, which belongs to the System swim lane of the added fragment. The task WaitForPossibleDelay is a wait task: basically, it performs no action but staying waiting for an amount of time. The amount of time is set to the exact value of the expected duration for the task whose execution time is to be monitored (i.e., GetPatientHabits in the current example). If we have to monitor the late execution for the task GetPatientHabits, and we know that the expected duration of GetPatientHabits is 30 minutes, the wait task WaitForPossibleDelay will simply stay waiting for 30 minutes.

Next, the OR join task, namely Delay in Figure 8.4, will be activated when either the task GetPatientHabits completes of when the task WaitForPossibleDelay completes. According to a process variable properly set by either task, the XOR fork task WithDelay can easily detect if the task GetPatientHabits of the plain process model completed within its expected duration or the wait task WaitForPossibleDelay completed before the task GetPatientHabits did. Thus, the fork task WithDelay can alternatively continue the execution of the plain process model, by scheduling the task GetBloodSamples, or force the execution of the fragment, by scheduling the task ManageDelay which takes care of properly managing the late execution of the task GetPatientHabits.

Again, it can be easily observed that mapping the late execution exception by a fragment within the plain flow of execution required to add two tasks (WaitForPossibleDelay and ManageDelay, namely) and three routing tasks (one diamond with a + sign inside, denoting an AND execution path, and two diamonds with an X sign inside, denoting two XOR execution paths).

The last example of exception mapping we consider here relates to asynchronous exceptions. Asynchronous exceptions are those exceptions which occur at any arbitrary stage of execution of the case: i.e., there is no way of knowing a priori what will be the state of the case at the time when the exception will have occurred. Such a requirement implies that the exception occurs independently of the fact that the task GetPatientData (or any other task) has started or not, or has completed or not. Consequently, the mapping of the asynchronous exception can't be coupled to any task of the plain process model, just because the occurrence of the exception is completely unrelated to every task.

The only way of mapping an asynchronous exception is that of starting the fragment which will serve as the asynchronous exception manager capturing

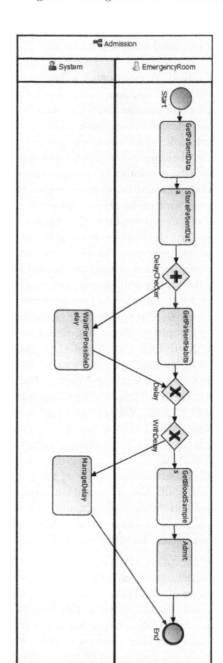

FIGURE 8.4 Example of a fragment inserted into the plain process model **Admission** to monitor the late execution of the task **GetPatientHabits**.

and managing the exception, as soon as the case starts. Thus, the mapping requires to launch the asynchronous exception manager in parallel to the first task.

The fragment is set up by a "sentinel" swim lane , which stays listening to capture the event as soon as it occurs: when the event is captured, the fragment will then manage it by the ActionExecutor swim lane. If no event is captured, the listening task waits for some time before re-activating itself. In fact, in the swim lane Sentinel the task DetectException checks if any exception has occurred: if more than one asynchronous exception is to be monitored, the task DetectException will check all of them. The task DetectException is non-suspensive, that is it instantaneously checks if any exception has occurred without staying waiting for the exception to occur.

If any exception is detected, the AnyException XOR fork task routes the execution to the task ExceptionHasBeenDetected, which stores all the required details about the captured exception, and then continues the execution by the DoAction task which performs all the required actions.

Instead, if no exception is detected, the AnyException XOR fork task routes the execution to the task Wait, which stays waiting for a given amount of time defined at customization time of the exception management unit. The selection of the proper waiting time for the Wait task is a very critical issue: in fact, a reduced waiting time (e.g., 2 minutes) permits the case to be informed about the occurrence of the exception within a small delay (in the average, the half of the waiting tine, that is 1 minute). However, a reduced waiting time implies that the sentinel swim lane and the task DetectException will be scheduled very often, thus increasing the workload to the system and reducing its overall performances. On the other side, a bigger waiting time (e.g., 30 minutes) permits the case to be informed about the exception with an average delay of 15 minutes. A bigger waiting time implies a less frequent activation of the DetectException task, and it will not introduce a considerable workload to the system.

If we consider the Admission process model of Figure 8.2, the patient may press a bed-side button to call a nurse: in fact, if the patient perceives that his/her conditions are worsening, or some sudden pain arises while waiting for the Admission process to be completed, he or she may invoke an intervention by the personnel of the emergency room. Such an event, and the related exception, are asynchronous, as they may occur at any arbitrary stage during the execution of the case. Thus, with reference to Figure 8.5, the task DetectException has to monitor if the bed-side panic button has been pressed: in case, the task ExceptionHasBeenDetected stores information about the alarm (e.g., bed number, patient name, date and time of occurrence of the event) and the task DoActions starts performing the proper actions (e.g., ringing a bell in the nurses' front-desk and waiting for a nurse to take care of the patient).

If more asynchronous events are to be monitored, the sentinel task DetectException has to test all the possible events in an OR pol-

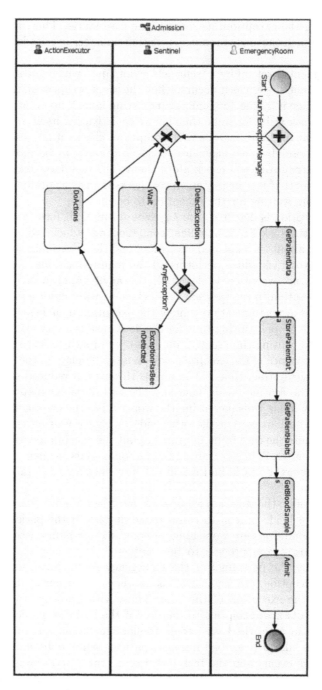

FIGURE 8.5 Example of a fragment inserted into the plain process model **Admission** to monitor asynchronous events during the execution of a case.

icy, and execute in parallel all the actions coupled to those events whose conditions returned TRUE. Thus, many sub-fragments of the tasks ExceptionHasBeenDeected and DoActions are to be defined, one sub-fragment for every possible event to be monitored. As a matter of fact, it can be easily observed that mapping an asynchronous exception manager within a plain process model may result in a challenging issue, and leading to an enriched process model which is hard to read and even harder to maintain.

8.4 CONCLUSIONS

In this chapter we focused on exceptions and their relevance for healthcare processes. An exception is an event that occurs during the execution of a process and can, possibly, force such an execution to deviate from the standard predefined execution path: the semantics of exceptions is not negligible for the correct execution of the process itself.

We considered several types of exceptions, and classified them by a proposed taxonomy. We also defined a methodology, i.e. a set of steps, criteria, and best practices to be followed in designing exceptions in healthcare processes: we also introduced the concept of mapping exceptions to activity diagrams, so that exception management can take place also on those process engines which do not come with a proper exception management unit.

EXERCISES

8.1 *Modeling.* Moving from the process model of Figure 8.2 depicted according to the BPMN notation, design the process model for a follow-up visit of a cardiological out-patient. Major activities include collecting heart rate, blood pressure, and weight, verifying compliance to prescribed therapies, confirming the therapy or assigning some new ones, and scheduling the next follow-up visit.

8.2 *Exception Modeling.* Consider an exception which monitors if the patient doesn't show up to the scheduled follow-up visit (hint: start by considering the example of trigger defined in Section 8.2.3). Which type of exception better models such a situation (hint: start by the taxonomy of exceptions defined in Figure 8.1)?

8.3 *Exception Definition.* Define the above exception according to the ECA paradigm (hint: start by considering the example of trigger defined in Section 8.2.3).

8.4 *Exception Mapping.* Map the above exception inside the activity graph (hint: start by considering the example of Figure 8.4).

GLOSSARY

BPMN: A standard way of graphically representing a process model. BPMN is developed by the standardizing organization OMG (Object Management Group) and endorsed by the Workflow Management Coalition (WfMC). The name stands for Business Process Modeling Notation. BPMN is not an executable or interpretable language: however, some process model editors enable the designer to graphically design the process model in BPMN and to save it in XPDL, which is an executable language.

ECA paradigm: A generic way of defining active behaviors of a computer system. A computer system features an active behavior when it can react to some events it is informed about.

ECA stands for *event, condition, action*: when an event is captured, a condition is evaluated and –if TRUE– the corresponding action is executed. Several ECA languages are defined by the literature.

Exception: Any event which may occur during the execution of a process instance, causing it to deviate from the predefined normal flow of execution.

Taxonomy of exceptions: A classification of exceptions, mainly based on the event which generates the exception itself.

XPDL: XML - Process Definition Language (XPDL) is an executable language for process models: it is standardized and recommended by the Workflow Management Coalition (WfMC).

Workflow Management Coalition: The Workflow Management Coalition (WfMC) is a nonprofit organization collecting experts, consultants, developers, users of Workflow Management Systems (WfMS).

Workflow Management System: A Workflow Management System (WfMS) is a software system supporting the coordinated execution of activities among different users within an organization.

FURTHER READING

Combi Carlo, Pozzi Giuseppe, Architectures for a Temporal Workflow Management System, *Proc. of the 19th Symposium on Applied Computing*, Nicosia, Cyprus, 2004 p. 659-666.

Weske Mathias, *Business Process Management: Concepts, Languages, Architectures*. Springer Publishing Company, 2010.

CHAPTER 9

Temporal Clinical Guidelines

Luca Anselma

University of Torino, Torino, Italy

Luca Piovesan

Universitt of Piemonte Orientale "A. Avogadro", Alessandria, Italy

Paolo Terenziani

University of Piemonte Orientale "A. Avogadro", Alessandria, Italy

CONTENTS

> Is this an hour for temporal
> affairs

W. Shakespeare

T HE notion of time deeply encompasses the way humans perceive and understand the world; thus, it is fundamental to support temporal information also in the computer-based treatment of clinical guidelines. This Chapter describes the management (representation and reasoning) of temporal phenomena in clinical guidelines.

9.1 INTRODUCTION

Time plays a fundamental role in the representation of guidelines, in the representation of patients' data and in the execution of the guidelines on specific patients. Regarding patients' data, it is worth noticing that most clinical data are intrinsically temporal and that it is not possible to interpret clinical data such as exam results and patients' symptoms without resorting to the time when such data hold.

Regarding clinical guidelines, in most therapies, for example, therapeutic actions have to be performed in a certain order, with certain delays between them and must have certain durations. Often such actions are periodic, i.e., they must be repeated regularly. Furthermore, it is also necessary to take into account implicit temporal constraints, such as the ones deriving from hierarchical/partonomic composition of the guideline and from the control-flow of actions.

These issues affect both the phase of acquisition of a clinical guideline, where time have to be represented, and the phase of execution of a clinical guideline, where a computer-based system may offer facilities such as compliance verification, query answering, what-if simulations.

Offering computerized support in dealing with the temporal constraints of clinical guidelines requires not only designing expressive representation formalisms able to capture the different phenomena sketched above, but also devising temporal reasoning mechanisms able to operate on the formalism both at acquisition time and at execution time.

The Artificial Intelligence community has proposed several formalisms to model and reason on temporal information, however the challenges posed by clinical guidelines require new formalisms and reasoning mechanisms. Indeed, representing and storing temporal information must be paired with suitable temporal reasoning techniques in order to be useful.

First, *temporal abstraction* can be required. Indeed, temporal patient data, as they are usually stored in clinical records, can be too low-level to be used in a guideline: for example, a guideline might require the occurrence of a certain temporal pattern in clinical data, and "raw" time-stamped data must be abstracted to be recognized as a temporal pattern.

Second, *temporal inference on the temporal constraints* of the clinical guideline is needed in the various phases of the life cycle of a clinical guideline. In the acquisition phase, it is necessary to check whether the temporal constraints in the guideline are consistent (indeed, if the temporal constraints were not satisfiable, it would not be possible to execute the guideline). In the execution phase, temporal inference is important to check whether the executed actions are temporally compliant with the guideline, to determine the next candidate action to be executed on the basis of the times of execution of the past actions and of the temporal constraints in the guideline.

The chapter is organized as follows. In Section 9.2, we introduce the representation of temporal information. In particular, first, in Section 9.2.1 we deal with patients' data, which are intrinsically temporal. Then in Section 9.2.2 we deal with the representation of clinical temporal knowledge for data interpretation (i.e., temporal abstraction) and finally in Section 9.2.3 we discuss the representation of temporal constraints about the actions in the clinical guidelines. In Section 9.3 we introduce some reasoning mechanisms on temporal information. In particular, in Section 9.3.1 we introduce some temporal constraint propagation mechanisms that can be exploited to provide some useful temporal facilities to the users of the clinical guideline systems. We introduce the basic framework of Simple Temporal Problems (Section 9.3.1.1), we introduce the temporal facilities (Section 9.3.1.2) to be provided and how Simple Temporal Problems are extended and exploited to provide such facilities (Section 9.3.1.3); finally we provide a general discussion of the main temporal reasoning frameworks in Artificial Intelligence (Section 9.3.1.4). In Section 9.3.2 we overview the main approaches to clinical temporal abstraction.

9.2 REPRESENTATION OF TIME IN CLINICAL GUIDELINES

9.2.1 Database Representation of Patients' Data

Clinical records are usually stored in relational databases and, since clinical data are intrinsically temporal, temporal information is a fundamental information to be stored.

For example, in a measurement, or in a laboratory test, at least three elements are important: the considered patient's parameter, the value assumed/measured for the parameter, and the time in which the particular information holds (sometimes represented with a time interval; see Example 9.1).

Example 9.1 *The patient's liver volume (parameter) has increased (value) in the time interval starting at day 21 and ending at day 38 (time interval in which the information holds).*

Over 20 years of research in the field of temporal databases have demonstrated that storing time requires a specific support and specific techniques and that the simple addition of some timestamp attributes such as the starting and ending times in which a tuple is valid is not sufficient, because many complex problems need to be tackled when designing, querying and updating time-varying data. The problem is that temporal attributes have a peculiar semantics and they cannot be treated as the non-temporal attributes. Despite often the issues raised by such a treatment receive an ad-hoc support at application level, it is worth to solve such issues in a principled way at the database level.

Let us consider, as an example, a temporal relational database with two temporal table $R1$ and $R2$. Let us assume that R1 and R2 are joined (as when an SQL query containing a "$R1$ JOIN $R2$ ON ..." clause is evaluated). What is the time of the tuples in the resulting table? Standard relational databases would double the temporal attributes and simply report together the times of the combined tuples, thus carrying not a significant information about the new tuples. In the area of temporal database there is a shared agreement that the resulting tuples should be associated with the *intersection* of the times of the original tuples. With standard non-temporal relational databases such result would be not obvious to be obtained by an application-level programmer. Other problems arise when a query contains projection, union, difference, intersection operations and aggregate functions.

These temporal aspects of clinical data are not strictly related with clinical guidelines and can be dealt with independently by temporal databases.

A temporal database can consist either of a sequence of versions of the data (a transaction-time database), of a history of the reality modeled by the database (a valid-time database), or of both. Most data models timestamp tuples (consider, e.g., TSQL2 [270]) and support bitemporal tuples with both transaction time (i.e., the time when data are inserted/deleted in the database) and valid time (i.e., the time when data hold in the world). For instance, supposing that the information of Example 9.1 has been inserted into the database at time 21 and that is still present in the database, its transaction time is $[21 \ldots Now]$ and its valid time is $[20 \ldots 38]$.

A consensus approach to temporal relational databases is TSQL2 [270], whose underlying semantics, BCDM (Bitemporal Conceptual Data Model) [134], has also been proven to be at the basis of several other temporal relational database approaches.

The problem of providing temporal support in databases is in general a domain-independent problem. However, clinical data possess some peculiarities which general database approaches do not address. For example, clinical data require support for temporal indeterminacy (e.g., "I don't know exactly when a symptom started"), for multiple granularities (e.g., data from medical visit obtained once a day versus temperature measured every hour), for abstraction of "raw" data (e.g., detect a trend in temperature from the data obtained in an intensive care unit), and for now-relative data. Some extensions of temporal relational databases to cover such issues have been proposed. For example, Chronus [72] and Chronus II [204] have focused their attention also on the management of temporal data. They are mostly an implementation of a subset of TSQL2 [270], with specific focus on valid time and on temporal indeterminacy [203]. The authors of [14] extended TSQL2 for dealing with indeterminacy in the valid time; the authors of [11] extended TSQL2 for supporting now-related data, and [10] for coping with data versioning.

9.2.2 Knowledge Representation for Temporal Abstraction

In many practical cases, the way in which clinical guidelines expect data is quite different from the way in which clinical data are stored in databases.

Indeed, clinical guidelines usually express conditions over patients' data that must occur, for instance, to make diagnostic or therapeutic decisions or to verify the preconditions of an action; however, conditions in clinical guidelines usually consider data at a higher granularity with respect to the one in which patients' data are generally stored in databases (see, e.g., Example 9.2).

Example 9.2 *If there was a period of high blood glucose level, lasting at least three days [...].*

In the case of Example 9.2, for instance, the database might not contain data about blood glucose levels with values like "high", nor data taken at each moment for three days. More probably, it contains *raw timestamped data* with the exact values of the measurements, taken few times a day, and the timestamps of the measure times (see, e.g., Example 9.3).

Example 9.3 *The triple ⟨"blood glucose level", 80, 21 ⟩ represents the value 80 (where the measure unit mg/dl is omitted) of the parameter "blood glucose level" at timestamp 21.*

Conditions can also be more complex (see, e.g., Example 9.6, describing the conditions to recognize a quiescent chronic graft-versus-host disease, a complication of the bone-marrow transplantation).

The example above clearly shows the difference between the level of abstraction of the conditions in clinical guidelines and the level of abstraction of the patients' data contained in databases. To bridge the gap between them, additional knowledge and additional temporal reasoning facilities (e.g., to transform two records of high blood glucose level at a distance of six hours in a unique time interval of six hours where the blood glucose level can considered high) are required. This is, in short, the goal of the *Temporal Abstraction*. In this section, we will describe the temporal knowledge needed to perform such a task, taking as an example the approach of the *Knowledge-based temporal abstraction* (KBTA) method [259, 261], adopted by Asbru [260] to provide support for the execution of clinical guidelines. In Section 9.3.2, we will describe how such a knowledge is exploited to perform temporal abstraction. Even if we use as example the KBTA approach, the model we sketch in this section is quite general, and provides an overview of part of the temporal knowledge[1] needed to support guidelines execution.

The KBTA approach identifies a set of basic concepts to model temporal knowledge:

Timestamps (roughly corresponding to the concept of *Time Points* in other approaches) are the basic temporal primitives. They belong to an ordered set of elements isomorphic to the positive integers. The symbols $-\infty$ and $+\infty$, are also considered, to denote the most remote past and the furthest future. There is a "zero-point" timestamp (called *reference time* in some approaches). The domain of timestamps must be associated at least with a lowest-granularity time unit (e.g., seconds) and, in case higher-granularity time units exist (e.g., minutes, hours), a function mapping higher-granularity timestamps into lowest granularity timestamps must be provided.

A **Time Interval** represents a convex set of timestamps. It is often denoted with the notation $[I_{Start}, I_{End}]$ where I_{Start} and I_{End} are, respectively, the starting and ending points of the interval.

The **Interpretation Context** (Context for short) represents a situation or a state relevant in the current task that can change the interpretation of data or influence the inferences on them (see Example 9.4).

Example 9.4 *When considering blood glucose levels, the context of a patient treated with insulin is relevant to correctly interpret data.*

A **Context Interval** is an association between a context and the time interval in which it holds (i.e., the span of time in which data are influenced by the specified context).

Events represent the occurrences of actions or process executions, or any other external thing that can potentially change the patient's status.

An **Event Interval** is the association between an event and a time interval in which the event occurs.

An event (but also a parameter or an abstraction goal described in the following) can *induce* one or more contexts (see Example 9.5). In the KBTA approach, this aspect is modeled through a **dynamic induction relation of a context interval (DIRC)**, which formally is a relation in which each member is a structure of the form $\langle \xi, \varphi, ss, se, es, ee \rangle$ (where ξ is the induced context, φ is the inducing element and ss, se, es, ee — where at least two elements must be valorized — denote the temporal distances between the starting/ending points of their intervals).

Example 9.5 *The event of administering azidothymidine (φ) induces a (potential) azidothymidine-toxicity interpretation context (ξ) that starts 2 weeks*

---

[1]For instance, a similar knowledge model has been adopted by the approach in [12] to detect and manage interactions among clinical guidelines for the treatment of patients affected by comorbidities.

after the beginning of the azidothymidine administration event (ss) and ends 4 weeks after the ending of that event (ee). The formal DIRC representing this situation is ⟨`AZT-TOXICITY, AZT, +2w, *, *, +4w`⟩.

A **Parameter** represents a (quantifiable) aspect of the patient's state (e.g., the blood glucose level) or, more in general, of the state of the world. Parameters can have *properties*, such as a description of their value domains (symbolic or numeric values, measurement units, and a measurement scale). A parameter can be associated with its *value*, and eventually *interpreted* over a context.

A **Parameter Interval** is the association of a parameter, a value and a possible interpretation context with a time interval or, in the degenerate case, a timestamp. Intuitively, it represents the span of time in which the parameter assumes the associated value, possibly interpreted over the context.

We can distinguish among two types of parameters: primitive and abstract ones. Basically, *primitive parameters* are raw data: they directly derive from an observation of patient's state (e.g., due to laboratory tests). On the other hand, *abstract parameters* are parameters deriving from an elaboration (i.e., the temporal abstraction task described in Section 9.3.2) of primitive ones. In [261], three main types of abstract parameters are identified: state, gradient and rate parameters.

A **State** is a classification of the value of a parameter. The admitted values for states are parameter- and task-specific. In case of abstractions of numeric values, it may belong to the set {`HIGH, LOW, NORMAL`}; in other cases, it can have a completely different domain (e.g., the value `MODERATE_ANEMIA` is admissible for the state abstraction Hemoglobin level state).

A **Gradient** is the direction of the parameters' change. Usually, the allowed values for the gradient parameter belong to the set {`DECREASING, INCREASING, SAME, NONINCREASING, NONDECREASING, NONMONOTONIC`} and further refinements.

A **Rate** is a classification of the rate of change of a parameter. The allowed values for the rate parameter belong to the set {`STABLE, STATIC, SLOW, FAST`} or to other domain-specific sets.

A particular type of abstraction parameter is the **temporal pattern**. Temporal patterns are abstractions of several other parameters, under specific contexts (see, e.g., Example 9.6)

Example 9.6 *A* `QUIESCENT-ONSET CHRONIC` *value of the parameter Graft-Versus-Host Disease (GVHD) is defined as a* `CHRONIC` *GVHD state starting at least 100 days after a bone-marrow transplantation event, but within 1 month of the end of a preceding* `ACUTE` *GVHD.*

Temporal patterns are usually the output of the temporal abstraction techniques, and the conditions expressed within clinical guidelines often require the occurrence of one or more temporal patterns in clinical data.

An **Abstraction Goal** is a proposition that denotes a particular goal or intention that is relevant to the temporal-abstraction task during some interval (e.g., the intention to control a diabetes patient's blood-glucose values). Intuitively, an abstraction goal represents the fact that an intention holds or that a goal should be achieved during the time interval over which it is interpreted.

An **Abstraction Goal Interval** is the association of an abstraction goal with a time interval in which the goal must be achieved.

The representation of these basic elements is not enough to represent the whole knowledge needed to perform temporal abstraction. In addition, a description of the relationships among these elements and of their behaviors over the time is needed. In particular, Shahar [259] identifies four types of knowledge: structural knowledge, classification knowledge, temporal semantic knowledge and temporal dynamic knowledge.

Structural knowledge represents the structural organization of the entities within the clinical domain. For instance, it models the relations between events and sub-events (see Example 9.7), contexts and sub-contexts (see Example 9.8), parameters (e.g., Hemoglobin level IS-A hematological parameter) and their abstractions and the properties of these elements (e.g., type of values, scale, units of measurement, range of the parameter Hemoglobin level).

Example 9.7 *(events and sub-events) The administration of azidothymidine, is a sub-event of the event CCTG-522 AIDS-treatment protocol (execution). In the approach by Shahar, this piece of knowledge is modeled through the* PART-OF *relation.*

Example 9.8 *(contexts and sub-contexts) Both the events in Example 9.7 induce one or some contexts. The potential context "azidothymidine toxicity" induced by the azidothymidine administration is a* SUBCONTEXT *of the context induced by the CCTG-522 AIDS-treatment protocol.*

A particular role is assumed by the relations modeling the fact that the values of one or more parameters can be abstracted into values of other (high-level) parameters (see Example 9.9). Besides the available abstractions, the structural knowledge contains also the knowledge about the qualitative dependencies (i.e., POSITIVELY PROPORTIONAL, NEGATIVELY PROPORTIONAL, AND NO MONOTONIC relations) describing the relations between the low-level parameters and the high-level abstracted ones.

A simple example of abstraction is the one occurring between a parameter representing the value of a laboratory measurement and the parameter representing the state abstracted from such a measurement. For instance,

Example 9.9 *The parameter Hemoglobin level (with numeric values, obtained from a blood examination) can be abstracted (relation* ABSTRACTED-INTO*) into the parameter Hemoglobin state (with values* LOW, MEDIUM, HIGH*).*

Classification knowledge maps the values of low-level parameters to values of abstracted parameters. Basically, it can be divided into vertical and horizontal classification knowledge. Vertical classification knowledge is needed for mapping contemporaneous parameter values into a value of an abstracted parameter (see Example 9.10). It can be usually represented through (classification) tables or functions.

Example 9.10 *Blood glucose level should be classified into a Blood glucose state (holding in the same span of time) LOW if lower than 70 mg/dl, HIGH if higher than 110 mg/dl, MEDIUM otherwise.*

On the other hand, horizontal classification knowledge represents the relations between consecutive meeting elements and their compositions. Elements can be values of the same parameter (see Example 9.11) or values of different parameters. Usually, in the first case, horizontal classification knowledge is modeled through horizontal inference tables with tuples of the form $\langle \pi, v_1, v_2, v_3, \xi \rangle$ where π is the involved parameter, v_1 and v_2 are the consecutive values, ξ (optional) models a context, and v_3 is the value assumed by π in the resulting composition.

Example 9.11 *Two consecutive intervals in which the parameter Blood pressure assumes the values INCREASING and DECREASING can be represented as an interval in which the parameter Blood pressure has the value NONMONOTONIC.*

Horizontal classification knowledge is also needed to classify complex temporal patterns as the one in Example 9.6.

Temporal semantic knowledge represents the inferential properties (i.e., the relations among propositions attached to intervals, and propositions attached to their subintervals) of the elements (e.g., downward-hereditary, concatenable, gestalt, universally diffusive) and their truth values.

Example 9.12 *(downward-hereditary property) Given an interval in which the Hemoglobin level has the value LOW, Hemoglobin level has the same value LOW in each sub-interval of the original one.*

Temporal dynamic knowledge, modeling the dynamic behavior of the parameters involved, such as expected persistence (validity) of a measurement both before and after that measurement was actually taken, the maximal gap between two intervals allowing their union, or the value of a minimal significant change within a certain interpretation context. Usually, temporal dynamic knowledge is represented with functions. For instance, the maximal gap between two intervals allowing their union is given by a function Δ, having as input the context, the parameter, the values of the two intervals and their length.

Example 9.13 *In some contexts, given two intervals, each 1 week long, of LOW Hemoglobin level, separated by a gap of a week, an abstraction such as "3 weeks of Hemoglobin level with value LOW" can be created.*

9.2.3 Representation of Temporal Constraints

Temporal constraints are important to represent the flow of actions in a clinical guideline. For example, some actions have to be performed in a temporal sequence, i.e., in a specified order establishing what is the next action to be executed, or in parallel, i.e., starting and/or ending concurrently. They can also be linked by more complex temporal relations. Examples of temporal relations are:

Example 9.14 *Action A must last* 10 *minutes (quantitative temporal constraint about durations)*

Example 9.15 *Action A_2 must start* 60 *minutes after the end of A_1 (quantitative temporal constraint about delays between actions).*

Such temporal constraints can possibly have some degree of "vagueness", as

Example 9.16 *Action A must last between* 10 *and* 20 *minutes (indeterminate quantitative temporal constraint about durations)*

and

Example 9.17 *Action A_2 must start no more than* 60 *minutes after the end of A_1 (indeterminate quantitative temporal constraint about delays between actions).*

Temporal relations can also be qualitative:

Example 9.18 *Action A_1 must be executed before A_2 (qualitative constraint).*

Also qualitative constraints can be indeterminate in the sense that more qualitative relations can be possible such as

Example 9.19 *Action A_2 must start at the same time or after A_1*

Moreover, certain actions can be repeated. Some temporal constraints are implicit and derive from the structure of the guideline. Let us consider the case where an action in the guideline is a composite action: its component actions have to be executed at the same time when the composite action is executed, even if there is no explicit temporal constraint stating it. Let us consider a fragment of a clinical guideline for the treatment of multiple myeloma:

Example 9.20 *The therapy for multiple myeloma is made by six cycles of five-day treatment, each one followed by a delay of 23 days (for a total time of 24 weeks). Within each cycle of five days, two inner cycles can be distinguished: the melphalan treatment, to be provided twice a day, for each of the five days, and the prednisone treatment, to be provided once a day, for each of the five days. These two treatments must be performed in parallel.*

In Example 9.20 there are two atomic actions, i.e., the administration of melphalan and the administration of prednisone. Such actions have to be repeated at regular times (melphalan administration twice a day and prednisone administration once a day). It is worth noticing that the guideline does not specify exactly at which time during the day they have to be administered, so that there is some imprecision in the temporal specification that has to be supported. The atomic actions are part of two composite actions, i.e., the prednisone treatment cycle and the melphalan treatment cycle. Each composite action has to be repeated in its turn for five days and the two composite actions have to be executed in parallel. In their turn each treatment cycle must be followed, before being repeated, by a delay of 23 days.

The example is paradigmatic, since it includes different types of constraints, such as qualitative and quantitative constraints, and periodic constraints on the repetitions.

Thus, the interplay between the different types of constraints has to be supported. For example, the interaction between composite and periodic events might be complex to represent and manage. Let us consider a composite periodic event with a temporal pattern that regards its components, which may, recursively, be composite and/or periodic events. For instance, in the example above, the administration of melphalan must respect the temporal pattern "twice a day, for 5 days", but such a pattern must be repeated for six cycles, each one followed by a delay of 23 days, since the melphalan treatment is part of the general therapy for multiple myeloma.

GLARE and Asbru are probably the two clinical guideline systems that devote more attention to the representation and management of temporal constraints.

The *GLARE (Guideline Acquisition, Representation and Execution)* system [9, 289, 290] is a domain-independent system for acquiring, representing and executing clinical guidelines. GLARE's temporal constraint language focuses on the specification of explicit constraints on the actions in the guideline.

In GLARE, a guideline is represented as a hierarchical graph, where nodes are the actions and arcs are the control relations linking them. GLARE distinguishes between *atomic* and *composite* actions (plans), where atomic actions represent simple steps in a CIG and plans represent actions that can be defined in terms of their components via the *has-part* relation.

The control relations establish which actions can be executed next and in what order. In particular, the *sequence* relation explicitly establishes what the following action to be executed is; the *alternative* relation describes which alternative paths stem from a decision action and the *repetition* relation states that an action has to be repeated several times. The *constrained* relation is used in order to express more complex temporal relations between actions. In GLARE it is possible to express precise and imprecise dates, durations, delays and complex forms of repetitions [13].

The representation of time in GLARE is based on a two-layer approach:

1. A high-level layer provides a high-level language to represent the temporal phenomena and to offer several temporal reasoning facilities;

2. The low-level layer consists of an internal representation of the temporal constraints, on which temporal constraint propagation algorithms operate.

Such a structure allows to provide an intuitive and high-level language which can be used for modeling temporal information; such a high-level language is automatically translated into the low-level language, which is more suitable for temporal reasoning (see the next section).

GLARE's temporal high-level language is designed with specific attention to modeling repeated actions, and in such a way that tractable temporal reasoning can be supported.

In GLARE dates can be expressed by the predicate $date(A, L_1, U_1, L_2, U_2)$, stating that the action A must start between dates L_1 and U_1 and end between dates L_2 and U_2. Precise dates can be expressed imposing $L1 = U1$ or $L2 = U2$. Please note that also unknown dates are allowed by imposing that the extremes assume value $-\infty$ or $+\infty$. Durations can be expressed by the predicate $duration(A, L, U)$, stating that the duration of action A must be included between L and U. Delay with the predicate $delay(P_1, P_2, L, U)$, stating that the delay between P_1 and P_2 must be between L and U, where P_1 and P_2 are time points (i.e., starting or ending points of actions). Also qualitative temporal constraints such as "before", "after", "during" are supported by GLARE. For example, the predicate $before(A, B)$ states that action A must be executed before B. The language supports all and only the qualitative constraints that can be mapped to conjunctions of STP constraints.

For instance, Examples 9.14–9.18 can be represented in GLARE as in the following (assuming a granularity of minutes).

- **Example 9.14'.** $duration(A, 10, 10)$

- **Example 9.15'.** $delay(A_1, A_2, 60, 60)$

- **Example 9.16'.** $duration(A, 10, 20)$

- **Example 9.17'.** $delay(A_1, A_2, 0, 60)$

- **Example 9.18'.** $before(A_1, A_2)$

In GLARE composite actions are represented with the predicate $partOf(A', A)$, stating that the action A' is part of the action A. As mentioned above, the part-of relation induces an implicit temporal constraint between the actions: the component action A' must be executed during the composite action A. Repeated actions are represented with the predicate $repetition(A, RSpec)$, to state that the (possibly composite) action A is repeated according to the repetition pattern $RSpec$. $RSpec$ consists of an arbitrary number of nestings of a quadruple of the form

$(NRep, ITime, RConstr, Cond)$. Roughly speaking, the $NRep$ component of the quadruple specifies the number of repetitions, $ITime$ represents the time span in which the repetitions must be included, $RConstr$ (which is optional) may impose a pattern that the repetitions must follow, and $Cond$ (which is optional) allows to express conditions that must hold so that the repetition can take place.

In particular, $RConstr$ can be $fromStart(min, max)$, representing a possibly imprecise delay between the start of the $ITime$ and the beginning of the first repetition, $toEnd(min, max)$, representing a possibly imprecise delay between the end of the last repetition and the end of the $ITime$, $inBetweenAll(min, max)$, representing a possibly imprecise delay between the end of each repetition and the start of the subsequent one, $inBetween((min_1, max_1), \ldots, (min_{nRep_i-1}, max_{nRep_i-1}))$, representing a possibly imprecise delays between each repetition and the subsequent one. Note that any pair (min_j, max_j) may be missing, for indicating that any delay between the jth repetition and the $(j+1)^{th}$ one is possible.

$Cond$ can be either $while(C)$ (where C is a Boolean predicate) stating that, when C becomes false, the repetition ends, and $onlyIf(C)$ (where C is a Boolean predicate) stating that, if C is true, the repetition may be performed and, if C is false, the repetition must not be performed and we can pass to the next repetition. Informally, the semantics of a quadruple $(NRep, ITime, RConstr, Cond)$ can be roughly described by the natural language sentence "repeat the action $NRep$ times in exactly $ITime$, if $Cond$ holds". For example, assuming the granularity of days, the fact that, in the Example 9.20, the melphalan treatment is composed by the action melphalan, which is administered twice a day, and such repetitions must be in its turn repeated five times in five days, can be represented as:

Example 9.20' $Repetition(melphalan, ((5, 5\ days), (2, 1\ days)))$.

As a further example, let us consider the following:

Example 9.21 *Intrathecal methotrexate must be administered 7 times during 88 weeks, never less than 10 weeks apart or more than 14 weeks apart.*

Example 9.21 can be represented with as

Example 9.21' $Repetition(IntrathecalMethotrexate,$
$((7, 88\ weeks, \{inBetweenAll(10\ weeks, 14weeks)\})))$.

GLARE also allows one to represent the time of execution of actions on specific patients using an instance-of relation. In such a way, instances of actions may "inherit" temporal constraints from the guideline they refer to. The predicate $instanceOf(I, A, p)$ represents the fact that I is an instance of the action A. If A is a repeated action, then it represents the fact that I is an instance of the pth repetition of A (if A is not a repeated action, $p = 1$).

Asbru [185, 260] proposes an expressive task-specific and intention-based representation language whose focus lies on the representation of explicit declarative temporal aspects of the guidelines. Asbru's temporal annotations allow to represent uncertainty in starting time, ending time and duration of a time interval. The temporal annotation supports multiple time lines by providing different reference annotations. A *reference annotation* can be an absolute reference point, a reference point with uncertainty (defined by an uncertainty region), a function (e.g., completion time) of a previously executed plan instance, or a domain-dependent time point variable (e.g., CONCEPTION). Uncertainty in the starting time, ending time and duration of a time interval can be represented as temporal displacements (shifts) from a reference annotation. Thus, a *temporal annotation* has the form $[[ESS, LSS], [EFS, LFS], [MinDu, MaxDu]]$ and represents the earliest starting shift (ESS), the latest starting shift (LSS), the earliest finishing shift (EFS), the latest finishing shift (LFS), the minimal duration ($MinDu$) and the maximal duration ($MaxDu$).

Let us consider the following example:

Example 9.22 *The plan GDM-II for the treatment of gestational diabetes mellitus of type II should be executed in a time interval starting between 0 and 8 weeks after the conception, finishing no earlier than 24 weeks after the conception, and lasting at least 18 weeks.*

Assuming a granularity of weeks, the temporal constraint in Example 9.22 between GDM-II and CONCEPTION can be represented with the time annotation $[[0, 8], [24, \_], [18, \_]]$, which has $ESS = 0$, $LSS = 8$, $EFS = 24$, $MinDu = 18$, and there is no restriction on LFS and $MaxDu$.

Asbru supports also repetitions through the notion of cyclical time points (e.g., MIDNIGHTS, representing the set of midnights, where each midnight occurs exactly at 0:00 a.m. every 24 hours) and cyclical time annotations (e.g., MORNINGS, which represents the set of mornings, where each morning starts at the earliest at 8:00 a.m., ends at the latest at 11:00 a.m., and lasts at least 30 minutes). For instance, assuming a granularity of hours,

Example 9.23 *The set of midnights is defined as MIDNIGHTS ← [0, 0, 24]*

Asbru allows the use of "shortcuts" for indicating the current time, whatever that time is, (using the symbol *NOW*) or the duration of the plan (using the symbol *). Thus, the Asbru notation enables the representation of interval-based intentions, states and prescribed actions with uncertainty regarding the start, the end and the duration, and the use of absolute, relative and even cyclical (with a predetermined granularity) reference annotations.

The actual implementation of the Asbru language can be achieved using several languages, such as through the Constraint based Pattern Specification Language CAPSUL [57].

Also various other clinical guideline systems provide support for representing temporal information in clinical guidelines. The InterMed project, a joint project of groups at Columbia, Harvard and Stanford universities, developed the GuideLine Interchange Format (GLIF) [36, 206]. GLIF used the Guideline Expression Language (GEL) [206] that is based on the Arden Syntax [209], later evolved in an object-oriented form GELLO [273].

A GEL temporal expression contemplates two main types of temporal expressions, both defining the frequency of a repetition and its duration: a *times expression* and a *every expression*. A times expression specifies that an event occurs a certain number of times within a certain interval (e.g., "two times a day"). An every expression specifies that an event occurs every fuzzy duration (e.g., every four hours). A *fuzzy duration* is a duration that has an associated before and after uncertainty period (e.g., a before and after uncertain period of half an hour results in a fuzzy duration of [3.5 hours, 4.5 hours]).

The GEL language supports temporal relations such as *is_within*, *preceding*, *following*, *surrounding*, *is_before*, *is_after*, *occurs_at* and *overlaps*.

GELLO is based on the Object Constraint Language and was adopted in 2005 as an international standard by HL7 and ANSI for a decision support language [126].

The GUIDE project [225] was developed at the University of Pavia, Italy. It is based on Petri nets and it integrates clinical guidelines with workflow management systems and electronic patient records. In GUIDE a Careflow monitors the patient's history, which is inserted by physicians; the physician is required to enter the patients' symptoms onset date, the time from the onset and the symptom persistence. This information is used by the system in simple temporal expressions such as: "if the time from the onset of symptoms is less than six hours".

PROforma was developed by Fox et al. [98, 283] at the Advanced Computation Laboratory of Cancer Research UK. PROforma supports four tasks: actions, plans, decisions and enquiries. A plan can contain a set of atomic tasks as actions, decisions and enquiries. A plan can also contain other plans. Guidelines are modeled as plans. Each plan may define scheduling constraints on the atomic tasks such as task duration and delays between two tasks. Moreover it is possible to define temporal constraints on plans, such as cycles with number of repetitions and durations.

DILEMMA and PRESTIGE [108], whose development was discontinued in 1999, model temporal constraints within conditions.

EON [195, 303] uses a temporal mediator, Tzolkin, i.e., an intermediate layer between a standard relational database and the EON guideline system. Tzolkin incorporates the RÉSUMÉ system, which provides temporal abstraction facilities over "raw" timestamped medical data, and Chronus, which provides a temporal extension to SQL. The Arden Syntax allows the representation of delays between a triggering event and the activation of a Medical Logic Module (MDL), and also between MDLs [264]. In [335] the authors proposed a rich ontology to deal with temporal information in clinical trial protocols, considering also relative and indeterminate temporal information and cyclical event patterns.

SAGE (Standards-Based Active Guideline Environment) [302] was developed by a consortium consisting of medical informatics groups at GE Healthcare, the University of Nebraska Medical Center, Intermountain Health Care, Apelon, Inc., Stanford University and the Mayo Clinic. It builds upon previous work on guideline modeling and in particular upon Asbru, GEM, GLIF, EON, PROforma, GUIDE and PRODIGY and it uses Protégé as a knowledge-engine platform. As expression language — and thus also as temporal expressions — it adopts GELLO, as GLIF [304].

9.3 REASONING ABOUT TIME IN CLINICAL GUIDELINES

Representing and *storing* temporal information regarding clinical guidelines and patients' data is not sufficient if support for *temporal reasoning* is not provided as well. Indeed, a complete automatic treatment of temporal constraints requires not only the design of expressive representation formalisms that capture temporal information in clinical guidelines, but it is also fundamental to pair such formalisms with temporal reasoning mechanisms. In addition to the temporal information explicitly represented as discussed in the previous section, it is necessary to take into account all the relevant knowledge, including the implicit one that can be obtained from the knowledge explicitly represented. We exemplify such concept in the following section regarding constraint propagation (Section 9.3.1), but it holds as well also for the other type of temporal reasoning we discuss, i.e., temporal abstraction (Section 9.3.2).

9.3.1 Constraint Propagation

9.3.1.1 Introduction to Constraint Propagation

Before introducing the temporal propagation algorithms, we briefly motivate the need for it. As an example, let us consider the following quantitative temporal constraints where A, B, and C are time points (such as starting/ending points of an action or a punctual event):

(i) A is 2 to 4 hours before B;

(ii) B is 2 to 4 hours before C;

(iii) A is 2 to 6 hours before C.

For example, suppose that the constraints (i), (ii), and (iii) are explicitly represented in a clinical guideline. Temporal reasoning can be used in order to infer the constraints implied by such constraints, such as

(iv) A is 4 to 6 hours before C

Inferring implied constraints is fundamental. For instance, suppose that an expert-physician wants to add a new constraint such as

(v) A is 2 hours before C

to the above ones. If no temporal reasoning is performed, such an addition would be accepted. However, the set $\{(i), (ii), (iii), (v)\}$ is not consistent, i.e., the guideline with such constraints is *not* executable at all. On the other hand, temporal reasoning can be adopted to propagate the constraints and detect the inconsistency, so that the system can reject the physician's update.

Clinical guidelines used in practice can include hundreds of actions, and contain various kinds of temporal constraints, so that humans cannot take into account and reason about all the temporal constraints. Thus, an automatic system which deals efficiently with them is fundamental. An automatic system can also grant some important properties such as *correctness* and *completeness* of the reasoning process.

Correctness, is, obviously, a mandatory property. Proving that a temporal reasoning algorithm is correct assures that it only infers constraints that are logically implied from the initial temporal constraints and that no wrong inference is made. For instance, an algorithm which is not correct could infer constraint (v) from the constraints (i), (ii), and (iii).

Notably, also the *completeness* property is a fundamental property. As a matter of facts, if the reasoning is not complete, the system is not able to grant to provide correct answers to temporal queries. Suppose, for instance, that the temporal reasoning algorithm is not complete, so that the constraint (iv) is not inferred by the system. Suppose also that a physician, operating on a patient, asks to the system how long she can wait to perform C (after the execution of A). The answer would be to wait between 2 and 6 hours, but, indeed, the guideline is *not* executable (respecting the temporal constraints) if the delay is 2 or 3 hours.

As an example, we now introduce a simple and widely adopted framework for temporal reasoning, the Simple Temporal Problem. In the next sections, we describe the temporal facilities that temporal reasoning can offer in the context of clinical guidelines, how some clinical guideline system offer temporal facilities by extending the basic temporal framework and then we discuss other approaches to temporal reasoning in the area of Artificial Intelligence.

The *Simple Temporal Problem* (henceforth STP) framework supports *correct and complete* temporal constraint propagation on bounds on differences constraints [76]. An STP constraint is a bounded difference of the form $c \leq x - y \leq d$, where x and y are temporal points and c and d are numbers whose domain can be either discrete or dense. The intuitive temporal interpretation of the constraint is that the temporal distance between the time points x and y is between c (minimum distance) and d (maximum distance). It is possible to specify also strict inequalities (i.e., $<$), and $-\infty$ and $+\infty$ can be used to denote infinite lower and upper bounds respectively (i.e., no lower or upper bound). An STP is a set of STP constraints, i.e., a conjunction of STP constraints.

Two representations are often used for STPs: graph and matrix. An STP is represented as a graph whose nodes correspond to the temporal points of the STP and the arcs are labeled with a weight representing the maximum temporal distance between the temporal points. A constraint $c \leq x - y \leq d$ is thus represented by two edges corresponding to the pair of inequalities $x - y \leq d$ and $y - x \leq c$. For short, usually the arcs are labeled with the interval $[c, d]$. Alternatively, an STP is represented as a matrix D of size $N \cdot N$ where N is the number of temporal points and where the element $D[x, y] = d$ represents the maximum distance d between the points x and y. The minimum distance c is represented as the maximum distance $D[y, x] = c$ between y and x.

Example 9.24 *Constraints (i), (ii), and (iii) can be represented as an STP containing three STP constraints $S = \{2 \leq B - A \leq 4, 2 \leq C - B \leq 4, 2 \leq C - A \leq 6\}$. In Fig. 9.1 S is represented both as a graph and in Table 9.1 as a matrix.*

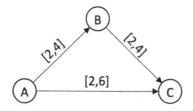

FIGURE 9.1 STP for constraints (i), (ii), and (iii) represented as a graph.

TABLE 9.1 STP for constraints (i), (ii), and (iii) represented as a matrix.

	A	B	C
A	0	4	6
B	-2	0	4
C	-2	-2	0

STP can also represent a fragment of the qualitative temporal constraints of the Allen's algebra called continuous pointizable constraints [139].

Example 9.25 *The qualitative constraint "A1 before A2" can be expressed as the STP constraint $-\infty < A1_{End} - A2_{Start} < 0$ where $A1_{End}$ and $A2_{Start}$ represent the ending point of A1 and the starting point of A2, respectively.*

Temporal reasoning on STP is performed by propagating the constraints. Such a propagation obtains the *minimal network*, which is the tightest equivalent STP, i.e., an STP where all pairwise temporal constraints are made explicit and correspond to the minimum and maximum allowed distances between each pair of points taking into account all the temporal constraints. An interesting feature of STP is that constraint propagation corresponds to computing the *all-pairs shortest paths* of the graph; an algorithm such as the classic Floyd-Warshall's one can be used [76]. Such an algorithm determines whether an STP is consistent by checking if after the propagation there are negative cycles. Floyd-Warshall's algorithm is shown below; in the algorithm $1 \ldots n$ denote the time points (e.g., starting/ending points of actions) and D the matrix of distances.

Floyd-Warshall's algorithm

```
1. for k:=1 to n do
2.   for i:=1 to n do
3.     for j:=1 to n do
4.       D[i,j]:=min(D[i,j],D[i,k]+D[k,j])
```

Floyd-Warshall's algorithm is *correct* and *complete* on STP, i.e., it performs all and only the correct inferences while propagating the STP constraints [76]. Its temporal computational cost is cubic in the number of time points.

Applying Floyd-Warshall's algorithm to the STP S in Example 9.24 allows one to determinate the minimal network of S, where it is made explicit that, if B occurs at least 2 hours after A and C at least 2 hours after B, C must occur at least 4 hours after A. This new STP constraint corresponds to constraint (iv) above and makes it evident that constraint (v) is not compatible to constraints (i), (ii), and (iii) (indeed, the intersection of the constraints (iv) and (v) is empty). In Figure 9.2 the minimal network for the STP S is represented both as a graph and in Table 9.2 as a matrix.

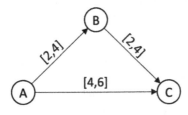

FIGURE 9.2 Minimal network for the STP related to constraints (i), (ii), and (iii) represented as a graph.

TABLE 9.2 Minimal network for the STP related to constraints (i), (ii), and (iii) represented as a matrix.

	A	B	C
A	0	4	6
B	-2	0	4
C	-4	-2	0

9.3.1.2 Temporal Facilities for Clinical Guidelines

A main task of temporal reasoning in clinical guidelines is that of checking the consistency of temporal constraints. Indeed, since, as said above, guidelines can consist of many actions, it cannot be taken for granted that the temporal constraints relating them are temporally consistent. As a consequence of an inconsistency, it would not be possible to consider reliable any information provided by the guideline, at least regarding time.

Performing temporal reasoning for checking the consistency of a guideline is useful in at least two phases of the lifecycle of a guideline: in the acquisition phase and in the execution phase.

During the *acquisition phase*, (a) the facility of checking the consistency of the temporal constraints in the guideline is useful to help the physician/knowledge engineer to ensure that it is possible to execute the guideline without violating the temporal constraints; in fact, if a guideline is not temporally consistent, there is no possible way to execute it.

During the *execution phase*, when a guideline is executed on a specific patient, (b) the facility of checking the consistency of both the temporal constraints of the guideline and the temporal constraints deriving from the guideline execution is useful to verify whether the execution temporally adheres to the guideline, important from the point of view of quality evaluation/assessment.

Moreover, in the execution phase, for scheduling purposes a guideline system can provide (c) a facility to assess when the next actions have to be performed, given the constraints in the whole guideline and given the time when the last actions in the guideline have been executed.

One of the main goals of guideline computer-based systems is to support decision making. In such a context, providing a (d) temporal query-answering facility is a crucial task. Such queries can be yes/no queries such as, e.g., "Is it correct to execute action A now, and action B within the next two hours?", or queries to obtain latest/earliest times such as, e.g., "When will I have to execute action A as early/late as possible?"

Another useful facility that can be provided to physicians by a guideline system is a (e) temporal "what if?" facility for expressing queries such as, e.g., "If I execute action A tomorrow, when can I execute action B?" or "If I execute actions A and B at the same time, when will the guideline's execution end?"

Still considering decision making, temporal reasoning can be profitably coupled with **(f) a facility to foresee the temporal consequences of choosing among different alternative paths in a guideline**, thus allowing physicians with a tool to discriminate among different alternatives of a decision by simulating the temporal consequences of each choice.

Last, but not least, temporal reasoning can be used in order to manage the **(g) controllability problem** for clinical guidelines execution. In short, in the general context in which one cannot assume that the duration of the execution of the guideline actions is totally under the control of the user-physician executing it, it is important to grant that, whatever the duration of a set of future actions will be, the guideline is still executable (respecting its temporal constraints).

9.3.1.3 Constraint Propagation in Clinical Guideline Systems

The most interesting clinical guideline systems that emphasize temporal reasoning are GLARE and Asbru, both based on STP. Since, to the best of our knowledge, specific temporal reasoning algorithms (other than STP) of Asbru have not been published, we mainly focus our discussion on GLARE.

As discussed in Section 9.2, for representing temporal information in clinical guidelines it is necessary to support possibly imprecise qualitative and qualitative temporal constraints, repetitions and the implicit temporal constraints deriving from a partonomic structure. Thus, it is not possible to simply adopt "as it is" a temporal reasoning approach such as STP.

GLARE uses, as the low-level layer temporal language, an extension of STP. In a certain sense, STP is used as an "assembly language" over which an expressive high-level temporal reasoning framework is built on top. Obviously, the gap between GLARE's high-level temporal language and STP is very large. Filling such a gap involves the design of suitable temporal reasoning algorithms to cope with the issues emerging from the treatment of clinical guidelines, as well as an extension of the STP framework itself. The basic idea in GLARE is to model the simple constraints such as durations, delays in STP, and to augment STP with a specific construct for dealing with repetitions. The topology of the clinical guidelines imposed by partonomic and periodicity constraints impose a tree structure (in other words, there cannot be a cycle in the part-of relations on in the periodicity specifications). Thus, the temporal information of a guideline can be represented as a labelled tree of STPs. The root of the tree is the STP which represents the constraints between all the actions in the guideline, except the components of repeated actions; the other nodes of the tree are the repeated actions and the repetition constraints are the labels of the edges of the tree.

The STP-tree corresponding to a guideline can be automatically con-

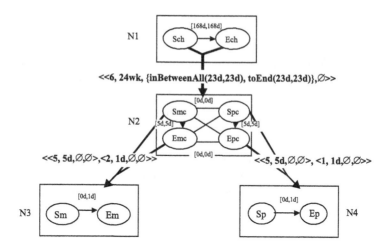

FIGURE 9.3 STP-tree for the multiple myeloma chemotherapy guideline in Example 9.20. Edges inside STPs represent STP constraints.
Edges between STPs represent repetitions. *Sch*, *Ech*, *Smc*, *Emc*, *Spc*,
Epc, *Sm*, *Em*, *Sp* and *Ep* stand for the starting (*S*) and ending (*E*)
points of chemotherapy, melphalan cycle, prednisone cycle, melphalan
treatment and prednisone treatment, respectively.

structed on the basis of the temporal constraints in the guideline expressed
using the high-level language.

For instance, in Figure 9.3, we show the STP-tree representing the temporal constraints in Example 9.20. In order to check the consistency of an STP-
tree (*facility (a)*), it is not sufficient to check separately the consistency of each
STP contained in its nodes. In such a case, in fact, the repetition/periodicity
information would be neglected. Temporal-consistency checking, thus, proceeds in a top-down fashion, starting from the root of the STP-tree toward
the leaves of the tree. For each node in the STP-tree (except the root, which
can be checked as a standard STP), the algorithm *STPTreeConsistency* in
the following is applied:

```
function STPTreeConsistency(X: STPNode,
                    ((NRep1, ITime1, RConstr1, Cond1),
                    ..., (NRepn, ITimen, RConstrn, Condn))
1. check that the repetition/periodicity constraint is
   well-formed (i.e., that repetitions nest properly)
2. compute Max, i.e. the maximum duration of a single
   repetition of X according to RSpec
3. impose in X that the maximum distance between each pair of
   points is less or equals Max
```

```
4. X := FloydWarshall(X)
5. if X = INCONSISTENT then return INCONSISTENT else return X
```

The algorithm, which is correct and complete, first checks whether the repetition constraint is well-formed, then computes the maximum duration of a repetition, adds such information to the STP in the node and finally propagates the temporal constraints.

GLARE also provides a correct and complete algorithm for checking the consistency of the execution of a guideline with respect to the related guideline, taking into account also the temporal constraints emerging from the execution of the actions on the specific patient (*facility (b)*). For representing such constraints, an additional STP is used containing the specific instances of the actions of the guidelines. Assuming, as in most approaches to clinical guidelines, that there is full observability of instances (i.e., that all the instances of actions which have been executed have been observed and inserted into the knowledge base), and that, for each instance, one knows the corresponding class of actions and/or repetition in the guidelines, the consistency check proceeds as follows.

IntegratedConsistency algorithm (described only informally):

1. Check that in the execution STP there are all and only the instances that the STP-tree predicts to be. Possible missing instances are hypothesized because they may happen in the future;

2. Inherit the repetition constraints and the temporal (non-periodic) constraints from the classes to the instances;

3. Propagate the temporal constraints on the execution STP, thus obtaining the minimal network;

4. Check whether the hypothesized instances expected in the future may actually start in the future (i.e., after NOW).

While the two algorithms described above implement the *facilities of consistency checking (a) and (b)* of Section 9.3.1.2, now we briefly sketch how the other temporal facilities can be provided exploiting the minimal network provided by the *IntegratedConsistency* algorithm.

First of all, to assess when the next actions have to be performed, given the constraints in the whole guideline and the time when the last actions in the guideline have been executed (*facility (c)*), it is possible to execute the following steps:

ObtainNextActions algorithm (described only informally):

1. Retrieve the set of candidate next actions through a navigation of the control-flow relations in the guideline;

2. Apply the algorithm the *IntegratedConsistency* algorithm to obtain the minimal network;

3. Retrieve the actions' possible execution-times from the minimal network (in the form of distances from the last-executed action, or from the origin of time).

The query-answering facility (*facility (d)*) can be efficiently implemented on the basis of the minimal network provided by the *IntegratedConsistency* algorithm along the lines discussed in [42] both to answer yes/no queries and/or to have in output the minimal distance between the instances of actions. To implement such a facility, once the minimal network has been computed, on the one hand the *queries to obtain the latest/earliest times* can be answered by directly inspecting the minimal network and returning the STP constraint between the involved actions. On the other hand, the *yes/no queries* can be answered by provisionally adding the query constraints to the minimal network, by propagating the constraints in a such new STP (to enhance the efficiency the locality properties proven in [41] can be exploited) and by finally inspecting the consistency of the resulting new minimal network.

By combining facility (c) with facility (d), temporal reasoning can also be used in an interactive way to determine schedules which are consistent with the temporal constraints (*facility (e)*). For example, given a pattern $A_1, \ldots, A_n$ of actions in a guideline, temporal reasoning can be used in order to answer queries such as "If I perform action A_1 today at 12 o'clock, when will I have to perform $A_2, \ldots, A_n$?", or "Is it OK if I perform A_1 today at 12, A_2 at 18 and A_3 at 20, and, if so, when will I have to perform A_4?"

GLARE provides physicians with a facility to compare paths from the temporal point of view (i.e., in order to find the maximal and minimal temporal duration of each path) (*facility (f)*) as follows:

ComparePaths algorithm:

1. For each path P_i to be compared:

   (a) Hypothesize the existence of an instance of each action in P_i which has not been executed yet

   (b) Apply the *IntegratedConsistency* algorithm to the (executed and hypothesized) actions in P_i, to determine the minimal network MN_i

   (c) Retrieve the minimal and maximal duration of P_i from MN_i

Last, but not least, the *controllability check* problem (*facility (g)*) has been studied, in the clinical guideline context, by Combi et al. [62]. Basically, in real world scenarios, it is possible that not all the durations of the actions to be executed in a guideline are under the control of the physicians (e.g., the duration of a treatment may depend on the patient's healing). To cope with such an aspect, a distinction must be introduced in STP between *contingent* (i.e., constraints whose effective duration will only be observed at execution time) and *free* constraints (i.e., whose instantiation is controlled by physicians). The resulting problem is an extension of STP called *Simple Temporal Network with*

Uncertainty (STNU) [322]. Controllability in STNU is the capability of finding at least a (possibly different) solution of an STNU for all possible durations of all contingent constraints and satisfying all temporal constraints. Controllability check algorithms restrict the range of free constraints (those controlled by physicians), until controllability is ensured.

The approach in [62] proposes a workflow-based formalism (*TNest*) to model clinical guidelines with contingent constraints. Given a clinical guideline modeled with TNest, it can be automatically mapped into STNU. Then, an algorithm to check the controllability of the STNU is adopted.

9.3.1.4 Constraint Propagation in Artificial Intelligence

In the community of Artificial Intelligence it is possible to identify two mainstreams in the research about temporal reasoning: approaches based on logic and approaches based on constraints. On the one hand, approaches based on logic — which we will not discuss further in this section — focus on the definition of general formalisms capturing the dynamic aspects of the world, and they adopt theorem proving to perform temporal reasoning (consider, e.g., [88, 24]). On the other hand, approaches based on constraints focus on the definition of representation formalisms and of constraint-propagation algorithms that deal specifically with (temporal constraints between) temporal entities (i.e., time points and time intervals), disregarding non-temporal information such as events and states taking place over such entities.

Several temporal constraint formalisms (and relative constraint propagation algorithms) have been proposed in the Artificial Intelligence literature. Such formalisms support various combinations of qualitative temporal constraints (i.e., constraints on the relative order of the events), of quantitative temporal constraints (i.e., constraints involving metric time) over temporal entities such as time points, time intervals or both.

Regarding *qualitative temporal constraints*, the Allen's Interval Algebra [5] is a fundamental approach. Allen identified the 13 basic qualitative relations between two time intervals (e.g., $I_1 \ BEFORE \ I_2$). In the Interval Algebra it is also possible to represent disjunctions of basic relations to express uncertainty (e.g., $I_1 \ BEFORE \ or \ DURING \ I_2$). Checking the consistency of a set of relations in the full Interval Algebra is NP-complete, thus either one limits oneself to small knowledge bases, or accepts a reasoning mechanism that is not complete and it does not draw all the possible inferences, or adopts another formalism.

Krokhin et al. [146] have provided a complete classification of the 18 maximal subsets of IA that are tractable (so that a polynomial algorithm exists). The most important fragment is the ORD-Horn subalgebra [197], which is the only one where all the 13 basic relations are admitted, although, obviously, not all the combinations of the basic relations are admitted.

If one considers as temporal entities time points instead of time intervals, the resulting Point Algebra [323] has three basic relations, i.e., $<$, $=$ and $>$,

and four non-basic relations, i.e., $\leq$, $\geq$, $\neq$ and $<=>$ (this last one is the universal relation). The Point Algebra is tractable. However, if one considers as temporal entities both time points and time intervals and devises a point-interval algebra where the five relations between a point and an interval are taken into account (i.e., before, after, starts, finishes and during), this resulting point-interval algebra is not tractable [323].

Considering *quantitative temporal constraints*, an influential approach is the one by Dechter et al. [76] already discussed in Section 9.3.1. In cases where disjunctions between bounds on difference are admitted (e.g., I_2 started 20–30 minutes *or* 50–60 minutes after the end of I_1), the problem, called Disjunctive Temporal Problem (DTP) [276], is in general NP-hard.

Some approaches have extended such fundamental works to treat also phenomena such as repetitions and periodicities (consider, e.g., [149, 188, 288]). For instance, [288] is an extension of Allen's Interval Algebra to consider also qualitative relations between periodic facts (e.g., "Between January 1, 1999 and December 31, 1999 on the first Monday of each month, Andrea went to the post office before going to work").

Other extensions to STP provide support for uncertainty [322], for probabilistic representation of uncertainty [300], for distributed computation [136] and an optimized treatment of DTP [276, 301].

The problem of *controllability* has been widely studied in the context of Simple Temporal Networks with Uncertainty (STNU) [322] and recently several approaches has been presented copying with controllability for workflow execution [62, 63, 65, 66].

9.3.2   Temporal Abstraction

As already mentioned, in many clinical domains, measurements about patients' conditions are collected in the form of raw timestamped data. Often, in particular in the cases of high-frequency/continuous patient monitoring (consider, for instance, patients hospitalized in intensive care units), large amounts of data are automatically generated in a quite short span of time. However, when they have to be used to perform decision making within clinical guidelines, such data are not very useful if kept in the form of raw timestamped data. On the one hand, considering, in the reasoning process, the whole amount of data can be difficult: a human physician can be easily overwhelmed by the number of considered data, while an automated decision support system can encounter computational problems in managing inputs of such sizes. On the other hand, a single, isolated, timestamped datum is often not very meaningful to identify the patient's condition. For instance, when making diagnoses, analyzing the trend of a parameter values over the time or recognizing the occurrence of a temporal pattern over more parameters is more useful for physicians. Furthermore, such kind of information may also have been discretized and associated with summarizing parameters. For instance, a set of consecutive blood glucose level measurements whose values are all below a given threshold can be associated with the predicate "blood glucose level low" or with the parameter "blood glucose level" with value "low", both valid over a determinate interval including all the timestamps of the original measurements. These higher-level concepts, which "summarize" sets of raw data over specific time intervals, are highly meaningful and easier to manage into the decision making process. They take the name of (temporal) *abstractions*.

Furthermore, to provide an effective summary, data cannot be analyzed in isolation with respect the context in which they have been collected. For instance, a "low" value for the blood glucose level has a completely different interpretation in a context of insulin drug treatment. For this reason, there is the need of identifying the *context intervals* (briefly contexts) representing homogeneous situations, and of limiting the inference mechanisms devoted to temporal abstraction to the data contained in the same context interval. Abstractions must be associated with the context intervals they belong to.

The set of temporal reasoning methodologies to abstract – from raw timestamped data – higher-level concepts (abstractions), associated to contexts, useful for specific goals takes the name of *Temporal Abstraction*.

Many different approaches to temporal abstraction have been proposed in the medical informatics literature (see, e.g., the surveys [16, 274]). The Knowledge Base Temporal Abstraction (KBTA) approach, implemented into the RÉSUMÉ system [259, 261] is particularly relevant in our context, since it specifically focuses on temporal abstractions for clinical guidelines. In the next subsection, we use such an approach to exemplify the temporal abstraction mechanisms and how they use the knowledge described in Section 9.2.2.

9.3.2.1 Temporal Abstraction Mechanisms

The approach in [261] suggests a further specification of the TA techniques. The general task of temporal abstraction can be decomposed into five different subtasks: temporal context restriction, vertical temporal inference, horizontal temporal inference, temporal interpolation, temporal pattern matching. The approaches providing support to temporal abstraction in medical informatics implicitly or explicitly perform some or all such subtasks. In the following, we briefly describe them.

Temporal context restriction creation. Abstractions are meaningful only within a relevant context interval. Thus, to support other temporal inference tasks in computing the most specific abstractions and to avoid computing abstractions for irrelevant contexts, there is the need to identify the most appropriate ones. In the KBTA approach, the context restriction creation is performed dynamically by the *context-forming mechanism* through the combinations of events, abstractions, goals of the abstraction process, and by combinations of existing interpretation contexts. DIRCs (see Section 9.2.2) are used to dynamically infer the induced contexts and their temporal intervals and Allen's algebra [5] is used to compute the relations between the intervals.

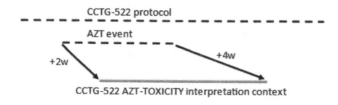

FIGURE 9.4 Example of context restriction creation.

In addition, also structural and classification knowledge (e.g., PART-OF and SUBCONTEXT relations) is used during the inference process.

Example 9.26 *In Figure 9.4 we show an example of context restriction. Given the azidothymidine administration (AZT) event, the AZT-TOXICITY interpretation context is inferred using the DIRC described in Example 9.5. On the other hand, the PART-OF relation (belonging to the structural knowledge) between the CCTG-522 protocol event and the AZT event (which is an action contained in the protocol) is used to create the CCTG-522 AZT-TOXICITY interpretation context (resulting from the intersection between the AZT-TOXICITY interpretation context and the context induced by the CCTG-522 protocol event).*

Vertical temporal inference. Given a context interval, the goal of vertical temporal inference is to abstract from low-level concepts and their time points or time intervals of occurrence, to more meaningful high-level concepts.

The KBTA approach performs vertical temporal inference through the *contemporaneous abstraction* mechanism. Basically, such mechanism performs two sub-tasks: *classification* and *computational transformation*. The first one classifies the value of a parameter into a state (e.g., from numeric values to "high", "medium" or "low"; see Example 9.27) according to the ABSTRACTED-INTO relations and the vertical classification knowledge. On the other hand, computational transformation (which can be considered as an extension of classification) performs abstraction on parameters: it maps one or more parameters and their values into the value of another, higher-level, parameter. Such a mechanism, which is very general, and might involve computing a given "black-box" function, exploits structural knowledge, classification knowledge and temporal dynamic knowledge.

Example 9.27 *The parameter "Hemoglobin blood level" with value 8.0 gr./100cc, occurring at a specific time point, can be abstracted into the parameter "Hemoglobin blood state" (accordingly to the ABSTRACTED-INTO relation) with value "low" (accordingly to the vertical classification knowledge), occurring at the same time point of the basic parameter.*

Horizontal temporal inference. The horizontal temporal inference task has the role to infer abstractions from similar-type clinical propositions, attached to different time intervals. In the KBTA approach, it is computed by the *temporal inference* mechanism, which can be divided into two submechanisms: *temporal-semantic inference* and *temporal horizontal inference*. Temporal-semantic inference accepts as input an abstraction and a context interval, or two abstraction intervals and returns an abstraction interpreted over the context interval, or a new super-interval of the two abstraction intervals using temporal semantic knowledge and Allen's algebra (see Example 9.28).

Example 9.28 *Given a week-long episode of coma (and the downward-hereditary property [265] of coma contained into temporal semantic knowledge), temporal-semantic inference can infer an abstraction of coma during each day included (STARTS, DURING, FINISHES Allen's relations) into the week.*

On the other hand, temporal horizontal inference determines (through the horizontal classification knowledge) the value of the join operation of two meeting abstraction intervals in the same context, where the same parameter has equal or different values.

Example 9.29 *Given two meeting intervals in the same context in which the same parameter assumes the values DECREASING and SAME, they can be concatenated into a NONINCREASING value.*

Temporal interpolation. The goal of temporal interpolation is to bridge gaps between disjoint time points or time intervals, to obtain longer intervals of persistence. The KBTA approach [259] distinguishes between two types of temporal interpolation depending on the input: *primary* and *secondary* interpolation. Primary interpolation abstracts the values of a parameter associated with time points into an abstraction associated to a time interval. Secondary interpolation takes as input data associated with time intervals (or time intervals and time points) and returns abstractions over super-intervals. Another distinction, orthogonal to the first one, is made considering the type of value to be assigned to the abstracted parameter. State type abstractions assign a specific value (e.g., "low"; see Example 9.30), gradient type abstractions associate a gradient (e.g., "increasing", "decreasing" and "same") and rate type abstractions classifies the rates of change (e.g., "stable", "slow") between two time points/intervals.

Example 9.30 *Two measurements of the parameter "Hemoglobin blood level" with value LOW (occurring at two different time points close enough) can be abstracted in a unique interval where the parameter "Hemoglobin blood level" assumes the value LOW.*

However, not all the data can be interpolated among them, and context-specific knowledge is required to perform such an operation. First, temporal semantic knowledge is needed to determinate whether, in the specific context, the input parameters are concatenable (i.e., *upward inheritance* [265] holds). An example of non-concatenable information is shown below.

Example 9.31 *Two consecutive episodes of 9 months of pregnancy cannot be abstracted in a 18 month single episode.*

In addition, two time points/intervals can be concatenated only if they are close enough in time. In the KBTA approach, the idea of "proximity" is given by a function Δ (belonging to the temporal dynamic knowledge) returning the maximal allowed gap to interpolate two time points/intervals. The calculation of Δ depends on the context, on the involved parameters and on the values assumed by the parameters. In case the actual gap is smaller than the maximal allowed gap, the original time points/intervals can be interpolated in one unique interval. The value of the abstraction is specified into the horizontal classification knowledge.

Temporal pattern matching. The task of temporal pattern matching recognizes predefined complex temporal patterns (such as the one in Example 9.32) using as input the abstractions deriving from previous subtasks. Basically, it extends temporal inference and temporal interpolation mechanisms by abstracting over multiple intervals and parameters, and typically reflects heuristic domain- and task-specific knowledge. The result are new abstractions within certain time intervals. Since most of the inferences has been already performed by previous mechanisms, the role of the temporal pattern matching is to classify the input abstractions using both structural and classification knowledge.

Example 9.32 *Detect a pattern such as a low white blood cell count lasting more than 2 weeks and starting within 0 to 4 weeks of a state of low Hemoglobin lasting more than 3 weeks.*

Temporal abstraction assumes a fundamental importance within the decision (both diagnostic and therapeutic) nodes, to compare the patient's data with the conditions expressed into the guideline. In addition, temporal abstraction can be also exploited to answer user physicians' complex queries.

Finally, we present an example (elaborated from an example of the work in [258]) that shows how the various TA mechanisms can be combined to produce useful abstractions. In the lower part of Figure 9.5, we show raw data regarding a patient during a prednisone/azathioprine (PAZ) protocol (PAZ protocol-administration event in figure) due to a bone-marrow transplantation (BMT event in the upper part of the figure). Two time series of raw data are shown: Platelet counts and Granulocyte counts. In the following, we briefly describe all the tasks executed by the TA mechanisms to infer the grade of Myelotoxicity starting from the given raw data.

1. The first step of abstraction is the creation of the adequate interpretation contexts. In the example, the interpretation context PAZ protocol is created by the context-forming mechanism starting from the contemporaneous PAZ protocol-administration event. The acute and chronic GVHD abstractions (AGVHD and CGVHD respectively) in this example are also inferred by TA mechanisms, with input parameters not shown in this example.

2. The next step is the vertical temporal inference performed by the contemporaneous abstraction: Platelet and Granulocyte counts are abstracted into the states Platelet toxicity and Granulocyte toxicity grades (P[n] and G[n] respectively, where n is the grade of toxicity) accordingly to specific thresholds. In the figure, for the sake of simplicity, we only show Platelet toxicity grades.

3. Then, points of the same grade of toxicity close enough are joined into intervals through primary temporal interpolation. After that, closed intervals of the same grade of toxicity are joined through secondary temporal interpolation (only the final result is shown in figure).

4. Finally, Myelotoxicity of grade n intervals (M[n]) are obtained (through computational transformation performing vertical inference) from intervals in which at least P[n] or G[n] holds.

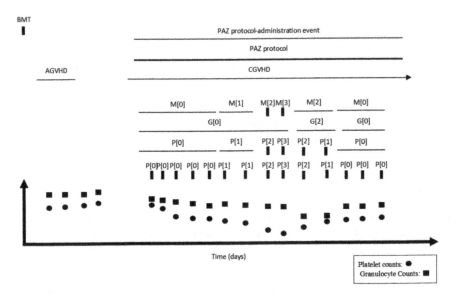

FIGURE 9.5 Example of composition of TA mechanisms. The figure has been elaborated from an example in [258].

On the architectural point of view, temporal abstraction is usually integrated into systems providing support to guideline execution through the use of *temporal-abstraction mediators* (see below). Basically, a temporal-abstraction mediator is a software layer placed between the guideline support system and the (temporal) database containing patient's raw data, providing temporal abstraction facilities.

EON [195, 303] and Asbru [260], for instance, use the temporal-abstraction mediator *Tzolkin* [201] as intermediate layer between a standard relational database and the guideline system. Tzolkin incorporates the *RÉSUMÉ* system, which provides temporal abstraction facilities over raw timestamped medical data (implementing the KBTA approach detailed in this section), and Chronus [72], which provides a temporal extension to SQL.

Another interesting approach is the *IDAN* approach [28]. IDAN provides a complete architecture in which a temporal abstraction computational component (implementing the KBTA approach) ALMA, provides support also to temporal constraints. A system using IDAN is *DeGeL* [262]. DeGeL support guideline specification, retrieval, application and quality assessment, by sending runtime queries to IDAN.

EXERCISES

9.1 *Representation.* Use the GLARE's high level language to represent Example 9.20.

9.2 *Constraint propagation.* Implement the Floyd–Warshall's all-pairs shortest paths algorithm in a programming language of your choice and use it to propagate the constraints of an STP $S_1 = \{(i), (ii), (iii)\}$ and an STP $S_2 = \{(i), (ii), (iii), (v)\}$, where (i), (ii), (iii), and (v) are the STP constraints in Section 9.3.1.

9.3 *Temporal abstraction.* Given the "insulin_administration" event starting at time 5pm and ending at 6pm, and the DIRC $\langle$insulin_effect, insulin_administration, +0.5h, *, *, +10h$\rangle$ draw in a timeline the context interval "insulin_effect".

GLOSSARY

Constraint propagation: A form of inference that tightens existing constraints removing values that are not consistent with the other constraints of the problem, thus providing an equivalent but "more explicit" constraint problem.

Interpretation Context: A situation or a state relevant in the current task that can change the interpretation of data or influence the inferences on them.

Reference Time: The "zero-point" timestamp.

Temporal abstraction: A form of knowledge-based temporal reasoning to infer, from low-level raw timestamped data, higher level meaningful concepts.

Temporal (binary) constraint: A temporal constraint is a relation between two temporal entities (time points or time intervals) that restricts that restricts the times when such entities can occur.

Temporal pattern: A temporal pattern is the definition over the time of a sequence of different (abstracted) parameters.

Time Interval: A convex set of timestamps. It is often denoted with the notation $[I_{Start}, I_{End}]$ where I_{Start} and I_{End} are, respectively, the starting and ending points of the interval.

Timestamp: Is the basic temporal primitive. Timestamps belong to an ordered set of elements isomorphic to the positive integers (plus the symbols $-\infty$ and $+\infty$, to denote the most remote past and the furthest future).

FURTHER READING

Terenziani Paolo, German Efrat, Shahar Yuval, The temporal aspects of clinical guidelines, *Studies in Health Technology and Informatics* 139:81–100, 2008.

Peleg Mor, Computer-interpretable clinical guidelines: A methodological review, *Journal of Biomedical Informatics* 46(4):744–763, August 2013.

Combi Carlo, Keravnou-Papailiou Elpida, Shahar Yuval, *Temporal information systems in medicine*, Springer, New York, 2010.

Adlassnig Klaus-Peter, Combi Carlo, Das Amar K., Keravnou-Papailiou Elpida, Pozzi Giuseppe, Temporal representation and reasoning in medicine: Research directions and challenges, *Artificial Intelligence in Medicine* 38(2):101–113, October 2006.

Bibliography

[1] Michael Adams, Arthur H. M. ter Hofstede, David Edmond, and Wil M. P. van der Aalst. Worklets: A service-oriented implementation of dynamic flexibility in workflows. In *On the Move to Meaningful Internet Systems 2006: CoopIS, DOA, GADA, and ODBASE, OTM Confederated International Conferences, CoopIS, DOA, GADA, and ODBASE 2006*, Montpellier, France, October 29 - November 3, 2006. Proceedings, Part I. 291–308, 2006.

[2] Arya Adriansyah. *Aligning Observed and Modeled Behavior*. PhD thesis, Eindhoven University of Technology, 2014.

[3] Arya Adriansyah and Joos C. A. M. Buijs. Mining process performance from event logs. In Marcello La Rosa and Pnina Soffer, editors, *Business Process Management Workshops - BPM 2012 International Workshops*, volume 132 of *Lecture Notes in Business Information Processing*, Tallinn, Estonia, September 3, 2012. Revised Papers. 217–218, 2012, Springer.

[4] Age-Related Eye Disease Study Research Group. The age-related eye disease study system for classifying age-related macular degeneration from stereoscopic color fundus photographs: the age-related eye disease study report number 6. *Am J Ophthalmol*, 132(5):668–681, Nov 2001.

[5] James F. Allen. Maintaining knowledge about temporal intervals. *Commun. ACM*, 26(11):832–843, 1983.

[6] American Academy of Ophthalmology Retina/Vitreous Panel. Preferred practice pattern guidelines: age-related macular degeneration. http://www.aao.org/preferred-practice-pattern/age-related-macular-degeneration-ppp-2015. Accessed: 2016-10-31.

[7] AMIA. *AMIA 2002, American Medical Informatics Association Annual Symposium*, San Antonio, TX, USA, November 9-13, 2002, 2002. AMIA.

[8] Winfried Amoaku, Susan Blakeney, Melissa Freeman, Richard Gale, Robert Johnston, Simon P. Kelly, Barbara McLaughlan, et al. Action on AMD. Optimising patient management: act now to ensure current and continual delivery of best possible patient care. *Eye (Lond)*, 26 Suppl 1:2–21, Feb 2012.

[9] Luca Anselma, Alessio Bottrighi, Gianpaolo Molino, Stefania Montani, Paolo Terenziani, and Mauro Torchio. Supporting knowledge-based decision making in the medical context: The GLARE approach. *IJKBO*, 1(1):42–60, 2011.

[10] Luca Anselma, Alessio Bottrighi, Stefania Montani, and Paolo Terenziani. Managing proposals and evaluations of updates to medical knowledge: Theory and applications. *Journal of Biomedical Informatics*, 46(2):363–376, 2013.

[11] Luca Anselma, Luca Piovesan, Abdul Sattar, Bela Stantic, and Paolo Terenziani. A comprehensive approach to 'now' in temporal relational databases: Semantics and representation. *IEEE Trans. Knowl. Data Eng.*, 28(10):2538–2551, 2016.

[12] Luca Anselma, Luca Piovesan, and Paolo Terenziani. Temporal detection and analysis of guideline interactions. *submitted*, 2016.

[13] Luca Anselma, Paolo Terenziani, Stefania Montani, and Alessio Bottrighi. Towards a comprehensive treatment of repetitions, periodicity and temporal constraints in clinical guidelines. *Artificial Intelligence in Medicine*, 38(2):171–195, 2006.

[14] Luca Anselma, Paolo Terenziani, and Richard T. Snodgrass. Valid-time indeterminacy in temporal relational databases: Semantics and representations. *IEEE Trans. Knowl. Data Eng.*, 25(12):2880–2894, 2013.

[15] Bhuma Anuradha, Suresh K Kumar, and Veera VC Reddy. Classification of cardiac signals using time domain methods. *ARPN Journal of Engineering and Applied Sciences*, 3(3):7–12, 2008.

[16] Juan Carlos Augusto. Temporal reasoning for decision support in medicine. *Artificial Intelligence in Medicine*, 33(1):1–24, 2005.

[17] Australia and Wayne Swan. *Australia to 2050: Future Challenges: The 2010 Intergenerational Report*. Commonwealth of Australia, 2010.

[18] Robert L. Avery, Sophie J. Bakri, Mark S. Blumenkranz, Alexander J. Brucker, Emmett T. Cunningham, Donald J. Dell'Amico, Pravin U. Dugel, et al. Intravitreal injection technique and monitoring: updated guidelines of an expert panel. *Retina*, 34 Suppl 12:1–1, Dec 2014.

[19] Clara Ayora, Victoria Torres, Barbara Weber, Manfred Reichert, and Vicente Pelechano. VIVACE: A framework for the systematic evaluation of variability support in process-aware information systems. *Information & Software Technology*, 57:248–276, 2015.

[20] Thomas Baier, Jan Mendling, and Mathias Weske. Bridging abstraction layers in process mining. *Inf. Syst.*, 46:123–139, 2014.

[21] Matt Barney. Motorala's second generation. *Six Sigma Forum Magazine*, 1(3):13–16, 2002.

[22] Ilan Beer, Eilon Barnea, Tamar Ziv, and Arie Admon. Improving large-scale proteomics by clustering of mass spectrometry data. *Proteomics*, 4(4):950–960, 2004.

[23] Zohra Bellahsene, Angela Bonifati, and Erhard Rahm, editors. *Schema Matching and Mapping*. Data-Centric Systems and Applications. Springer, 2011.

[24] Johan Van Benthem. *The Logic of Time: a Model-Theoretic Investigation into the Varieties of Temporal Ontology and Temporal Discourse*, volume 156. Springer Science & Business Media, 2013.

[25] Chiara Biagi, Valentino Conti, Nicola Montanaro, Mauro Melis, Elena Buccellato, M. Donati, Anna Covezzoli, et al. Comparative safety profiles of intravitreal bevacizumab, ranibizumab and pegaptanib: the analysis of the who database of adverse drug reactions. *Eur J Clin Pharmacol*, 70(12):1505–1512, Dec 2014.

[26] Michael Binder, Wolfgang Dorda, Georg Duftschmid, Reinhold Dunkl, Karl Anton Fröschl, Walter Gall, Wilfried Grossmann, et al. On analyzing process compliance in skin cancer treatment: An experience report from the evidence-based medical compliance cluster (EBMC2). In Jolita Ralyté, Xavier Franch, Sjaak Brinkkemper, and Stanislaw Wrycza, editors, *Advanced Information Systems Engineering - 24th International Conference, CAiSE 2012, Gdansk, Poland, June 25-29, 2012. Proceedings*, volume 7328 of *Lecture Notes in Computer Science*. 398–413, Springer, 2012.

[27] Alan C. Bird, Neil M. Bressler, Susan B. Bressler, Iain H. Chisholm, Gabriel Coscas, Matthew D. Davis, Paulus T.V.M. de Jong, et al. An international classification and grading system for age-related maculopathy and age-related macular degeneration. the international arm epidemiological study group. *Surv Ophthalmol*, 39(5):367–374, Mar-Apr 1995.

[28] David Boaz and Yuval Shahar. Idan: A distributed temporal-abstraction mediator for medical databases. In Dojat et al. [79], 21–30.

[29] Brigitte Boeckmann, Amos Bairoch, Rolf Apweiler, Marie-Claude Blatter, Anne Estreicher, Elisabeth Gasteiger, Maria J Martin, et al. The swiss-prot protein knowledgebase and its supplement trembl in 2003. *Nucleic Acids Research*, 31(1):365–370, 2003.

[30] Stephan Bögel, Hannes Schlieter, and Werner Esswein. Compliance check of health care process models. In Vallabh Sambamurthy and

Mohan Tanniru, editors, *A Renaissance of Information Technology for Sustainability and Global Competitiveness. 17th Americas Conference on Information Systems, AMCIS 2011*, Detroit, Michigan, USA, August 4-8 2011. 2011, Association for Information Systems.

[31] Rantham Prabhakara Jagadeesh Chandra Bose, Ronny S. Mans, and Wil M. P. van der Aalst. Wanna improve process mining results? In *IEEE Symposium on Computational Intelligence and Data Mining, CIDM 2013*, Singapore, 16-19 April, 2013. 127–134, 2013, IEEE.

[32] Rantham Prabhakara Jagadeesh Chandra Bose, Ronny S. Mans, and Wil M. P. van der Aalst. Wanna improve process mining results? It's high time we consider data quality issues seriously. Technical Report BPM-13-02, BPM Center Report, http://bpmcenter.org/wp-content/uploads/reports/2013/BPM-13-02.pdf, 2013.

[33] Rantham Prabhakara Jagadeesh Chandra Bose, Wil M. P. van der Aalst, Indre Zliobaite, and Mykola Pechenizkiy. Handling concept drift in process mining. In Haralambos Mouratidis and Colette Rolland, editors, *Advanced Information Systems Engineering - 23rd International Conference, CAiSE 2011*, volume 6741 of *Lecture Notes in Computer Science*, London, UK, June 20-24, 2011. Proceedings. 391–405, 2011, Springer.

[34] David G. Bostwick. Radiofrequency identification specimen tracking in anatomical pathology: Pilot study of 1067 consecutive prostate biopsies. *Annals of Diagnostic Pathology*, 17(5):391–402, 2013.

[35] Gregory W. Botteron and Josepeh M. Smith. A technique for measurement of the extent of spatial organization of atrial activation during atrial fibrillation in the intact human heart. *IEEE Trans. Biomed. Engineering*, 42(6):579–586, 1995.

[36] Aziz A. Boxwala, Mor Peleg, Samson W. Tu, Omolola Ogunyemi, Qing T. Zeng, Dongwen Wang, Vimla L. Patel, et al. GLIF3: a representation format for sharable computer-interpretable clinical practice guidelines. *Journal of Biomedical Informatics*, 37(3):147–161, 2004.

[37] Richard Braun, Hannes Schlieter, Martin Burwitz, and Werner Esswein. BPMN4CP: Design and implementation of a BPMN extension for clinical pathways. In *IEEE International Conference on Bioinformatics and Biomedicine (BIBM)*. IEEE, 9–16, 2014.

[38] Ross J. Brechner, Philip J. Rosenfeld, J. Daniel Babish, and Stuart Caplan. Pharmacotherapy for neovascular age-related macular degeneration: an analysis of the 100 *Am J Ophthalmol*, 151(5):887–895, May 2011.

[39] David M. Brown, Peter K. Kaiser, Mark Michels, Gisele Soubrane, Jeffrey S. Heier, Robert Y. Kim, Judy P. Sy, et al. Ranibizumab versus verteporfin for neovascular age-related macular degeneration. *N Engl J Med*, 355(14):1432–1444, Oct 2006.

[40] Melissa M. Brown, Gary C. Brown, Heidi C. Brown, and Jonathan Peet. A value-based medicine analysis of ranibizumab for the treatment of subfoveal neovascular macular degeneration. *Ophthalmology*, 115(6):1039–1045, Jun 2008.

[41] Vittorio Brusoni, Luca Console, and Paolo Terenziani. On the computational complexity of querying bounds on differences constraints. *Artif. Intell.*, 74(2):367–379, 1995.

[42] Vittorio Brusoni, Luca Console, Paolo Terenziani, and Barbara Pernici. Later: Managing temporal information efficiently. *IEEE Expert*, 12(4):56–64, 1997.

[43] CaboLabs. EHR committer. https://github.com/ppazos/ EHRCommitter. Accessed: 2016-10-31.

[44] CaboLabs. EHR server. https://github.com/ppazos/ cabolabs-ehrserver. Accessed: 2016-10-31.

[45] CaboLabs. OpenEHR-OPT project source code repository. https: //github.com/ppazos/openEHR-OPT. Accessed: 2016-10-31.

[46] CaboLabs. OpenEHR-skeleton example code repository. https:// github.com/ppazos/openEHR-skeleton. Accessed: 2016-10-31.

[47] Mario Cannataro, Giovanni Cuda, Marco Gaspari, Sergio Greco, Giuseppe Tradigo, and Pierangelo Veltri. The eipeptidi tool: enhancing peptide discovery in icat-based LC MS/MS experiments. *BMC Bioinformatics*, 8, 2007.

[48] Mario Cannataro, Pietro Hiram Guzzi, Giuseppe Tradigo, and Pierangelo Veltri. On the choice of centralized vs decentralized systems for EPR in hospitals. *SIGHIT Record*, 2(1):19, 2012.

[49] Mario Cannataro, Domenico Talia, Giuseppe Tradigo, Paolo Trunfio, and Pierangelo Veltri. SIGMCC: A system for sharing meta patient records in a peer-to-peer environment. *Future Generation Comp. Syst.*, 24(3):222–234, 2008.

[50] Jorge S. Cardoso, Jan Mendling, Gustaf Neumann, and Hajo A. Reijers. A discourse on complexity of process models. In Johann Eder and Schahram Dustdar, editors, *Business Process Management Workshops, BPM 2006 International Workshops, BPD, BPI, ENEI, GPWW,*

DPM, semantics4ws, volume 4103 of *Lecture Notes in Computer Science*, Vienna, Austria, September 4-7, 2006, Proceedings. 117–128, 2006, Springer.

[51] Fabio Casati, Silvana Castano, Maria Grazia Fugini, Isabelle Mirbel, and Barbara Pernici. Using patterns to design rules in workflows. *IEEE Trans. Software Eng.*, 26(8):760–785, 2000.

[52] Fabio Casati, Stefano Ceri, Stefano Paraboschi, and Giuseppe Pozzi. Specification and Implementation of Exceptions in Workflow Management Systems. *ACM Trans. Database Syst.*, 24(3):405–451, 1999.

[53] Fabio Casati, Stefano Ceri, Barbara Pernici, and Giuseppe Pozzi. Conceptual Modelling of WorkFlows. In Mike P. Papazoglou, editor, *OOER*, volume 1021 of *Lecture Notes in Computer Science*. 341–354, Springer, 1995.

[54] Fabio Casati and Giuseppe Pozzi. Modeling Exceptional Behaviors in Commercial Workflow Management Systems. In *CoopIS*. 127–138, IEEE Computer Society, 1999.

[55] Francisco Castells, Raquel Cervigon, and Jose Millet. On the preprocessing of atrial electrograms in atrial fibrillation: understanding botteron's approach. *Pacing and Clinical Electrophysiology*, 37(2):133–143, 2014.

[56] Antonio Cerasa, Francesco Fera, Maria Cecilia Gioia, Maria Liguori, Luca Passamonti, Giuseppe Nicoletti, Loredana Vercillo, et al. Adaptive cortical changes and the functional correlates of visuo-motor integration in relapsing-remitting multiple sclerosis. *Brain Research Bulletin*, 69(6):597–605, 2006.

[57] Shubha Chakravarty and Yuval Shahar. CAPSUL: A constraint-based specification of repeating patterns in time-oriented data. *Ann. Math. Artif. Intell.*, 30(1-4):3–22, 2000.

[58] Carolina Ming Chiao, Vera Künzle, and Manfred Reichert. Object-aware process support in healthcare information systems: Requirements, conceptual framework and examples. *Int'l Journal on Advances in Life Sciences*, 5(1 & 2):11–26, July 2013.

[59] Jan Claes, Irene T. P. Vanderfeesten, Frederik Gailly, Paul Grefen, and Geert Poels. The structured process modeling theory (SPMT) a cognitive view on why and how modelers benefit from structuring the process of process modeling. *Information Systems Frontiers*, 17(6):1401–1425, 2015.

[60] The Workflow Management Coalition. Terminology and glossary WFMC-TC-1011. `http://www.wfmc.org/standards/docs/TC-1011_term_glossary_v3.pdf`, February 1999.

[61] Anne L. Coleman, Fei Yu, Kristine E. Ensrud, Katie L. Stone, Jane A. Cauley, Kathryn L. Pedula, Marc C. Hochberg, and Carol M. Mangione. Impact of age-related macular degeneration on vision-specific quality of life: Follow-up from the 10-year and 15-year visits of the study of osteoporotic fractures. *Am J Ophthalmol*, 150(5):683–691, Nov 2010.

[62] Carlo Combi, Mauro Gambini, Sara Migliorini, and Roberto Posenato. Representing business processes through a temporal data-centric workflow modeling language: An application to the management of clinical pathways. *IEEE Trans. Systems, Man, and Cybernetics: Systems*, 44(9):1182–1203, 2014.

[63] Carlo Combi, Luke Hunsberger, and Roberto Posenato. An algorithm for checking the dynamic controllability of a conditional simple temporal network with uncertainty - revisited. In Joaquim Filipe and Ana L. N. Fred, editors, *Agents and Artificial Intelligence - 5th International Conference, ICAART 2013*, volume 449 of *Communications in Computer and Information Science*, Barcelona, Spain, February 15-18, 2013. Revised Selected Papers. 314–331, 2013, Springer.

[64] Carlo Combi, Barbara Oliboni, Alessandro Zardiniy, and Francesca Zerbato. Seamless design of decision-intensive care pathways. In *2016 IEEE International Conference on Healthcare Informatics, ICHI 2016*, Chicago, IL, USA, October 4-7, 2016. 35–45, 2016, IEEE Computer Society.

[65] Carlo Combi and Roberto Posenato. Towards temporal controllabilities for workflow schemata. In Nicolas Markey and Jef Wijsen, editors, *TIME 2010 - 17th International Symposium on Temporal Representation and Reasoning*, Paris, France, 6-8 September 2010. 129–136, 2010, IEEE Computer Society.

[66] Carlo Combi and Giuseppe Pozzi. Towards Temporal Information in Workflow Systems. In Stefano Spaccapietra, Salvatore T. March, and Yahiko Kambayashi, editors, *ER (Workshops)*, volume 2503 of *Lecture Notes in Computer Science*. 13–25, Springer, 2002.

[67] Carlo Combi and Giuseppe Pozzi. Architectures for a temporal workflow management system. In Hisham Haddad, Andrea Omicini, Roger L. Wainwright, and Lorie M. Liebrock, editors, *SAC*. 659–666, ACM, 2004.

[68] Raffaele Conforti, Marcello La Rosa, and Arthur H. M. ter Hofstede. Filtering out infrequent behavior from business process event logs. *IEEE Transactions on Knowledge and Data Engineering*, (accepted for publication), 2016. doi:10.1109/TKDE.2016.2614680.

[69] Jay Cousins and Tony Stewart. What is business process design and why should I care? http://www.rivers-family.info/resources/RivCom-WhatIsBPD-WhyShouldICare.pdf, September 2002.

[70] Peter Crampton, Roshan Perera, Sue Crengle, Antony Dowell, Philippa Howden-Chapman, Robin Kearns, Tom Love, et al. What makes a good performance indicator? Devising primary care performance indicators for New Zealand. *The New Zealand Medical Journal*, 117(119):1–12, 2004.

[71] Alan F. Cruess, Gergana Zlateva, Xiao Xu, Gisele Soubrane, Daniel Pauleikhoff, Andrew Lotery, Jordi Mones, et al. Economic burden of bilateral neovascular age-related macular degeneration: multi-country observational study. *Pharmacoeconomics*, 26(1):57–73, 2008.

[72] Amar K. Da and Mark A. Musen. A temporal query system for protocol-directed decision support. *Methods of information in medicine*, 33(4):358–370, 1994.

[73] Peter Dadam and Manfred Reichert. The ADEPT project: a decade of research and development for robust and flexible process support. *Computer Science - R&D*, 23(2):81–97, 2009.

[74] Peter Dadam, Manfred Reichert, and Klaus Kuhn. *Clinical Workflows— The Killer Application for Process-oriented Information Systems?*, 36–59. Springer London, 2000.

[75] Andrew G. Davies, Dwayne Conway, Scott Reid, Arnold R. Cowen, and Mohan Sivananthan. Assessment of coronary stent deployment using computer enhanced X-ray images-validation against intravascular ultrasound and best practice recommendations. *Catheterization and Cardiovascular Interventions*, 81(3):419–427, 2013.

[76] Rina Dechter, Itay Meiri, and Judea Pearl. Temporal constraint networks. *Artif. Intell.*, 49(1-3):61–95, 1991.

[77] Sayed Mehdi Hejazi Dehaghani and Nafiseh Hajrahimi. Which factors affect software projects maintenance cost more? *Acta Informatica Medica*, 21(1):63–66, 2013.

[78] Tom DeMarco. *Controlling Software Projects: Management, Measurement, and Estimates*. Prentice Hall PTR, Upper Saddle River, NJ, USA, 1986.

[79] Michel Dojat, Elpida T. Keravnou, and Pedro Barahona, editors. *Artificial Intelligence in Medicine, 9th Conference on Artificial Intelligence in Medicine in Europe, AIME 2003*, volume 2780 of *Lecture Notes in Computer Science*, Protaras, Cyprus, October 18-22, 2003, Proceedings, 2003. Springer.

[80] Marlon Dumas, Marcello La Rosa, Jan Mendling, and Hajo A. Reijers. *Fundamentals of Business Process Management*. Springer, 2013.

[81] Marlon Dumas, Wil M. P. van der Aalst, and Arthur H. M. Ter Hofstede. *Process-Aware Information Systems: Bridging People and Software through Process Technology*. John Wiley & Sons, 2005.

[82] Reinhold Dunkl, Karl Anton Fröschl, Wilfried Grossmann, and Stefanie Rinderle-Ma. Assessing medical treatment compliance based on formal process modeling. In Andreas Holzinger and Klaus-Martin Simonic, editors, *Information Quality in e-Health - 7th Conference of the Workgroup Human-Computer Interaction and Usability Engineering of the Austrian Computer Society, USAB 2011*, volume 7058 of *Lecture Notes in Computer Science*, Graz, Austria, November 25-26, 2011. Proceedings. 533–546, 2011, Springer.

[83] Schahram Dustdar, José Luiz Fiadeiro, and Amit P. Sheth, editors. *Business Process Management, 4th International Conference, BPM 2006*, volume 4102 of *Lecture Notes in Computer Science*, Vienna, Austria, September 5-7, 2006, Proceedings, 2006. Springer.

[84] Matthew B. Dwyer, George S. Avrunin, and James C. Corbett. Patterns in property specifications for finite-state verification. In Barry W. Boehm, David Garlan, and Jeff Kramer, editors, *Proceedings of the 1999 International Conference on Software Engineering, ICSE' 99*, Los Angeles, CA, USA, May 16-22, 1999. 411–420, 1999, ACM.

[85] Johann Eder and Walter Liebhart. The workflow activity model WAMO. In *CoopIS*, 87–98, 1995.

[86] Aitor Eguzkiza, Jesús D. Trigo, Miguel Martínez-Espronceda, Luis Serrano, and José Andonegui. Formalize clinical processes into electronic health information systems: Modelling a screening service for diabetic retinopathy. *Journal of Biomedical Informatics*, 56:112–126, 2015.

[87] Ramez Elmasri and Shamkant B. Navathe. *Fundamentals of Database Systems*. 3rd edition, Addison-Wesley-Longman, 2000.

[88] Ernest Allen Emerson. Temporal and modal logic. In *Handbook of Theoretical Computer Science, Volume B: Formal Models and Sematics (B)*, 995–1072. Elsevier, 1990.

[89] Xavier J. Fagan and Salmaan Al-Qureshi. Intravitreal injections: a review of the evidence for best practice. *Clin. Experiment. Ophthalmol.*, 41(5):500–507, Jul 2013.

[90] Walid Fdhila, Manuel Gall, Stefanie Rinderle-Ma, Juergen Mangler, and Conrad Indiono. Classification and formalization of instance-spanning constraints in process-driven applications. In Marcello La Rosa, Peter Loos, and Oscar Pastor, editors, *Business Process Management - 14th International Conference, BPM 2016*, volume 9850 of *Lecture Notes in*

Computer Science, Rio de Janeiro, Brazil, September 18-22, 2016. Proceedings. 348–364, 2016, Springer.

[91] Walid Fdhila, Conrad Indiono, Stefanie Rinderle-Ma, and Manfred Reichert. Dealing with change in process choreographies: Design and implementation of propagation algorithms. *Inf. Syst.*, 49:1–24, 2015.

[92] Walid Fdhila, Stefanie Rinderle-Ma, David Knuplesch, and Manfred Reichert. Change and compliance in collaborative processes. In *2015 IEEE International Conference on Services Computing, SCC 2015*, New York City, NY, USA, June 27 - July 2, 2015. 162–169, 2015, IEEE.

[93] Ivan P. Fellegi and Alan B. Sunter. A theory for record linkage. *Journal of the American Statistical Association*, 64(328):1183–1210, December 1969.

[94] Norman E. Fenton and Shari Lawrence Pfleeger. *Software Metrics: A Rigorous and Practical Approach*. 2nd edition, PWS Publishing Co., Boston, MA, USA, 1998.

[95] Simona Ferrante, Stefano Bonacina, Giuseppe Pozzi, Francesco Pinciroli, and Sara Marceglia. A design methodology for medical processes. *Applied Clinical Informatics*, 7(1):191–210, 2016.

[96] Kathrin Figl. Comprehension of procedural visual business process models - a literature review. *Business & Information Systems Engineering*, 59, 2017.

[97] Kathrin Figl, Jan Mendling, and Mark Strembeck. The influence of notational deficiencies on process model comprehension. *J. AIS*, 14(6):1, 2013.

[98] John Fox, Nicky Johns, and Ali Rahmanzadeh. Disseminating medical knowledge: the proforma approach. *Artificial Intelligence in Medicine*, 14(1-2):157–182, 1998.

[99] Douglas B. Fridsma. Health informatics: our domain, our challenge. *Journal of the American Medical Informatics Association*, 23(6):1202–1202, 2016.

[100] Anne E. Fung, Geeta A. Lalwani, Philip J. Rosenfeld, Sander R. Dubovy, Stephan Michels, William J. Feuer, Carmen A. Puliafito, et al. An optical coherence tomography-guided, variable dosing regimen with intravitreal ranibizumab (lucentis) for neovascular age-related macular degeneration. *Am J Ophthalmol*, 143(4):566–583, Apr 2007.

[101] Stacey B. Gabriel, Stephen F. Schaffner, Huy Nguyen, Jamie M. Moore, Jessica Roy, Brendan Blumenstiel, John Higgins, et al. The structure of haplotype blocks in the human genome. *Science*, 296(5576):2225–2229, 2002.

[102] Claus Garbe, Ketty Peris, Axel Hauschild, Philippe Saiag, Mark Middleton, Alain Spatz, Jean-Jacques Grob, et al. Diagnosis and treatment of melanoma: European consensus-based interdisciplinary guideline. *European Journal of Cancer*, 46(2):270–283, 2010.

[103] Manuel Garcia-Goñi, Cristina Hernández-Quevedo, Roberto Nusño-Solinís, and Francesco Paolucci. Pathways towards chronic care-focused healthcare systems: Evidence from Spain. *Health Policy*, 108(2–3):236 – 245, 2012.

[104] Andrew Gemino and Yair Wand. A framework for empirical evaluation of conceptual modeling techniques. *Requir. Eng.*, 9(4):248–260, 2004.

[105] Dimitrios Georgakopoulos, Mark F. Hornick, and Amit P. Sheth. An overview of workflow management: From process modeling to workflow automation infrastructure. *Distributed and Parallel Databases*, 3(2):119–153, 1995.

[106] Geoffrey K. Gill and Chris F. Kemerer. Cyclomatic complexity density and software maintenance productivity. *IEEE Trans. Software Eng.*, 17(12):1284–1288, 1991.

[107] Luise Göbel. A framework of process redesign heuristics in healthcare. Master's thesis, School of Business and Economics, Humboldt-Universität zu Berlin, Germany, March 2012.

[108] Colin Gordon, Ian Herbert, and Peter Johnson. Knowledge representation and clinical practice guidelines: the DILEMMA and PRESTIGE projects. *Srudies in Health Technology and Informatics*, 511–515, 1996.

[109] Maria Adela Grando, Mor Peleg, Marc Cuggia, and David Glasspool. Patterns for collaborative work in health care teams. *Artificial Intelligence in Medicine*, 53(3):139–160, 2011.

[110] Maria Adela Grando, Mor Peleg, and David Glasspool. A goal-oriented framework for specifying clinical guidelines and handling medical errors. *Journal of Biomedical Informatics*, 43(2):287–299, 2010.

[111] Paul W. P. J. Grefen and Jochem Vonk. A taxonomy of transactional workflow support. *Int. J. Cooperative Inf. Syst.*, 15(1):87–118, 2006.

[112] Ulrike Greiner, Robert Mueller, Erhard Rahm, Jan Ramsch, Barbara Heller, and Markus Loeffler. Adaptflow: protocol-based medical treatment using adaptive workflows. *Methods of Information in Medicine*, 44(1):80–88, 2005.

[113] Richard Grol and Jeremy M. Grimshaw. Evidence-based implementation of evidence-based medicine. *The Joint Commission Journal on Quality Improvement*, 25(10):503–513, 1999.

[114] Wilfried Grossmann and Stefanie Rinderle-Ma. *Fundamentals of Business Intelligence*. Data-Centric Systems and Applications. Springer, 2015.

[115] Christian W. Günther, Manfred Reichert, and Wil M. P. van der Aalst. Supporting flexible processes with adaptive workflow and case handling. In *17th IEEE International Workshops on Enabling Technologies: Infrastructures for Collaborative Enterprises, WETICE 2008*, Rome, Italy, June 23-25, 2008, Proceedings. 229–234, 2008.

[116] Omesh P. Gupta, Gary Shienbaum, Avni H. Patel, Christopher Fecarotta, Richard S. Kaiser, and Carl D. Regillo. A treat and extend regimen using ranibizumab for neovascular age-related macular degeneration clinical and economic impact. *Ophthalmology*, 117(11):2134–2140, Nov 2010.

[117] Claus Hagen and Gustavo Alonso. Flexible exception handling in the OPERA process support system. In *Proceedings of the 18th International Conference on Distributed Computing Systems*, Amsterdam, The Netherlands, May 26-29, 1998. 526–533, 1998, IEEE Computer Society.

[118] Cornelia Haisjackl, Irene Barba, Stefan Zugal, Pnina Soffer, Irit Hadar, Manfred Reichert, Jakob Pinggera, and Barbara Weber. Understanding declare models: strategies, pitfalls, empirical results. *Software and System Modeling*, 15(2):325–352, 2016.

[119] Alena Hallerbach, Thomas Bauer, and Manfred Reichert. Context-based configuration of process variants. In *3rd International Workshop on Technologies for Context-Aware Business Process Management (TCoB 2008)*, 31–40, June 2008.

[120] Alena Hallerbach, Thomas Bauer, and Manfred Reichert. Guaranteeing soundness of configurable process variants in provop. In *2009 IEEE Conference on Commerce and Enterprise Computing, CEC 2009*, Vienna, Austria, July 20-23, 2009. 98–105, 2009.

[121] Alena Hallerbach, Thomas Bauer, and Manfred Reichert. Capturing variability in business process models: the provop approach. *Journal of Software Maintenance*, 22(6-7):519–546, 2010.

[122] Jennifer B. Hassell, Ecosse L. Lamoureux, and Jill E. Keeffe. Impact of age related macular degeneration on quality of life. *Br J Ophthalmol*, 90(5):593–596, May 2006.

[123] Kristiina Häyrinen, Kaija Saranto, and Pirkko Nykänen. Definition, structure, content, use and impacts of electronic health records: A review of the research literature. *I. J. Medical Informatics*, 77(5):291–304, 2008.

[124] Sallie M. Henry and Dennis G. Kafura. Software structure metrics based on information flow. *IEEE Trans. Software Eng.*, 7(5):510–518, 1981.

[125] Peter Hibbert, Natalie Hannaford, Janet Long, Jenny Plumb, and Jeffrey Braithwaite. *Final Report: Performance Indicators Used Internationally to Report Publicly on Health Organisations and Local Health Systems*. Australian Institute of Health Innovation, 2013.

[126] HL7. HL7 ver. 3 standard: GELLO, a common expression language, rel. 2. `http://www.hl7.org/implement/standards/product_brief.cfm?product_id=5`, 2016.

[127] Payam Homayounfar. Process mining challenges in hospital information systems. In Maria Ganzha, Leszek A. Maciaszek, and Marcin Paprzycki, editors, *Federated Conference on Computer Science and Information Systems - FedCSIS 2012*, Wroclaw, Poland, 9-12 September 2012, Proceedings. 1135–1140, 2012.

[128] Geoffrey R. Hung and Quynh Doan. Assessment of the reliability of active radiofrequency identification technology for patient tracking in the pediatric emergency department. *Pediatric Emergency Care*, 29(2):162–164, 2013.

[129] Emanuel F. Petricoin III, Ali M. Ardekani, Ben A. Hitt, Peter J. Levine, Vincent A. Fusaro, Seth M. Steinberg, Gordon B. Mills, et al. Use of proteomic patterns in serum to identify ovarian cancer. *The Lancet*, 359(9306):572–577, 2002.

[130] Ciro Indolfi, Mario Cannataro, Pierangelo Veltri, and Giuseppe Tradigo. Cartesio: A software tool for pre-implant stent analyses. In *Computational Science - ICCS 2009, 9th International Conference*, Baton Rouge, LA, USA, May 25-27, 2009, Proceedings, Part I. 810–818, 2009.

[131] ITU Telecommunication Standardization Sector (ITU-T). ITU-T technology watch report: e-health standards and interoperability. `http://www.itu.int/dms_pub/itu-t/oth/23/01/T23010000170001PDFE.pdf`, 2012. Accessed: 2016-10-31.

[132] John T. James. A new, evidence-based estimate of patient harms associated with hospital care. *Journal of Patient Safety*, 9(3):122–128, 2013.

[133] Monique Jansen-Vullers and Hajo A. Reijers. Business process redesign in healthcare: Towards a structured approach. *Information Systems and Operational Research*, 43(4):321–339, 2005.

[134] Christian S. Jensen and Richard T. Snodgrass. Semantics of time-varying information. *Inf. Syst.*, 21(4):311–352, 1996.

[135] Kurt Jensen and Wil M. P. van der Aalst, editors. *Transactions on Petri Nets and Other Models of Concurrency II, Special Issue on Concurrency in Process-Aware Information Systems*, volume 5460 of *Lecture Notes in Computer Science*. Springer, 2009.

[136] James C. Boerkoel Jr. and Edmund H. Durfee. Distributed reasoning for multiagent simple temporal problems. *J. Artif. Intell. Res. (JAIR)*, 47:95–156, 2013.

[137] Stephen H. Kan. *Metrics and Models in Software Quality Engineering*. 2nd edition, Addison-Wesley Longman Publishing Co., Inc., Boston, MA, USA, 2002.

[138] Robert S. Kaplan and David P. Norton. The balanced scorecard - measures that drive performance. *Harvard Business Review*, 70(1):71–79, 1992.

[139] Henry Kautz, Peter van Beek, and Marc Vilain. Constraint propagation algorithms: A revised report. *Qualitative Reasoning about Physical Systems*, 373–381, 1990.

[140] Tom Kehler, editor. *Proceedings of the 5th National Conference on Artificial Intelligence*. Morgan Kaufmann, 1986.

[141] Ellen Kilsdonk, Linda W. P. Peute, and Monique W. M. Jaspers. Factors influencing implementation success of guideline-based clinical decision support systems: A systematic review and gaps analysis. *I. J. Medical Informatics*, 98:56–64, 2017.

[142] Michelle J. Kincade, Richard A. Abrams, Serguei V. Astafiev, Gordon L. Shulman, and Maurizio Corbetta. An event-related functional magnetic resonance imaging study of voluntary and stimulus-driven orienting of attention. *The Journal of Neuroscience*, 25(18):4593–4604, 2005.

[143] Ronald Klein, Chiu-Fang Chou, Barbara E. K. Klein, Xinzhi Zhang, Stacy M. Meuer, and Jinan B. Saaddine. Prevalence of age-related macular degeneration in the us population. *Arch Ophthalmol*, 129(1):75–80, Jan 2011.

[144] Ned Kock, Jacques Verville, Azim Danesh-Pajou, and Dorrie DeLuca. Communication flow orientation in business process modeling and its effect on redesign success: Results from a field study. *Decision Support Systems*, 46(2):562–575, 2009.

[145] Ivo Kocur and Serge Resnikoff. Visual impairment and blindness in europe and their prevention. *Br J Ophthalmol*, 86(7):716–722, Jul 2002.

[146] Andrei A. Krokhin, Peter Jeavons, and Peter Jonsson. Reasoning about temporal relations: The tractable subalgebras of allen's interval algebra. *J. ACM*, 50(5):591–640, 2003.

[147] Vera Künzle and Manfred Reichert. Philharmonicflows: towards a framework for object-aware process management. *Journal of Software Maintenance*, 23(4):205–244, 2011.

[148] Vera Künzle, Barbara Weber, and Manfred Reichert. Object-aware business processes: Fundamental requirements and their support in existing approaches. *IJISMD*, 2(2):19–46, 2011.

[149] Peter B. Ladkin. Time representation: A taxonomy of internal relations. In Kehler [140], 360–366.

[150] Linda M. Laird and Carol M. Brennan. *Software Measurement and Estimation: A Practical Approach.* 1st edition, Wiley-IEEE Computer Society Pr, 2006.

[151] Geetika T. Lakshmanan, Paul T. Keyser, and Songyun Duan. Detecting changes in a semi-structured business process through spectral graph analysis. In Serge Abiteboul, Klemens Böhm, Christoph Koch, and Kian-Lee Tan, editors, *Workshops Proceedings of the 27th International Conference on Data Engineering, ICDE 2011*, Hannover, Germany, April 11-16, 2011. 255–260, 2011, IEEE Computer Society.

[152] Geeta A. Lalwani, Philip J. Rosenfeld, Anne E. Fung, Sander R. Dubovy, Stephen Michels, William Feuer, Janet L. Davis, et al. A variable-dosing regimen with intravitreal ranibizumab for neovascular age-related macular degeneration: year 2 of the PrONTO study. *Am J Ophthalmol*, 148(1):43–58, Jul 2009.

[153] Leslie Lamport. *LaTeX - A Document Preparation System: User's Guide and Reference Manual.* Second edition, Pearson/Prentice Hall, 1994.

[154] Eric S. Lander, Lauren M. Linton, Bruce Birren, Chad Nusbaum, Michael C. Zody, Jennifer Baldwin, Keri Devon, et al. Initial sequencing and analysis of the human genome. *Nature*, 409(6822):860–921, 2001.

[155] Beth Lanham and Pamela Maxson-Cooper. Is Six Sigma the answer for nursing to reduce medical errors? *Nursing Economics*, 21(1):39–41, 2003.

[156] Andreas Lanz, Manfred Reichert, and Barbara Weber. Process time patterns: A formal foundation. *Inf. Syst.*, 57:38–68, 2016.

[157] Andreas Lanz, Barbara Weber, and Manfred Reichert. Time patterns for process-aware information systems. *Requir. Eng.*, 19(2):113–141, 2014.

[158] Ralf Laue and Jan Mendling. Structuredness and its significance for correctness of process models. *Inf. Syst. E-Business Management*, 8(3):287–307, 2010.

[159] Martin Lawrence and Frede Olesen. Indicators of quality in healthcare. *European Journal of General Practice*, 3(3):103–108, 1997.

[160] Peter Lawrence, editor. *Workflow Handbook 1997, Workflow Management Coalition*. John Wiley & Sons, New York, NY, USA, 1997.

[161] Sander J. J. Leemans, Dirk Fahland, and Wil M. P. van der Aalst. Process and deviation exploration with inductive visual miner. In Lior Limonad and Barbara Weber, editors, *Proceedings of the BPM Demo Sessions 2014 Co-located with the 12th International Conference on Business Process Management (BPM 2014)*, volume 1295 of *CEUR Workshop Proceedings*, Eindhoven, The Netherlands, September 10, 2014. 46, 2014, CEUR-WS.org.

[162] Richard Lenz and Manfred Reichert. IT support for healthcare processes - premises, challenges, perspectives. *Data Knowl. Eng.*, 61(1):39–58, 2007.

[163] Leonard A. Leonard, Barry M. Farr, Robert J. Sherertz, Issam I .Raad, Naoimi O'Grady, JoAnn S. Harris, and Donald E. Craven. Guidelines for the management of intravascular catheter-related infections. *Infection Control & Hospital Epidemiology*, 22(04):222–242, 2001.

[164] Henrik Leopold, Rami-Habib Eid-Sabbagh, Jan Mendling, Leonardo Guerreiro Azevedo, and Fernanda Araujo Baião. Detection of naming convention violations in process models for different languages. *Decision Support Systems*, 56:310–325, 2013.

[165] Henrik Leopold, Jan Mendling, and Artem Polyvyanyy. Supporting process model validation through natural language generation. *IEEE Trans. Software Eng.*, 40(8):818–840, 2014.

[166] Chen Li, Manfred Reichert, and Andreas Wombacher. Mining business process variants: Challenges, scenarios, algorithms. *Data Knowl. Eng.*, 70(5):409–434, 2011.

[167] Thorsten Loeffeler, Ruediger Striemer, and Wolfgang Dieters. A framework for identification, classification and IT support of semi-structured business processes. *Knowledge and Process Management*, 5(1):51–57, 1998.

[168] Robert J. Luttman, Glenn L. Laffel, and Steven D. Pearson. Using PERT/CPM to design and improve clinical processes. *Quality Management in Health Care*, 3(2):1–13, 1995.

[169] Linh Thao Ly, Fabrizio Maria Maggi, Marco Montali, Stefanie Rinderle-Ma, and Wil M. P. van der Aalst. Compliance monitoring in business processes: Functionalities, application, and tool-support. *Inf. Syst.*, 54:209–234, 2015.

[170] Linh Thao Ly, Stefanie Rinderle-Ma, and Peter Dadam. Semantic correctness in adaptive process management systems. In Dustdar et al. [83], 193–208.

[171] Linh Thao Ly, Stefanie Rinderle-Ma, and Peter Dadam. Design and verification of instantiable compliance rule graphs in process-aware information systems. In Barbara Pernici, editor, *Advanced Information Systems Engineering, 22nd International Conference, CAiSE 2010*, volume 6051 of *Lecture Notes in Computer Science*, Hammamet, Tunisia, June 7-9, 2010. Proceedings. 9–23, 2010, Springer.

[172] Douglas A. M. Lyall, Adrian Tey, Barny Foot, Stuart T. D. Roxburgh, Meena Virdi, Chris Robertson, and Caroline J. MacEwen. Postintravitreal anti-VEGF endophthalmitis in the united kingdom: incidence, features, risk factors, and outcomes. *Eye (Lond)*, 26(12):1517–1526, Dec 2012.

[173] Nicholas John Mackintosh. *Conditioning and Associative Learning.* Clarendon Press Oxford, 1983.

[174] Fabrizio Maria Maggi, Michael Westergaard, Marco Montali, and Wil M. P. van der Aalst. Runtime verification of ltl-based declarative process models. In Sarfraz Khurshid and Koushik Sen, editors, *Runtime Verification - Second International Conference, RV 2011*, volume 7186 of *Lecture Notes in Computer Science*, San Francisco, CA, USA, September 27-30, 2011, Revised Selected Papers. 131–146, 2011, Springer.

[175] Claudia Manfredi. Adaptive noise energy estimation in pathological speech signals. *IEEE Trans. Biomed. Engineering*, 47(11):1538–1543, 2000.

[176] Ronny S. Mans, Wil M. P. van der Aalst, and Rob J. B. Vanwersch. *Process Mining in Healthcare - Evaluating and Exploiting Operational Healthcare Processes.* Springer Briefs in Business Process Management. Springer, 2015.

[177] Ronny S. Mans, Wil M. P. van der Aalst, Rob J. B. Vanwersch, and Arnold J. Moleman. Process mining in healthcare: Data challenges when answering frequently posed questions. In Richard Lenz, Silvia Miksch, Mor Peleg, Manfred Reichert, David Riaño, and Annette ten Teije, editors, *Process Support and Knowledge Representation in Health Care - BPM 2012 Joint Workshop, ProHealth 2012/KR4HC 2012*, volume 7738 of *Lecture Notes in Computer Science*, Tallinn, Estonia, September 3, 2012, Revised Selected Papers. 140–153, 2012, Springer.

[178] Catalina Martínez-Costa, Marcos Menárguez Tortosa, and Jesualdo Tomás Fernández-Breis. An approach for the semantic interoperability of ISO EN 13606 and OpenEHR archetypes. *Journal of Biomedical Informatics*, 43(5):736–746, 2010.

[179] Stefan Matl, Richard Brosig, Maximilian Baust, Nassir Navab, and Stefanie Demirci. Vascular image registration techniques: A living review. *Medical Image Analysis*, 35:1–17, 2017.

[180] Matrix Science. Mascot website. http://www.matrixscience.com. Accessed: 2017-01-17.

[181] Jan Mendling. *Metrics for Process Models: Empirical Foundations of Verification, Error Prediction, and Guidelines for Correctness*, volume 6 of *Lecture Notes in Business Information Processing*. Springer, 2008.

[182] Jan Mendling, Hajo A. Reijers, and Jan Recker. Activity labeling in process modeling: Empirical insights and recommendations. *Inf. Syst.*, 35(4):467–482, 2010.

[183] Jan Mendling, Hajo A. Reijers, and Wil M. P. van der Aalst. Seven process modeling guidelines (7PMG). *Information & Software Technology*, 52(2):127–136, 2010.

[184] Jan Mendling, Laura Sánchez-González, Félix García, and Marcello La Rosa. Thresholds for error probability measures of business process models. *Journal of Systems and Software*, 85(5):1188–1197, 2012.

[185] Silvia Miksch, Yuval Shahar, and Peter Johnson. Asbru: a task-specific, intention-based, and time-oriented language for representing skeletal plans. In *Proceedings of the 7th Workshop on Knowledge Engineering: Methods & Languages (KEML-97)*. Milton Keynes, UK, The Open University, Milton Keynes, UK, 9–19, 1997.

[186] Ministry of Health and Social Policy. Official documentation website of the NHS EHR system from Spain (in Spanish). http://www.msssi.gob.es/profesionales/hcdsns/home.htm. Accessed: 2016-10-31.

[187] Mohamed A. Mneimneh, Edwin E. Yaz, Michael T. Johnson, and Richard J. Povinelli. An adaptive Kalman filter for removing baseline wandering in ECG signals. In *2006 Computers in Cardiology*. IEEE, 253–256, 2006.

[188] Robert A. Morris, William D. Shoaff, and Lina Khatib. Domain-independent temporal reasoning with recurring events. *Computational Intelligence*, 12:450–477, 1996.

[189] Ali M. Mosadeghrad. Obstacles to TQM success in health care systems. *International Journal of Health Care Quality Assurance*, 26(2):147–173, 2013.

[190] Philipp S. Muether, Robert Hoerster, Manuel M. Hermann, Bernd Kirchhof, and Sascha Fauser. Long-term effects of ranibizumab treatment delay in neovascular age-related macular degeneration. *Graefes Arch Clin Exp Ophthalmol*, 251(2):453–458, Feb 2013.

[191] Richard Müller and Andreas Rogge-Solti. BPMN for healthcare processes. In *Proceedings of the 3rd Central-European Workshop on Services and their Composition (ZEUS 2011)*, Karlsruhe, Germany. 2011.

[192] Nicolas Mundbrod, Florian Beuter, and Manfred Reichert. Supporting knowledge-intensive processes through integrated task lifecycle support. In *19th IEEE International Enterprise Distributed Object Computing Conference, EDOC 2015*, Adelaide, Australia, September 21-25, 2015. 19–28, 2015.

[193] Nicolas Mundbrod, Gregor Grambow, Jens Kolb, and Manfred Reichert. Context-aware process injection - enhancing process flexibility by late extension of process instances. In *On the Move to Meaningful Internet Systems: OTM 2015 Conferences - Confederated International Conferences: CoopIS, ODBASE, and C&TC 2015*, Rhodes, Greece, October 26-30, 2015, Proceedings. 127–145, 2015.

[194] Nicolas Mundbrod, Jens Kolb, and Manfred Reichert. Towards a system support of collaborative knowledge work. In *Business Process Management Workshops – BPM 2012 International Workshops*, 31–42, 2012.

[195] Mark A. Musen, Samson W. Tu, Amar K. Das, and Yuval Shahar. Synthesis of research: EON: A component-based approach to automation of protocol-directed therapy. *JAMIA*, 3(6):367–388, 1996.

[196] Isao Nakata, Kenji Yamashiro, Hideo Nakanishi, Yumiko Akagi-Kurashige, Masahiro Miyake, Akitaka Tsujikawa, Fumihiko Matsuda, et al. Prevalence and characteristics of age-related macular degeneration in the japanese population: the nagahama study. *Am J Ophthalmol*, 156(5):1002–1009, Nov 2013.

[197] Bernhard Nebel and Hans-Jürgen Bürckert. Reasoning about temporal relations: A maximal tractable subclass of allen's interval algebra. *J. ACM*, 42(1):43–66, 1995.

[198] Martin M. Nentwich, Yazmin Yactayo-Miranda, Fabian Schwarzbach, Armin Wolf, Anselm Kampik, and Herminia Mino-de-Kaspar. Endophthalmitis after intravitreal injection: decreasing incidence and clinical outcome-8-year results from a tertiary ophthalmic referral center. *Retina*, 34(5):943–950, May 2014.

[199] Hoang Nguyen, Marlon Dumas, Marcello La Rosa, Fabrizio Maria Maggi, and Suriadi Suriadi. Mining business process deviance: A quest for accuracy. In Robert Meersman, Hervé Panetto, Tharam S. Dillon, Michele Missikoff, Lin Liu, Oscar Pastor, Alfredo Cuzzocrea, and Timos K. Sellis, editors, *On the Move to Meaningful Internet Systems: OTM 2014 Conferences - Confederated International Conferences: CoopIS, and ODBASE 2014*, volume 8841 of *Lecture Notes in Computer*

Science, Amantea, Italy, October 27-31, 2014, Proceedings. 436–445, 2014, Springer.

[200] Hoang Nguyen, Marlon Dumas, Arthur H. M. ter Hofstede, Marcello La Rosa, and Fabrizio Maria Maggi. Business process performance mining with staged process flows. In Selmin Nurcan, Pnina Soffer, Marko Bajec, and Johann Eder, editors, *Advanced Information Systems Engineering - 28th International Conference, CAiSE 2016*, volume 9694 of *Lecture Notes in Computer Science*, Ljubljana, Slovenia, June 13-17, 2016. Proceedings. 167–185, 2016, Springer.

[201] John H. Nguyen, Yuval Shahar, Samson W. Tu, Amar K. Das, and Mark A. Musen. Integration of temporal reasoning and temporal-data maintenance into a reusable database mediator to answer abstract, time-oriented queries: The tzolkin system. *J. Intell. Inf. Syst.*, 13(1-2):121–145, 1999.

[202] Ocean Informatics. The openEHR Clinical Knowledge Manager (CKM). http://www.openehr.org/ckm. Accessed: 2016-10-31.

[203] Martin J. O'Connor, Samson W. Tu, and Mark A. Musen. Representation of temporal indeterminacy in clinical databases. In *AMIA 2000, American Medical Informatics Association Annual Symposium*, Los Angeles, CA, USA, November 4-8, 2000. 2000, AMIA.

[204] Martin J. O'Connor, Samson W. Tu, and Mark A. Musen. The chronus II temporal database mediator. In *AMIA 2002, American Medical Informatics Association Annual Symposium* [7].

[205] OECD. *Health at a Glance 2015: OECD Indicators*. OECD Publishing, Paris, 2015. http://dx.doi.org/10.1787/health_glance-2015-en.

[206] Omolola Ogunyemi. The guideline expression language (GEL) user's guide. Technical report, Technical Report, DSG-TR-2000-001, 2000, Decision Systems Group, Boston, MA, 2000.

[207] Alejandro Oliver-Fernandez, Jeff Bakal, Shaun Segal, Gaurav K. Shah, Ashish Dugar, and Sanjay Sharma. Progression of visual loss and time between initial assessment and treatment of wet age-related macular degeneration. *Can J Ophthalmol*, 40(3):313–319, Jun 2005.

[208] Allan Paivio. Mental imagery in associative learning and memory. *Psychological review*, 76(3):241, 1969.

[209] Mor Peleg, Omolola Ogunyemi, Samson W. Tu, Aziz A. Boxwala, Qing T. Zeng, Robert A. Greenes, and Edward H. Shortliffe. Using features of arden syntax with object-oriented medical data models for guideline modeling. In *AMIA 2001, American Medical Informatics Association Annual Symposium*, Washington, DC, USA, November 3-7, 2001. 2001, AMIA.

[210] Mor Peleg, Judith Somekh, and Dov Dori. A methodology for eliciting and modeling exceptions. *Journal of Biomedical Informatics*, 42(4):736–747, 2009.

[211] Mor Peleg and Samson W. Tu. Design patterns for clinical guidelines. *Artificial Intelligence in Medicine*, 47(1):1–24, 2009.

[212] Brian T. Pentland, Jan Recker, and George M. Wyner. Rediscovering handoffs. *Academy of Management Discoveries*, 2017.

[213] María Martínez Pérez, Mariano Cabrero Canosa, José Ramon Vizoso Hermida, Lino Carrajo García, Daniel Llamas Gómez, Guillermo Vázquez González, and Isabel Martín Herranz. Application of RFID technology in patient tracking and medication traceability in emergency care. *Journal Medical Systems*, 36(6):3983–3993, 2012.

[214] Razvan Petrusel, Jan Mendling, and Hajo A. Reijers. Task-specific visual cues for improving process model understanding. *Information & Software Technology*, 79:63–78, 2016.

[215] Razvan Petrusel, Jan Mendling, and Hajo A. Reijers. How visual cognition influences process model comprehension. *Decision Support Systems*, 2017.

[216] Jakob Pinggera, Pnina Soffer, Dirk Fahland, Matthias Weidlich, Stefan Zugal, Barbara Weber, Hajo A. Reijers, and Jan Mendling. Styles in business process modeling: an exploration and a model. *Software and System Modeling*, 14(3):1055–1080, 2015.

[217] Azzurra Pini, Ross Brown, and Moe Thandar Wynn. Process vizualisation techniques for multi-perspective process comparisons. In *Proceedings of Asia Pacific Business Process Management: Third Asia Pacific Conference, AP-BPM 2015*, volume 219 of *LNBIP*. 183–197, Springer Verlag, 2015.

[218] Fabian Pittke, Henrik Leopold, and Jan Mendling. Automatic detection and resolution of lexical ambiguity in process models. *IEEE Trans. Software Eng.*, 41(6):526–544, 2015.

[219] Artem Polyvyanyy, Luciano García-Bañuelos, Dirk Fahland, and Mathias Weske. Maximal structuring of acyclic process models. *Comput. J.*, 57(1):12–35, 2014.

[220] Wichian Prechaiswadi and Parham Porouhan. Process model and bottleneck mining in on-line peer-review systems. *SpringerPlus*, 4(1):1, August 2015.

[221] Johannes Prescher, Siegfried Schefer-Wenzl, Anne Baumgrass, and Mark Strembeck andJan Mendling. Towards a comprehensive complexity assessment of RBAC models. *EMISA Forum*, 34(2):12–23, 2014.

[222] Elena Prokofyeva and Eberhart Zrenner. Epidemiology of major eye diseases leading to blindness in europe: a literature review. *Ophthalmic Res*, 47(4):171–188, 2012.

[223] Rüdiger Pryss, Nicolas Mundbrod, David Langer, and Manfred Reichert. Supporting medical ward rounds through mobile task and process management. *Inf. Syst. E-Business Management*, 13(1):107–146, 2015.

[224] Shaun Purcell, Benjamin Neale, Kathe Todd-Brown, Lori Thomas, Manuel A.R. Ferreira, David Bender, Julian Maller, et al. PLINK: a tool set for whole-genome association and population-based linkage analyses. *The American J. of Human Genetics*, 81(3):559–575, 2007.

[225] Silvana Quaglini, Mario Stefanelli, Giordano Lanzola, Vincenzo Caporusso, and Silvia Panzarasa. Flexible guideline-based patient careflow systems. *Artificial Intelligence in Medicine*, 22(1):65–80, 2001.

[226] Jan Recker, Michael Rosemann, Peter F. Green, and Marta Indulska. Do ontological deficiencies in modeling grammars matter? *MIS Quarterly*, 35(1):57–79, 2011.

[227] Carl D. Regillo, David M. Brown, Prema Abraham, Huibin Yue, Tsontcho Ianchulev, Susan Schneider, Naveed Shams, and PIER Study Group. Randomized, double-masked, sham-controlled trial of ranibizumab for neovascular age-related macular degeneration: PIER study year 1. *Am J Ophthalmol*, 145(2):239–248, Feb 2008.

[228] David H. Rehkopf, Benjamin W. Domingue, and Mark R. Cullen. The geographic distribution of genetic risk as compared to social risk for chronic diseases in the united states. *Biodemography and Social Biology*, 62(1):126–142, 2016.

[229] Manfred Reichert. What BPM technology can do for healthcare process support. In *Artificial Intelligence in Medicine - 13th Conference on Artificial Intelligence in Medicine, AIME 2011*, Bled, Slovenia, July 2-6, 2011. Proceedings. 2–13, 2011.

[230] Manfred Reichert. Process and data: Two sides of the same coin? In *On the Move to Meaningful Internet Systems: OTM 2012, Confederated International Conferences: CoopIS, DOA-SVI, and ODBASE 2012*, Rome, Italy, September 10-14, 2012. Proceedings, Part I. 2–19, 2012.

[231] Manfred Reichert and Peter Dadam. ADEPT$_{flex}$-supporting dynamic changes of workflows without losing control. *J. Intell. Inf. Syst.*, 10(2):93–129, 1998.

[232] Manfred Reichert and Peter Dadam. Enabling adaptive process-aware information systems with ADEPT2. In Jorge Cardoso and Wil M.P.

van der Aalst, editors, *Handbook of Research on Business Process Modeling*, 173–203. Information Science Reference, Hershey, New York, March 2009.

[233] Manfred Reichert, Peter Dadam, and Thomas Bauer. Dealing with forward and backward jumps in workflow management systems. *Software and System Modeling*, 2(1):37–58, 2003.

[234] Manfred Reichert, Alena Hallerbach, and Thomas Bauer. Lifecycle management of business process variants. In Jan vom Brocke and Michael Rosemann, editors, *Handbook on Business Process Management 1, Introduction, Methods, and Information Systems, 2nd Ed.*, International Handbooks on Information Systems, 251–278. Springer, 2015.

[235] Manfred Reichert, Stefanie Rinderle-Ma, and Peter Dadam. On the common support of workflow type and instance changes under correctness constraints. In *On The Move to Meaningful Internet Systems 2003: CoopIS, DOA, and ODBASE - OTM Confederated International Conferences, CoopIS, DOA, and ODBASE 2003*, Catania, Sicily, Italy, November 3-7, 2003. 407–425, 2003.

[236] Manfred Reichert, Stefanie Rinderle-Ma, and Peter Dadam. Flexibility in process-aware information systems. In *T. Petri Nets and Other Models of Concurrency* [135], 115–135.

[237] Manfred Reichert and Barbara Weber. *Enabling Flexibility in Process-Aware Information Systems — Challenges, Methods, Technologies*. Springer, 2012.

[238] Hajo A. Reijers, Thomas Freytag, Jan Mendling, and Andreas Eckleder. Syntax highlighting in business process models. *Decision Support Systems*, 51(3):339–349, 2011.

[239] Hajo A. Reijers and Jan Mendling. A study into the factors that influence the understandability of business process models. *IEEE Trans. Systems, Man, and Cybernetics, Part A*, 41(3):449–462, 2011.

[240] Hajo A. Reijers, Jan Mendling, and Remco M. Dijkman. Human and automatic modularizations of process models to enhance their comprehension. *Inf. Syst.*, 36(5):881–897, 2011.

[241] David Riaño, Richard Lenz, and Manfred Reichert, editors. *Knowledge Representation for Health Care - HEC 2016 International Joint Workshop, KR4HC/ProHealth 2016*, volume 10096 of *Lecture Notes in Computer Science*, Munich, Germany, September 2, 2016, Revised Selected Papers, 2017. Springer.

[242] Stefanie Rinderle-Ma, Manfred Reichert, and Peter Dadam. Flexible support of team processes by adaptive workflow systems. *Distributed and Parallel Databases*, 16(1):91–116, 2004.

[243] Stefanie Rinderle-Ma, Manfred Reichert, and Peter Dadam. On dealing with structural conflicts between process type and instance changes. In *Business Process Management: Second International Conference, BPM 2004*, Potsdam, Germany, June 17-18, 2004. Proceedings. 274–289, 2004.

[244] Andreas Rogge-Solti, Ronny Mans, Wil M. P. van der Aalst, and Mathias Weske. Improving documentation by repairing event logs. In Janis Grabis, Marite Kirikova, Jelena Zdravkovic, and Janis Stirna, editors, *The Practice of Enterprise Modeling - 6th IFIP WG 8.1 Working Conference, PoEM 2013*, volume 165 of *Lecture Notes in Business Information Processing*, Riga, Latvia, November 6-7, 2013, Proceedings. 129–144, 2013, Springer.

[245] Marcello La Rosa, Wil M. P. van der Aalst, Marlon Dumas, and Arthur H. M. ter Hofstede. Questionnaire-based variability modeling for system configuration. *Software and System Modeling*, 8(2):251–274, 2009.

[246] Philip J. Rosenfeld, David M. Brown, Jeffrey S. Heier, David S. Boyer, Peter K. Kaiser, Carol Y. Chung, Robert Y. Kim, and MARINA Study Group. Ranibizumab for neovascular age-related macular degeneration. *N Engl J Med*, 355(14):1419–1431, Oct 2006.

[247] Anne Rozinat and Wil M. P. van der Aalst. Decision mining in ProM. In Dustdar et al. [83], 420–425.

[248] Geary A. Rummler and Alan P. Brache. *Improving Performance: How to Manage the White Space in the Organization Chart.* Jossey-Bass, 1995.

[249] Ravi Sachidanandam, David Weissman, Steven C Schmidt, Jerzy M Kakol, Lincoln D Stein, Gabor Marth, Steve Sherry, et al. A map of human genome sequence variation containing 1.42 million single nucleotide polymorphisms. *Nature*, 409(6822):928–933, 2001.

[250] Shazia Wasim Sadiq, Guido Governatori, and Kioumars Namiri. Modeling control objectives for business process compliance. In Gustavo Alonso, Peter Dadam, and Michael Rosemann, editors, *Business Process Management, 5th International Conference, BPM 2007*, volume 4714 of *Lecture Notes in Computer Science*, Brisbane, Australia, September 24-28, 2007, Proceedings. 149–164, 2007, Springer.

[251] Ferenc B. Sallo, Tunde Peto, Irene Leung, Wen Xing, Catey Bunce, and Alan C. Bird. The international classification system and the progression of age-related macular degeneration. *Curr Eye Res*, 34(3):238–240, Mar 2009.

[252] Reza Sameni, Mohammad B Shamsollahi, Christian Jutten, and Massoud Babaie-Zade. Filtering noisy ecg signals using the extended kalman

filter based on a modified dynamic ecg model. In *Computers in Cardiology, 2005*. IEEE, 1017–1020, 2005.

[253] Hubert Scheuerlein, Falk Rauchfuss, Yves Dittmar, Rüdiger Molle, Torsten Lehmann, Nicole Pienkos, and Utz Settmacher. New methods for clinical pathways—business process modeling notation (BPMN) and tangible business process modeling (t.BPM). *Langenbeck's Archives of Surgery*, 397(5):755–761, 2012.

[254] Hendrik P.N. Scholl, Robert W. Massof, and Sheila West. *Ophthalmology and the Ageing Society*. Essentials in Ophthalmology. Springer Berlin Heidelberg, 2013.

[255] Stefan Schönig, Cristina Cabanillas Stefan Jablonski, and Jan Mendling. A framework for efficiently mining the organisational perspective of business processes. *Decision Support Systems*, 89:87–97, 2016.

[256] Loay Sehwail and Camille DeYong. Six Sigma in healthcare. *Leadership in Health Services*, 16(4):1–5, 2003.

[257] Arik Senderovich, Andreas Rogge-Solti, Avigdor Gal, Jan Mendling, and Avishai Mandelbaum. The ROAD from sensor data to process instances via interaction mining. In Selmin Nurcan, Pnina Soffer, Marko Bajec, and Johann Eder, editors, *Advanced Information Systems Engineering - 28th International Conference, CAiSE 2016*, volume 9694 of *Lecture Notes in Computer Science*, Ljubljana, Slovenia, June 13-17, 2016. Proceedings. 257–273, 2016, Springer.

[258] Yuval Shahar. *A Knowledge-based Method for Temporal Abstraction of Clinical Data*. PhD thesis, Stanford University, Stanford, CA, USA, 1994.

[259] Yuval Shahar. A framework for knowledge-based temporal abstraction. *Artif. Intell.*, 90(1-2):79–133, 1997.

[260] Yuval Shahar, Silvia Miksch, and Peter D. Johnson. The asgaard project: a task-specific framework for the application and critiquing of time-oriented clinical guidelines. *Artificial Intelligence in Medicine*, 14(1-2):29–51, 1998.

[261] Yuval Shahar and Mark A. Musen. Knowledge-based temporal abstraction in clinical domains. *Artificial Intelligence in Medicine*, 8(3):267–298, 1996.

[262] Yuval Shahar, Ohad Young, Erez Shalom, Alon Mayaffit, Robert Moskovitch, Alon Hessing, and Maya Galperin. DEGEL: A hybrid, multiple-ontology framework for specification and retrieval of clinical guidelines. In Dojat et al. [79], 122–131.

[263] Erez Shalom, Yuval Shahar, and Eitan Lunenfeld. An architecture for a continuous, user-driven, and data-driven application of clinical guidelines and its evaluation. *Journal of Biomedical Informatics*, 59:130–148, 2016.

[264] Eric H. Sherman, George Hripcsak, Justin Starren, Robert A. Jenders, and Paul Clayton. Using intermediate states to improve the ability of the arden syntax to implement care plans and reuse knowledge. In *Proceedings of the Annual Symposium on Computer Application in Medical Care*. American Medical Informatics Association, 238, 1995.

[265] Yoav Shoham. Temporal logics in AI: semantical and ontological considerations. *Artif. Intell.*, 33(1):89–104, 1987.

[266] Luigi Siciliani, Valerie Moran, and Michael Borowitz. Measuring and comparing health care waiting times in OECD countries. *Health Policy*, 118(3):292–303, 2014.

[267] Pradeep K. Sinha, Gaur Sunder, Prashant Bendale, Manisha Mantri, and Atreya Dande. *Electronic Health Record: Standards, Coding Systems, Frameworks, and Infrastructures*. 1st edition, Wiley-IEEE Press, 2012.

[268] Douglas S. Smink, Jonathan A. Finkelstein, Barbara M. Garcia Peña, Michael Shannon, George A. Taylor, and Steven J. Fishman. Diagnosis of acute appendicitis in children using a clinical practice guideline. *Journal of Pediatric Surgery*, 39(3):458–463, 2004.

[269] Scott M. Smith and Geral S. Albaum. *Fundamentals of Marketing Research*. Sage Publications, Thousand Oaks, Calif, 2005.

[270] Richard T. Snodgrass, editor. *The TSQL2 Temporal Query Language*. Kluwer, 1995.

[271] Alexandru Soceanu, Alexandru Egner, and Florica Moldoveanu. Towards interoperability of ehealth system networked components. In *2013 19th International Conference on Control Systems and Computer Science*, 147–154, May 2013.

[272] Minseok Song and Wil M. P. van der Aalst. Towards comprehensive support for organizational mining. *Decision Support Systems*, 46(1):300–317, 2008.

[273] Margarita Sordo, Omolola Ogunyemi, Aziz A. Boxwala, and Robert A. Greenes. GELLO: an object-oriented query and expression language for clinical decision support: AMIA 2003 open source expo. In *AMIA 2003, American Medical Informatics Association Annual Symposium*, Washington, DC, USA, November 8-12, 2003. 2003, AMIA.

[274] Michael Stacey and Carolyn McGregor. Temporal abstraction in intelligent clinical data analysis: A survey. *Artificial Intelligence in Medicine*, 39(1):1–24, 2007.

[275] Bruder F. Stapleton, James Hendricks, Patrick Hagan, and Mark DelBeccaro. Modifying the Toyota Production System for continuous performance improvement in an academic children's hospital. *Pediatric Clinics of North America*, 56(4):799–813, 2009.

[276] Kostas Stergiou and Manolis Koubarakis. Backtracking algorithms for disjunctions of temporal constraints. *Artif. Intell.*, 120(1):81–117, 2000.

[277] Stanley Smith Stevens. On the theory of scales of measurement. *Science*, 103(2684):677–680, 1946.

[278] Jovan Stevovic, Jun Li, Hamid Reza Motahari-Nezhad, Fabio Casati, and Giampaolo Armellin. Business process management enabled compliance-aware medical record sharing. *IJBPIM*, 6(3):201–223, 2013.

[279] Kathleen Strong, Phil Trickett, Ian Titulaer, and Kuldeep Bhatia. *Health in Rural and Remote Australia: The First Report of the Australian Institute of Health and Welfare on Rural Health*. Australian Institute of Health and Welfare, Canberra, Australia, 1998.

[280] Suriadi Suriadi, R. Andrews, Arthur H. M. ter Hofstede, and Moe Thandar Wynn. Event log imperfection patterns for process mining: Towards a systematic approach to cleaning event logs. *Inf. Syst.*, 64:132–150, 2017.

[281] Suriadi Suriadi, Ronny S. Mans, Moe Thandar Wynn, Andrew Partington, and Jonathan Karnon. Measuring patient flow variations: A cross-organisational process mining approach. In Chun Ouyang and Jae-Yoon Jung, editors, *Asia Pacific Business Process Management - Second Asia Pacific Conference AP-BPM 2014*, volume 181 of *Lecture Notes in Business Information Processing*, Brisbane, QLD, Australia, July 3-4, 2014. Proceedings. 43–58, 2014, Springer.

[282] Suriadi Suriadi, Chun Ouyang, Wil M. P. van der Aalst, and Arthur H. M. ter Hofstede. Event interval analysis: Why do processes take time? *Decision Support Systems*, 79:77–98, 2015.

[283] David R. Sutton and John Fox. Application of information technology: The syntax and semantics of the proforma guideline modeling language. *JAMIA*, 10(5):433–443, 2003.

[284] Keith D. Swenson, Nathaniel Palmer, and Max J. Pucher. *How Knowledge Workers Get Things Done: Real-World Adaptive Case Management*, 93–100. Future Strategies Inc., 2012.

[285] Mehmet T. Taner, Bülent Sezen, and Jiju Antony. An overview of Six Sigma applications in healthcare industry. *International Journal of Health Care Quality Assurance*, 20(4):329–340, 2007.

[286] Frederick Winslow Taylor. *The Principles of Scientific Management.* Harper & Row, Publishers, New York, NY, USA, 1911.

[287] Claire L. Temple, Shirley A. Huchcroft, and Walley J. Temple. The natural history of appendicitis in adults. a prospective study. *Annals of Surgery*, 221(3):278–281, 1995.

[288] Paolo Terenziani. Integrating calendar dates and qualitative temporal constraints in the treatment of periodic events. *IEEE Trans. Knowl. Data Eng.*, 9(5):763–783, 1997.

[289] Paolo Terenziani, Gianpaolo Molino, and Mauro Torchio. A modular approach for representing and executing clinical guidelines. *Artificial Intelligence in Medicine*, 23(3):249–276, 2001.

[290] Paolo Terenziani, Stefania Montani, Alessio Bottrighi, Gianpaolo Molino, and Mauro Torchio. Applying artificial intelligence to clinical guidelines: the GLARE approach. *Studies in Health Technology and Informatics*, 139:273–282, 2008.

[291] The Business Process Management Notation. BPMN - website, 2012. http://www.bpmn.org.

[292] The EN 13606 association. Clinical information model manager (CIMM). http://cimm.en13606.org/. Accessed: 2016-10-31.

[293] The Object Management Group. OMG - website, 2016. http://www.omg.org.

[294] The Workflow Management Coalition. WfMC - website, 2012. http://www.wfmc.org.

[295] ThermoFisher Scientific. Applied biosystems website. http://www.appliedbiosystems.com/. Accessed: 2017-01-17.

[296] Warren S. Torgerson. *Theory and Methods of Scaling.* Wiley, New York, NY, USA, 1958.

[297] Giuseppe Tradigo, Pierangelo Veltri, Mario Cannataro, and Francesco Fera. Stimare: A software tool supporting visual stimuli definition and analysis in magnetic resonance. In *Proceedings of the Twenty-Second IEEE International Symposium on Computer-Based Medical Systems, August 3-4, 2009*, Albuquerque, New Mexico, USA. 1–5, 2009.

[298] Giuseppe Tradigo, Pierangelo Veltri, and Sergio Greco. Geomedica: managing and querying clinical data distributions on geographical database systems. *Procedia Computer Science*, 1(1):979–986, 2010.

[299] Marina Trkman, Jan Mendling, and Marjan Krisper. Using business process models to better understand the dependencies among user stories. *Information & Software Technology*, 71:58–76, 2016.

[300] Ioannis Tsamardinos. A probabilistic approach to robust execution of temporal plans with uncertainty. In Ioannis P. Vlahavas and Constantine D. Spyropoulos, editors, *Methods and Applications of Artificial Intelligence, Second Hellenic Conference on AI, SETN 2002*, volume 2308 of *Lecture Notes in Computer Science*, Thessaloniki, Greece, April 11-12, 2002, Proceedings. 97–108, 2002, Springer.

[301] Ioannis Tsamardinos and Martha E. Pollack. Efficient solution techniques for disjunctive temporal reasoning problems. *Artif. Intell.*, 151(1-2):43–89, 2003.

[302] Samson W. Tu, James R. Campbell, Julie Glasgow, Mark A. Nyman, Robert C. McClure, James C. McClay, Craig G. Parker, et al. Synthesis of research paper: The SAGE guideline model: Achievements and overview. *JAMIA*, 14(5):589–598, 2007.

[303] Samson W. Tu and Mark Musen et al. Modeling data and knowledge in the EON guideline architecture. *Studies in Health Technology and Informatics*, –(1):280–284, 2001.

[304] Samson W. Tu and Julie Glasgow. The SAGE guideline model technical specification. Technical Report 1243, Stanford Medical Informatics, Stanford University, 2006.

[305] Wil M. P. van der Aalst. Process-aware information systems: Lessons to be learned from process mining. In *Trans. Petri Nets and Other Models of Concurrency* [135], 1–26.

[306] Wil M. P. van der Aalst. *Process Mining - Discovery, Conformance and Enhancement of Business Processes.* Springer, 2011.

[307] Wil M. P. van der Aalst. *Process Mining – Data Science in Action, Second Edition.* Springer, 2016.

[308] Wil M. P. van der Aalst, Arya Adriansyah, Ana Karla Alves de Medeiros, Franco Arcieri, Thomas Baier, Tobias Blickle, Rantham Prabhakara Jagadeesh Chandra Bose, et al. Process mining manifesto. In Florian Daniel, Kamel Barkaoui, and Schahram Dustdar, editors, *Business Process Management Workshops - BPM 2011 International Workshops*, volume 99 of *Lecture Notes in Business Information Processing*, Clermont-Ferrand, France, August 29, 2011, Revised Selected Papers, Part I. 169–194, 2011, Springer.

[309] Wil M. P. van der Aalst, Alexander Dreiling, Florian Gottschalk, Michael Rosemann, and Monique H. Jansen-Vullers. Configurable process models as a basis for reference modeling. In *Business Process Management Workshops, BPM 2005 International Workshops, BPI, BPD, ENEI, BPRM, WSCOBPM, BPS*, 512–518, 2005.

[310] Wil M. P. van der Aalst and Schahram Dustdar. Process mining put into context. *IEEE Internet Computing*, 16(1):82–86, 2012.

[311] Wil M. P. van der Aalst, Shengnan Guo, and Pierre Gorissen. Comparative process mining in education: An approach based on process cubes. In Paolo Ceravolo, Rafael Accorsi, and Philippe Cudré-Mauroux, editors, *Data-Driven Process Discovery and Analysis - Third IFIP WG 2.6,2.12 International Symposium, SIMPDA 2013*, volume 203 of *Lecture Notes in Business Information Processing*, Riva del Garda, Italy, August 30, 2013, Revised Selected Papers. 110–134, 2013, Springer.

[312] Wil M. P. van der Aalst, Niels Lohmann, and Marcello La Rosa. Ensuring correctness during process configuration via partner synthesis. *Inf. Syst.*, 37(6):574–592, 2012.

[313] Wil M. P. van der Aalst, Maja Pesic, and Helen Schonenberg. Declarative workflows: Balancing between flexibility and support. *Computer Science — R&D*, 23(2):99–113, 2009.

[314] Wil M. P. van der Aalst, Hajo A. Reijers, and Minseok Song. Discovering social networks from event logs. *Computer Supported Cooperative Work*, 14(6):549–593, 2005.

[315] Wil M. P. van der Aalst, Arthur H. M. ter Hofstede, Bartek Kiepuszewski, and Alistair P. Barros. Workflow patterns. *Distributed and Parallel Databases*, 14(1):5–51, 2003.

[316] Wil M. P. van der Aalst, Arthur H. M. ter Hofstede, and Mathias Weske. Business process management: A survey. In Wil M. P. van der Aalst, Arthur H. M. ter Hofstede, and Mathias Weske, editors, *Business Process Management, International Conference, BPM 2003*, volume 2678 of *Lecture Notes in Computer Science*, Eindhoven, The Netherlands, June 26-27, 2003, Proceedings. 1–12, 2003, Springer.

[317] Wil M. P. van der Aalst, Ton Weijters, and Laura Maruster. Workflow mining: Discovering process models from event logs. *IEEE Trans. Knowl. Data Eng.*, 16(9):1128–1142, 2004.

[318] Jan Martijn E. M. van der Werf, Boudewijn F. van Dongen, Cor A. J. Hurkens, and Alexander Serebrenik. Process discovery using integer linear programming. *Fundam. Inform.*, 94(3-4):387–412, 2009.

[319] Boudewijn F. van Dongen and Arya Adriansyah. Process mining: Fuzzy clustering and performance visualization. In Stefanie Rinderle-Ma, Shazia Wasim Sadiq, and Frank Leymann, editors, *Business Process Management Workshops, BPM 2009 International Workshops*, volume 43 of *Lecture Notes in Business Information Processing*, Ulm, Germany, September 7, 2009. Revised Papers. 158–169, 2009, Springer.

[320] Jussi Vanhatalo, Hagen Völzer, and Jana Koehler. The refined process structure tree. *Data Knowl. Eng.*, 68(9):793–818, 2009.

[321] Rob J. B. Vanwersch, Khurram Shahzad, Irene T. P. Vanderfeesten, Kris Vanhaecht, Paul W. P. J. Grefen, Liliane Pintelon, Jan Mendling, et al. A critical evaluation and framework of business process improvement methods. *Business & Information Systems Engineering*, 58(1):43–53, 2016.

[322] Thierry Vidal and Hélène Fargier. Handling contingency in temporal constraint networks: from consistency to controllabilities. *J. Exp. Theor. Artif. Intell.*, 11(1):23–45, 1999.

[323] Marc B. Vilain and Henry A. Kautz. Constraint propagation algorithms for temporal reasoning. In Kehler [140], 377–382.

[324] Nicholas P. Vitalari. Knowledge as a basis for expertise in systems analysis: An empirical study. *MIS Quarterly*, 9(3):221–241, 1985.

[325] Patrizia Vizza, Antonio Curcio, Giuseppe Tradigo, Ciro Indolfi, and Pierangelo Veltri. A framework for the atrial fibrillation prediction in electrophysiological studies. *Computer Methods and Programs in Biomedicine*, 120(2):65–76, 2015.

[326] Jan vom Brocke, Sarah Zelt, and Theresa Schmiedel. Considering context in business process management: The BPM context framework. *bptrends.com*, 2015.

[327] Barbara Weber, Manfred Reichert, Jan Mendling, and Hajo A. Reijers. Refactoring large process model repositories. *Computers in Industry*, 62(5):467–486, 2011.

[328] Barbara Weber, Manfred Reichert, and Stefanie Rinderle-Ma. Change patterns and change support features - enhancing flexibility in process-aware information systems. *Data Knowl. Eng.*, 66(3):438–466, 2008.

[329] Barbara Weber, Manfred Reichert, and Werner Wild. Case-base maintenance for ccbr-based process evolution. In *Advances in Case-Based Reasoning, 8th European Conference, ECCBR 2006*, 106–120, 2006.

[330] Barbara Weber, Manfred Reichert, Werner Wild, and Stefanie Rinderle-Ma. Balancing flexibility and security in adaptive process management systems. In *On the Move to Meaningful Internet Systems 2005: CoopIS, DOA, and ODBASE, OTM Confederated International Conferences CoopIS, DOA, and ODBASE 2005*, Agia Napa, Cyprus, October 31 - November 4, 2005, Proceedings, Part I. 59–76, 2005.

[331] Barbara Weber, Stefanie Rinderle-Ma, Werner Wild, and Manfred Reichert. Ccbr-driven business process evolution. In *Case-Based Reasoning, Research and Development, 6th International Conference, on Case-Based Reasoning, ICCBR 2005*, 610–624, 2005.

[332] Ingo Weber and Jan Mendling. A vision of experimental process improvement. In Paolo Ceravolo and Stefanie Rinderle-Ma, editors, *Proceedings of the 5th International Symposium on Data-driven Process Discovery and Analysis (SIMPDA 2015)*, volume 1527 of *CEUR Workshop Proceedings*, Vienna, Austria, December 9-11, 2015. 127–130, 2015, CEUR-WS.org.

[333] Sual N. Weingart, Ross M. Wilson, Robert W. Gibberd, and Bernadette Harrison. Epidemiology of medical error. *Western Journal of Medicine*, 172(6):390–393, 2000.

[334] Anton J.M. Weitjers, Wil M. P. van der Aalst, and Ana Karla Alves De Medeiros. Process mining with the heuristics miner algorithm. Technical Report WP 166, Technische Universiteit Eindhoven, 2006. https://pdfs.semanticscholar.org/1cc3/d62e27365b8d7ed6ce93b41c193d0559d086.pdf.

[335] Chunhua Weng, Michael G. Kahn, and John H. Gennari. Temporal knowledge representation for scheduling tasks in clinical trial protocols. In *AMIA 2002, American Medical Informatics Association Annual Symposium* [7].

[336] Mathias Weske. *Business Process Management: Concepts, Languages, Architectures.* Springer, 2007.

[337] Sabrina T. Wong and Sandra Reagan. Patient perspectives on primary health care in rural communities: Effects of geography on access, continuity and efficiency. *Rural and Remote Health*, 9(1142), 2009. http://www.rrh.org.au/articles/subviewnew.asp?ArticleID=1142.

[338] Kim Wüllenweber, Daniel Beimborn, Tim Weitzel, and Wolfgang König. The impact of process standardization on business process outsourcing success. *Information Systems Frontiers*, 10(2):211–224, 2008.

[339] XML Process Definition Language (XPDL). XPDL - website, 2012. http://www.xpdl.org.

[340] Francesca Zerbato, Barbara Oliboni, Carlo Combi, Manuel Campos, and Jose M. Juarez. BPMN-based representation and comparison of clinical pathways for catheter-related bloodstream infections. In Prabhakaran Balakrishnan, Jaideep Srivatsava, Wai-Tat Fu, Sanda M. Harabagiu, and Fei Wang, editors, *2015 International Conference on Healthcare Informatics, ICHI 2015*. 346–355, IEEE Computer Society, 2015.

[341] Xiao-Yu Zhang, Xiao-Fan Guo, Shao-Dan Zhang, Jing-Na He, Cao-Yu Sun, Yin Zou, Han-Si Bi, and Yang Qu. Comparison of bevacizumab and ranibizumab in age-related macular degeneration: a systematic review and meta-analysis. *Int J Ophthalmol*, 7(2):355–364, 2014.

Index